THE AMAZING SPIDER-MAN

BASED ON THE FILM *THE AMAZING SPIDER-MAN*
STORY BY JAMES VANDERBILT
SCREENPLAY BY JAMES VANDERBILT, STEVE KLOVES & ALVIN SARGENT

WRITER **TOM COHEN** PENCILER **NEIL EDWARDS**

INKERS **RICK MAGYAR, RICK KETCHAM, MARK PENNINGTON, ROLAND PARIS, LORENZO RUGGIERO**

COLORIST **VERONICA GANDINI** LETTERER **JEFF ECKLEBERRY**

PRODUCTION **MAYELA GUTIERREZ** ASSISTANT EDITOR **JON MOISAN** EDITOR **SANA AMANAT**

EDITOR IN CHIEF **AXEL ALONSO** CHIEF CREATIVE OFFICER **JOE QUESADA**
PUBLISHER **DAN BUCKLEY** EXECUTIVE PRODUCER **ALAN FINE**

SPECIAL THANKS TO CIRA SIMS, WILL CORONA PILGRIM AND KEVIN FEIGE

AMAZING SPIDER-MAN: THE MOVIE. Contains material originally published in magazine form as AMAZING SPIDER-MAN: THE MOVIE #1-2. First printing 2012. ISBN# 978-0-7851-6499-9. Published by MARVEL WORLDWIDE, INC., a subsidiary of MARVEL ENTERTAINMENT, LLC. OFFICE OF PUBLICATION: 135 West 50th Street, New York, NY 10020. Copyright © 2012 Marvel Characters, Inc. All rights reserved. The Amazing Spider-Man, the Movie © 2012 CPII. $9.99 per copy in the U.S. and $10.99 in Canada (GST #R127032852); Canadian Agreement #40668537. All characters featured in this issue and the distinctive names and likenesses thereof, and all related indicia are trademarks of Marvel Characters, Inc. No similarity between any of the names, characters, persons, and/or institutions in this magazine with those of any living or dead person or institution is intended, and any such similarity which may exist is purely coincidental. **Printed in the U.S.A.** ALAN FINE, EVP - Office of the President, Marvel Worldwide, Inc. and EVP & CMO Marvel Characters B.V.; DAN BUCKLEY, Publisher & President - Print, Animation & Digital Divisions; JOE QUESADA, Chief Creative Officer; TOM BREVOORT, SVP of Publishing; DAVID BOGART, SVP of Operations & Procurement, Publishing; C.B. CEBULSKI, SVP & Associate Publisher, Publishing; C.B. CEBULSKI, SVP of Creator & Content Development; DAVID GABRIEL, SVP of Publishing Sales & Circulation; MICHAEL PASCIULLO, SVP of Brand Planning & Communications; JIM O'KEEFE, VP of Operations & Logistics; DAN CARR, Executive Director of Publishing Technology; SUSAN CRESPI, Editorial Operations Manager; ALEX MORALES, Publishing Operations Manager; STAN LEE, Chairman Emeritus. For information regarding advertising in Marvel Comics or on Marvel.com, please contact John Dokes, SVP Integrated Sales and Marketing, at jdokes@marvel.com. For Marvel subscription inquiries, please call 800-217-9158. **Manufactured between 5/17/2012 and 6/5/2012 by QUAD/GRAPHICS, DUBUQUE, IA, USA.**

10 9 8 7 6 5 4 3 2 1

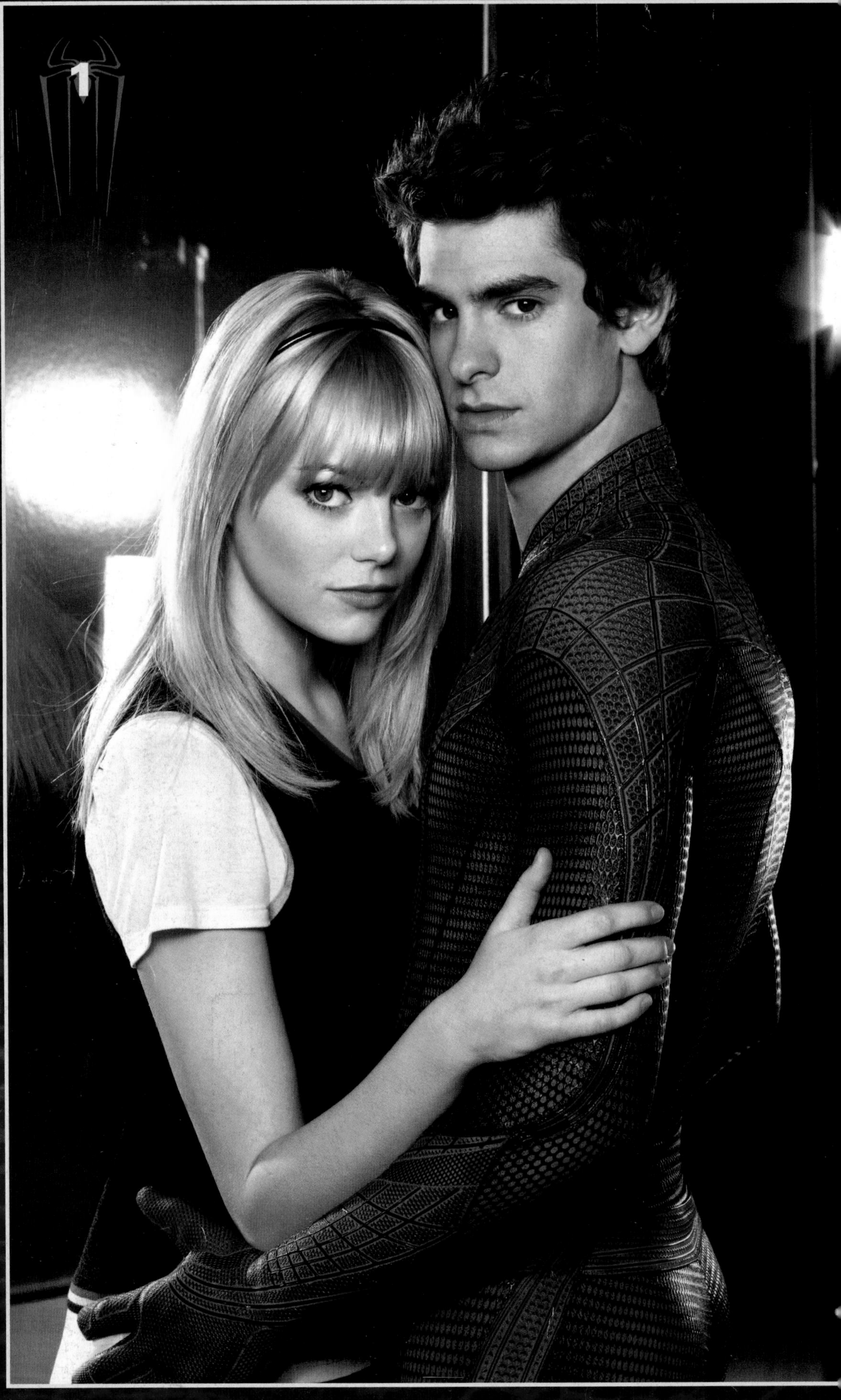

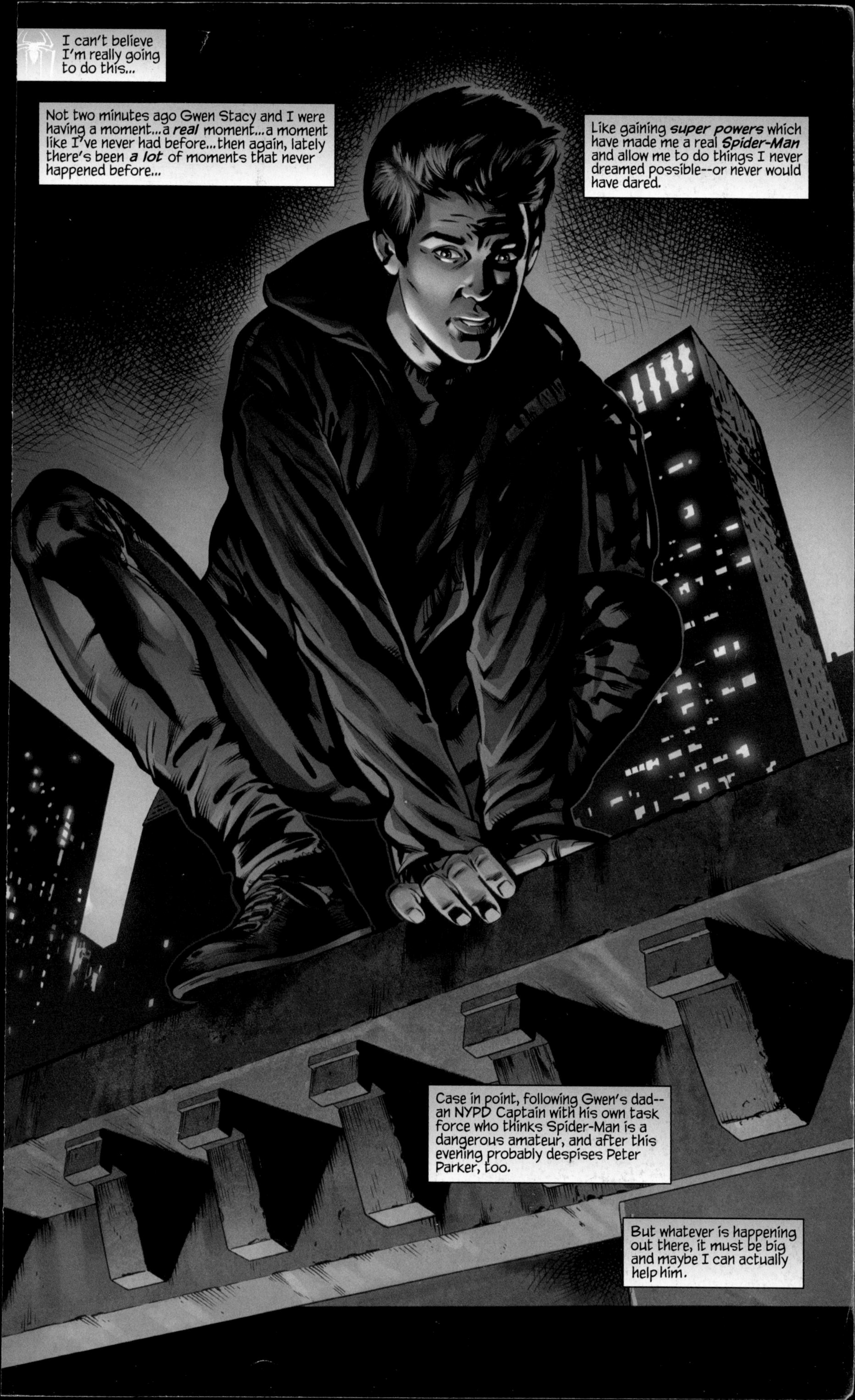
I can't believe I'm really going to do this...
Not two minutes ago Gwen Stacy and I were having a moment...a *real* moment...a moment like I've never had before...then again, lately there's been *a lot* of moments that never happened before...
Like gaining *super powers* which have made me a real *Spider-Man* and allow me to do things I never dreamed possible--or never would have dared.
Case in point, following Gwen's dad--an NYPD Captain with his own task force who thinks Spider-Man is a dangerous amateur, and after this evening probably despises Peter Parker, too.
But whatever is happening out there, it must be big and maybe I can actually help him.

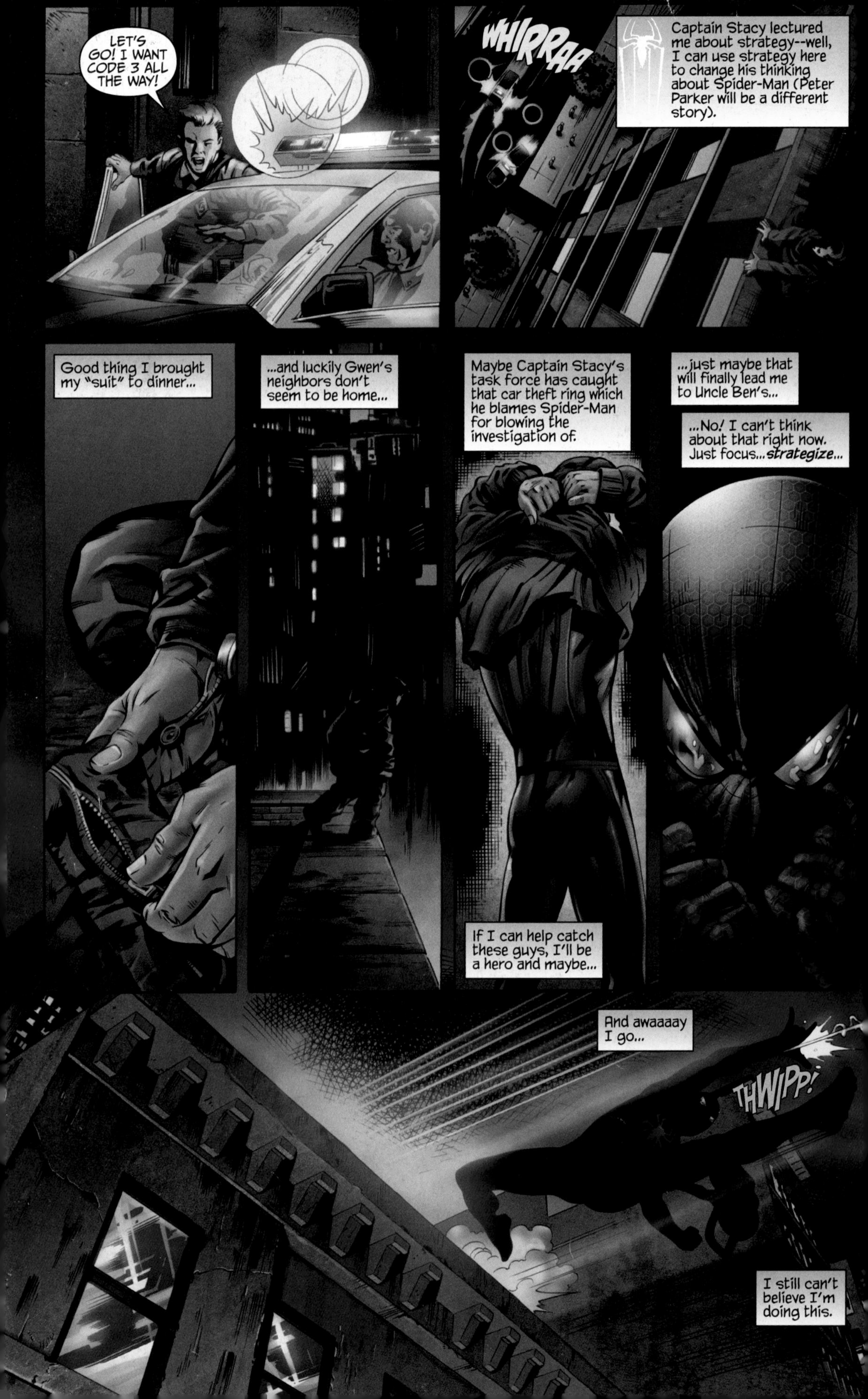
LET'S GO! I WANT CODE 3 ALL THE WAY!
WHIRRAA
Captain Stacy lectured me about strategy--well, I can use strategy here to change his thinking about Spider-Man (Peter Parker will be a different story).
Good thing I brought my "suit" to dinner...
...and luckily Gwen's neighbors don't seem to be home...
Maybe Captain Stacy's task force has caught that car theft ring which he blames Spider-Man for blowing the investigation of.
If I can help catch these guys, I'll be a hero and maybe...
...just maybe that will finally lead me to Uncle Ben's...
...No! I can't think about that right now. Just focus...*strategize*...
And awaaaay I go...
THWIPP!
I still can't believe I'm doing this.

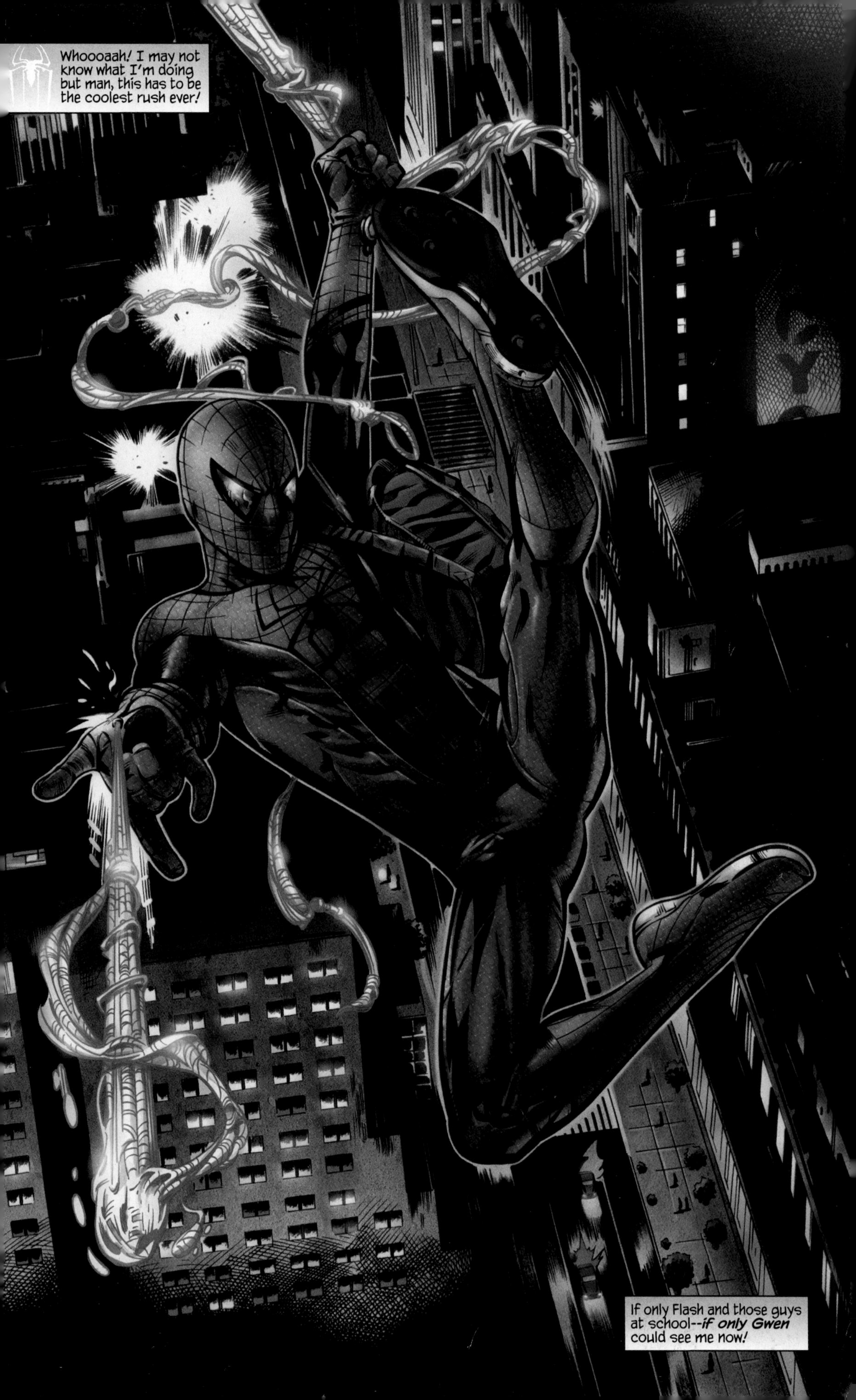
Whoooaah! I may not know what I'm doing but man, this has to be the coolest rush ever!
If only Flash and those guys at school--*if only Gwen* could see me now!

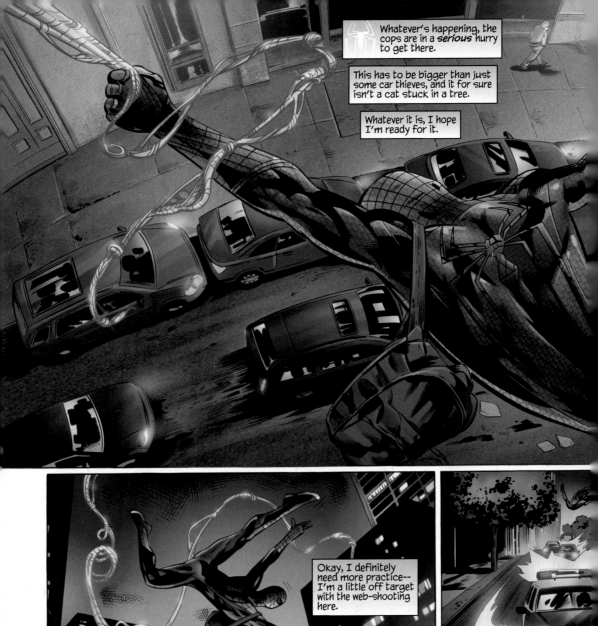

Whatever's happening, the cops are in a *serious* hurry to get there.

This has to be bigger than just some car thieves, and it for sure isn't a cat stuck in a tree.

Whatever it is, I hope I'm ready for it.

Okay, I definitely need more practice-- I'm a little off target with the web-shooting here.

I have to be honest, I'm feeling more than a little nervous.

Not only do I have no idea what I'm getting into but what if I mess this up, too? Sheesh, Captain Stacy will *really* hate me then.

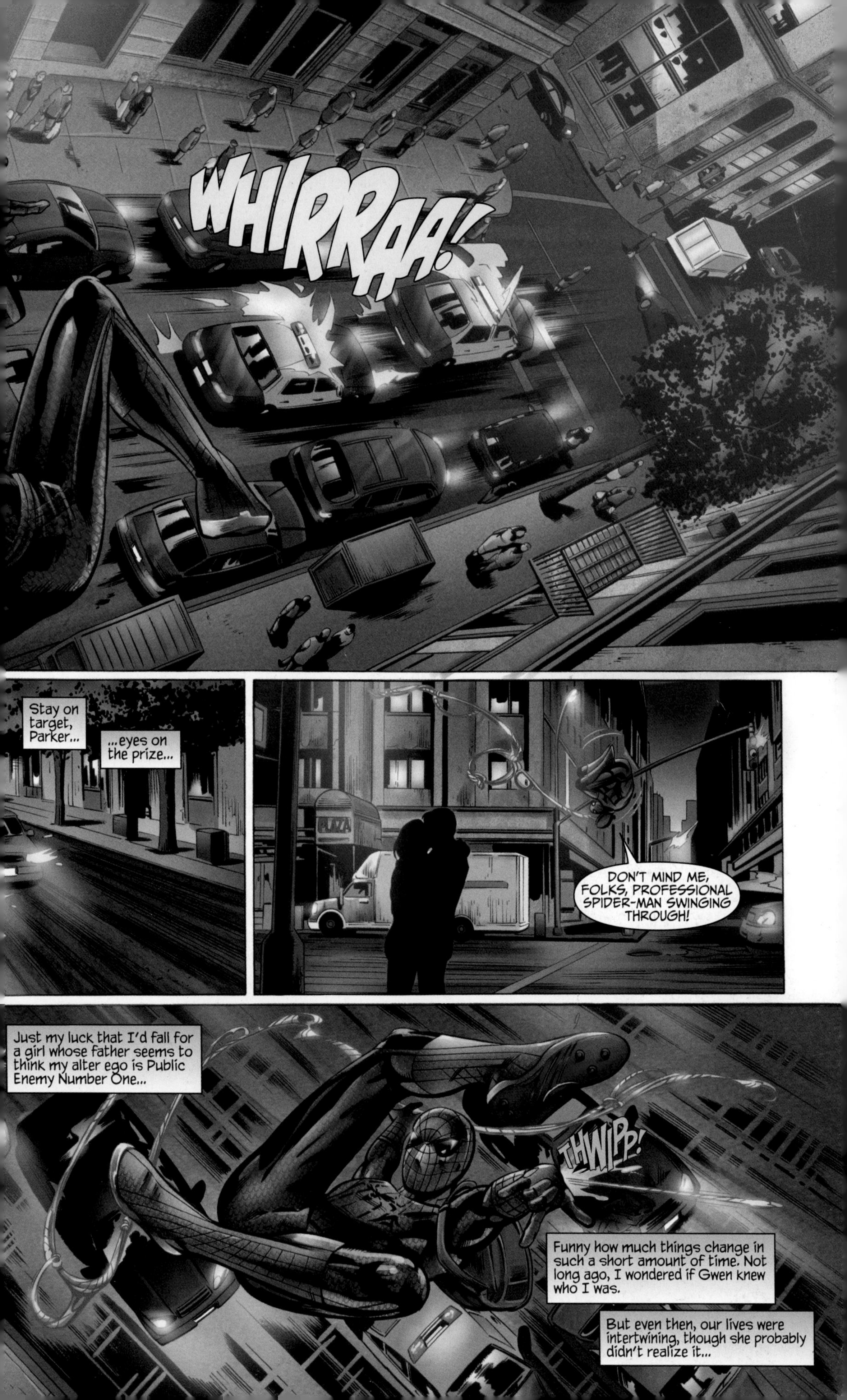
WHIRRAA!
Stay on target, Parker...
...eyes on the prize...
PLAZA
DON'T MIND ME, FOLKS, PROFESSIONAL SPIDER-MAN SWINGING THROUGH!
Just my luck that I'd fall for a girl whose father seems to think my alter ego is Public Enemy Number One...
THWIPP!
Funny how much things change in such a short amount of time. Not long ago, I wondered if Gwen knew who I was.
But even then, our lives were intertwining, though she probably didn't realize it...

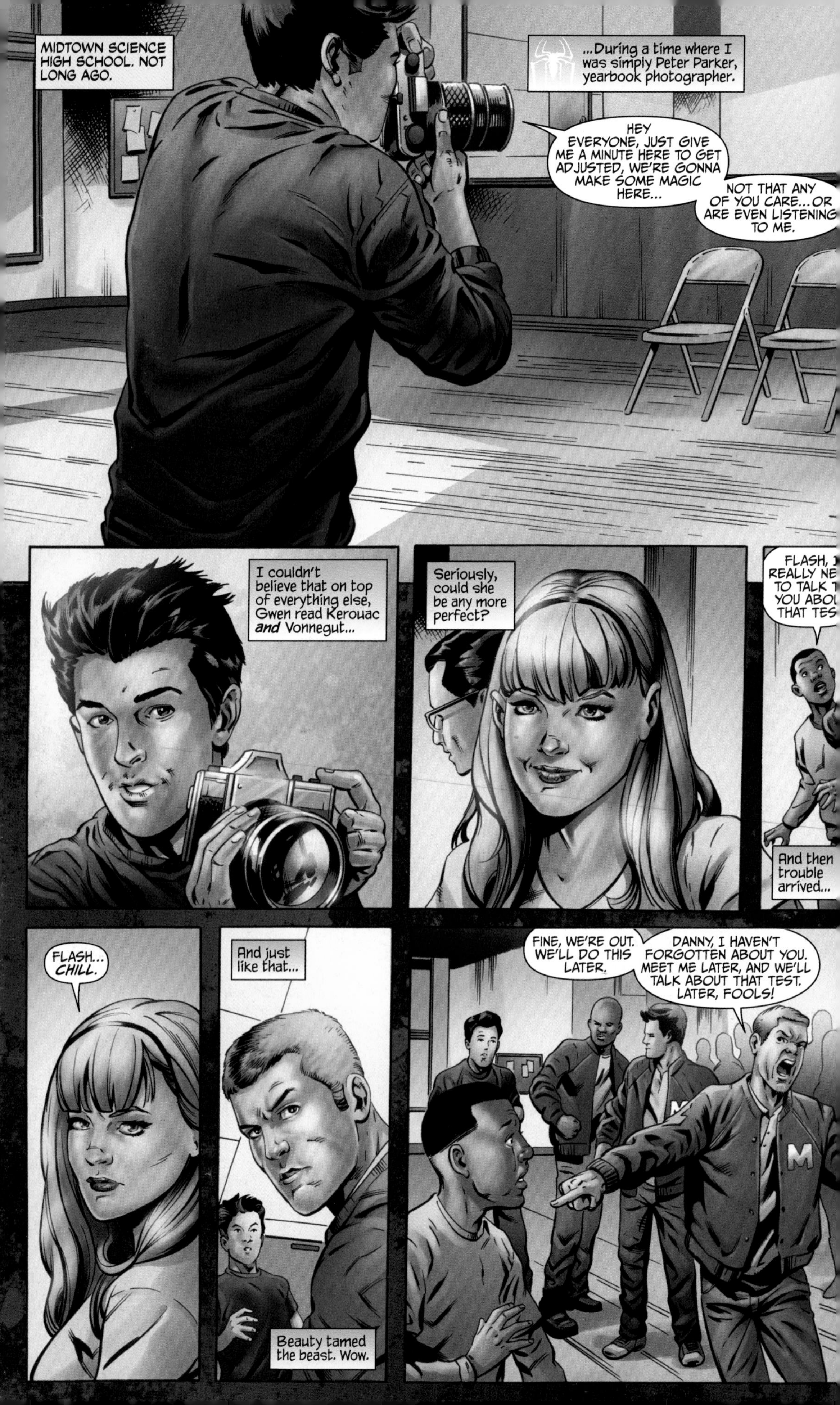
MIDTOWN SCIENCE HIGH SCHOOL. NOT LONG AGO.
...During a time where I was simply Peter Parker, yearbook photographer.
HEY EVERYONE, JUST GIVE ME A MINUTE HERE TO GET ADJUSTED, WE'RE GONNA MAKE SOME MAGIC HERE...
NOT THAT ANY OF YOU CARE...OR ARE EVEN LISTENING TO ME.
I couldn't believe that on top of everything else, Gwen read Kerouac *and* Vonnegut...
Seriously, could she be any more perfect?
And then trouble arrived...
FLASH... *CHILL*.
And just like that...
Beauty tamed the beast. Wow.
FINE, WE'RE OUT. WE'LL DO THIS LATER.
DANNY, I HAVEN'T FORGOTTEN ABOUT YOU. MEET ME LATER, AND WE'LL TALK ABOUT THAT TEST. LATER, FOOLS!

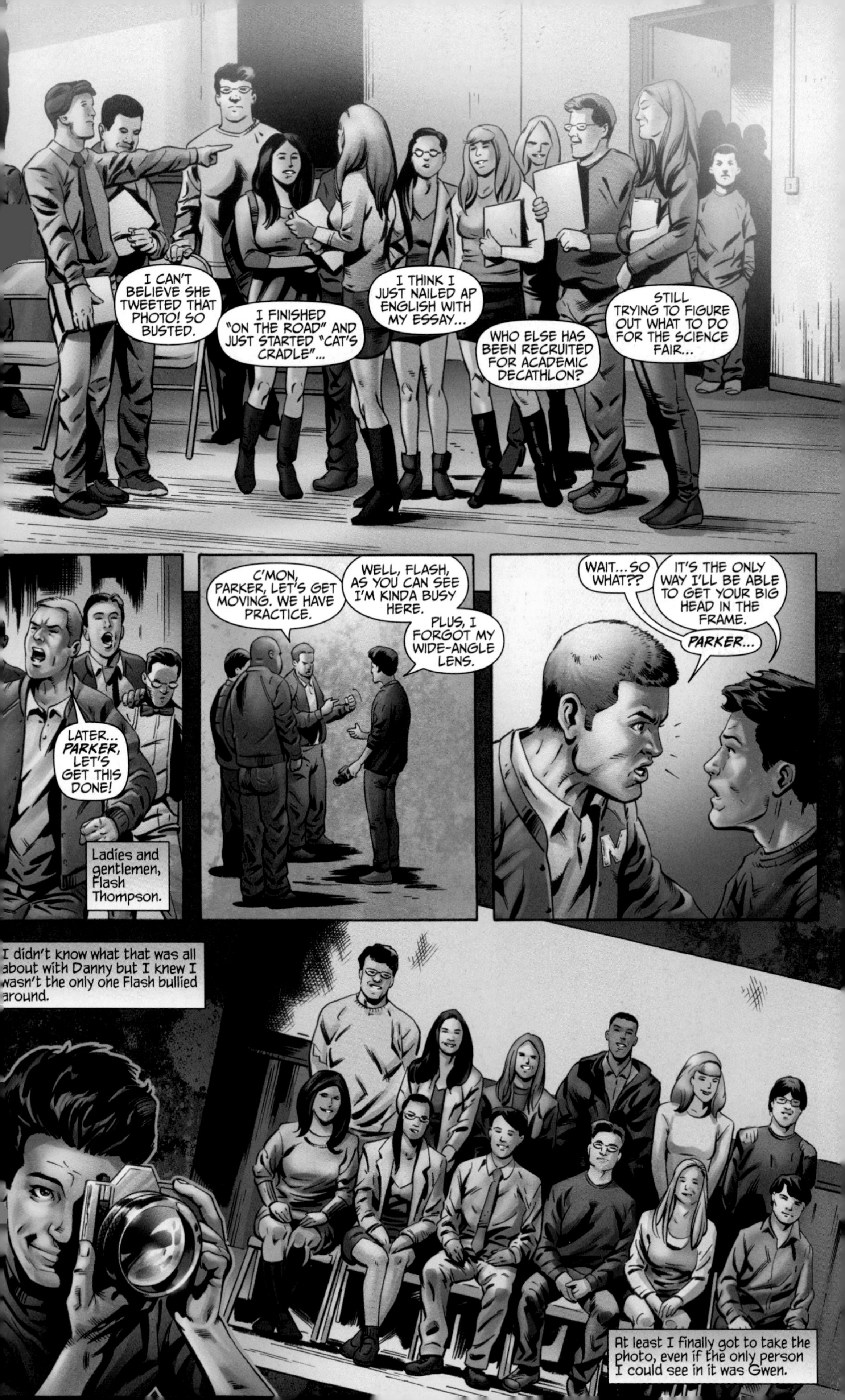
I CAN'T BELIEVE SHE TWEETED THAT PHOTO! SO BUSTED.
I FINISHED "ON THE ROAD" AND JUST STARTED "CAT'S CRADLE"...
I THINK I JUST NAILED AP ENGLISH WITH MY ESSAY...
WHO ELSE HAS BEEN RECRUITED FOR ACADEMIC DECATHLON?
STILL TRYING TO FIGURE OUT WHAT TO DO FOR THE SCIENCE FAIR...
LATER... PARKER, LET'S GET THIS DONE!
Ladies and gentlemen, Flash Thompson.
C'MON, PARKER, LET'S GET MOVING. WE HAVE PRACTICE.
WELL, FLASH, AS YOU CAN SEE I'M KINDA BUSY HERE.
PLUS, I FORGOT MY WIDE-ANGLE LENS.
WAIT... SO WHAT??
IT'S THE ONLY WAY I'LL BE ABLE TO GET YOUR BIG HEAD IN THE FRAME.
PARKER...
I didn't know what that was all about with Danny but I knew I wasn't the only one Flash bullied around.
At least I finally got to take the photo, even if the only person I could see in it was Gwen.

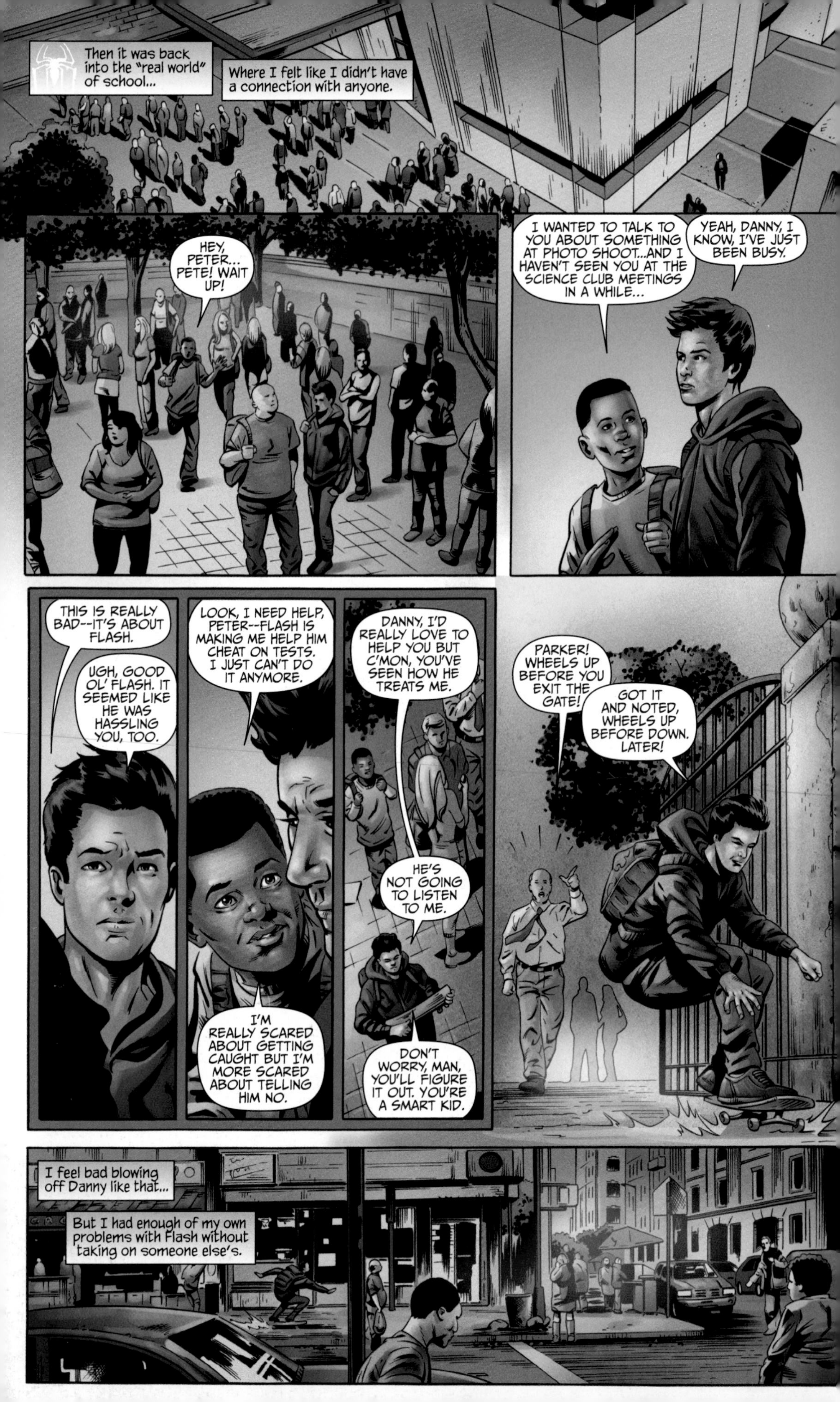

Then it was back into the "real world" of school...
Where I felt like I didn't have a connection with anyone.
HEY, PETER... PETE! WAIT UP!
I WANTED TO TALK TO YOU ABOUT SOMETHING AT PHOTO SHOOT...AND I HAVEN'T SEEN YOU AT THE SCIENCE CLUB MEETINGS IN A WHILE...
YEAH, DANNY, I KNOW, I'VE JUST BEEN BUSY.
THIS IS REALLY BAD--IT'S ABOUT FLASH.
UGH, GOOD OL' FLASH. IT SEEMED LIKE HE WAS HASSLING YOU, TOO.
LOOK, I NEED HELP, PETER--FLASH IS MAKING ME HELP HIM CHEAT ON TESTS. I JUST CAN'T DO IT ANYMORE.
I'M REALLY SCARED ABOUT GETTING CAUGHT BUT I'M MORE SCARED ABOUT TELLING HIM NO.
DANNY, I'D REALLY LOVE TO HELP YOU BUT C'MON, YOU'VE SEEN HOW HE TREATS ME.
HE'S NOT GOING TO LISTEN TO ME.
DON'T WORRY, MAN, YOU'LL FIGURE IT OUT. YOU'RE A SMART KID.
PARKER! WHEELS UP BEFORE YOU EXIT THE GATE!
GOT IT AND NOTED, WHEELS UP BEFORE DOWN. LATER!
I feel bad blowing off Danny like that...
But I had enough of my own problems with Flash without taking on someone else's.

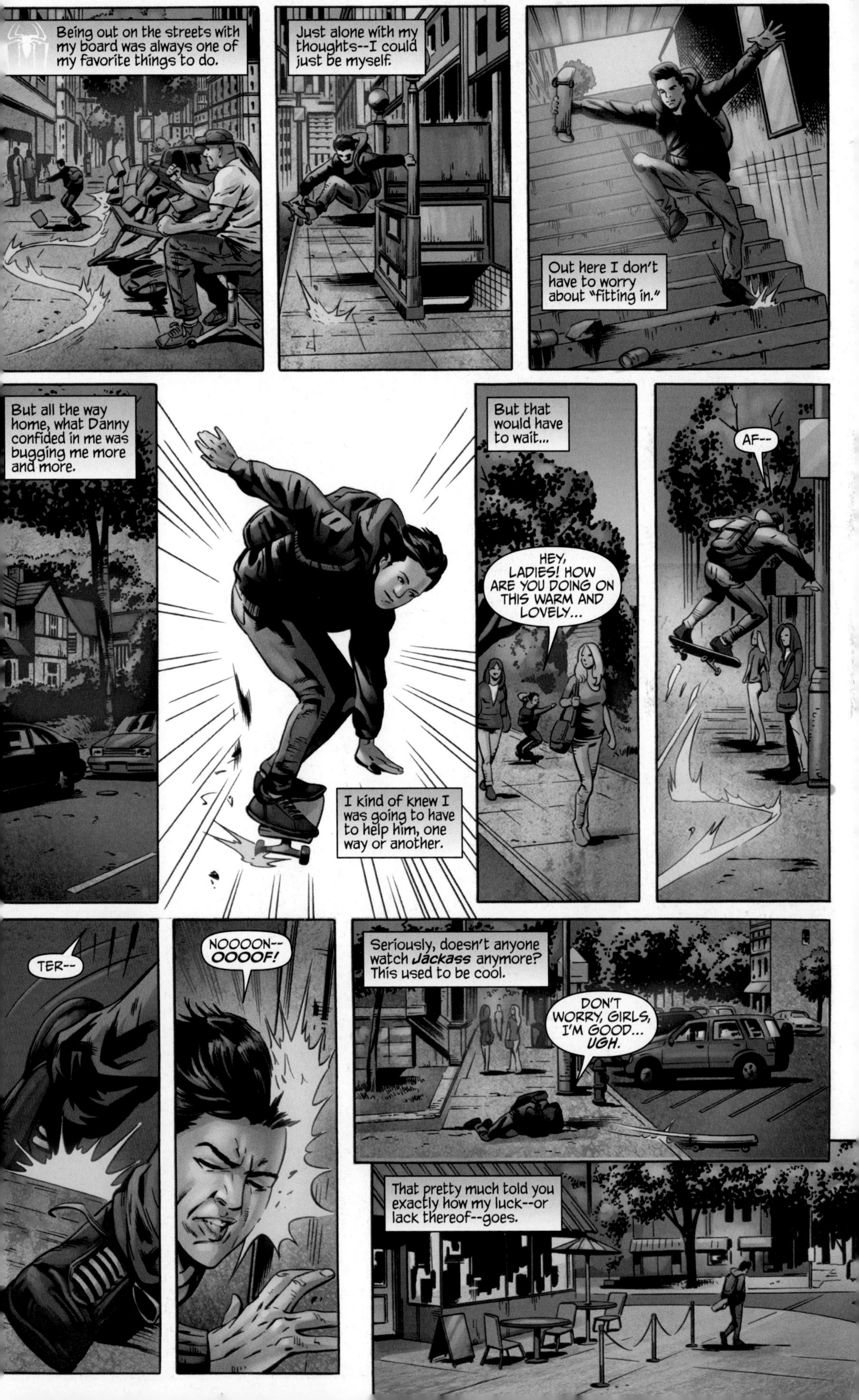
Being out on the streets with my board was always one of my favorite things to do.
Just alone with my thoughts--I could just be myself.
Out here I don't have to worry about "fitting in."
But all the way home, what Danny confided in me was bugging me more and more.
I kind of knew I was going to have to help him, one way or another.
But that would have to wait...
HEY, LADIES! HOW ARE YOU DOING ON THIS WARM AND LOVELY...
AF--
TER--
NOOOON--OOOOF!
Seriously, doesn't anyone watch Jackass anymore? This used to be cool.
DON'T WORRY, GIRLS, I'M GOOD... UGH.
That pretty much told you exactly how my luck--or lack thereof--goes.

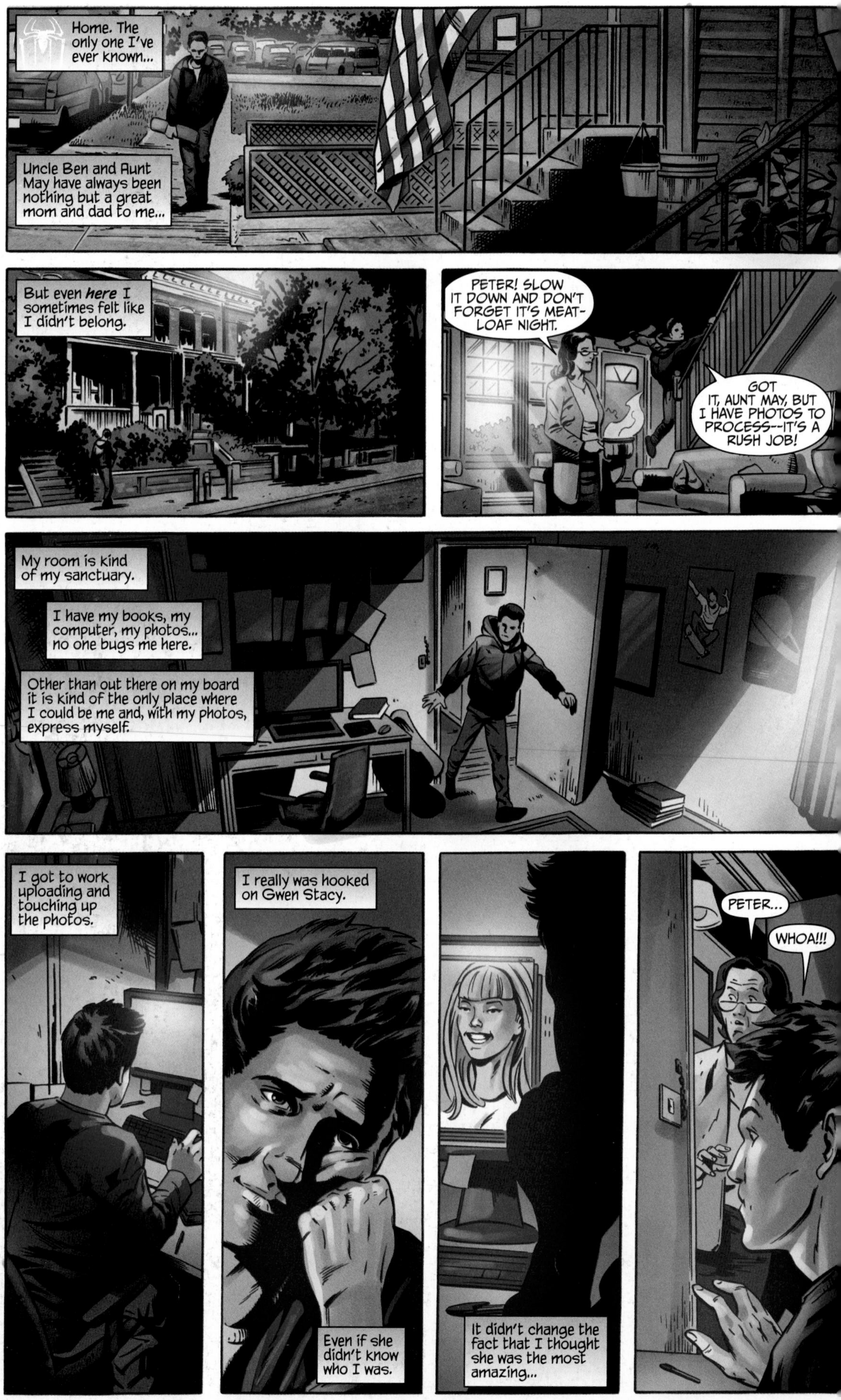
Home. The only one I've ever known...
Uncle Ben and Aunt May have always been nothing but a great mom and dad to me...
But even *here* I sometimes felt like I didn't belong.
PETER! SLOW IT DOWN AND DON'T FORGET IT'S MEAT-LOAF NIGHT.
GOT IT, AUNT MAY, BUT I HAVE PHOTOS TO PROCESS--IT'S A RUSH JOB!
My room is kind of my sanctuary.
I have my books, my computer, my photos... no one bugs me here.
Other than out there on my board it is kind of the only place where I could be me and, with my photos, express myself.
I got to work uploading and touching up the photos.
I really was hooked on Gwen Stacy.
Even if she didn't know who I was.
It didn't change the fact that I thought she was the most amazing...
PETER...
WHOA!!!

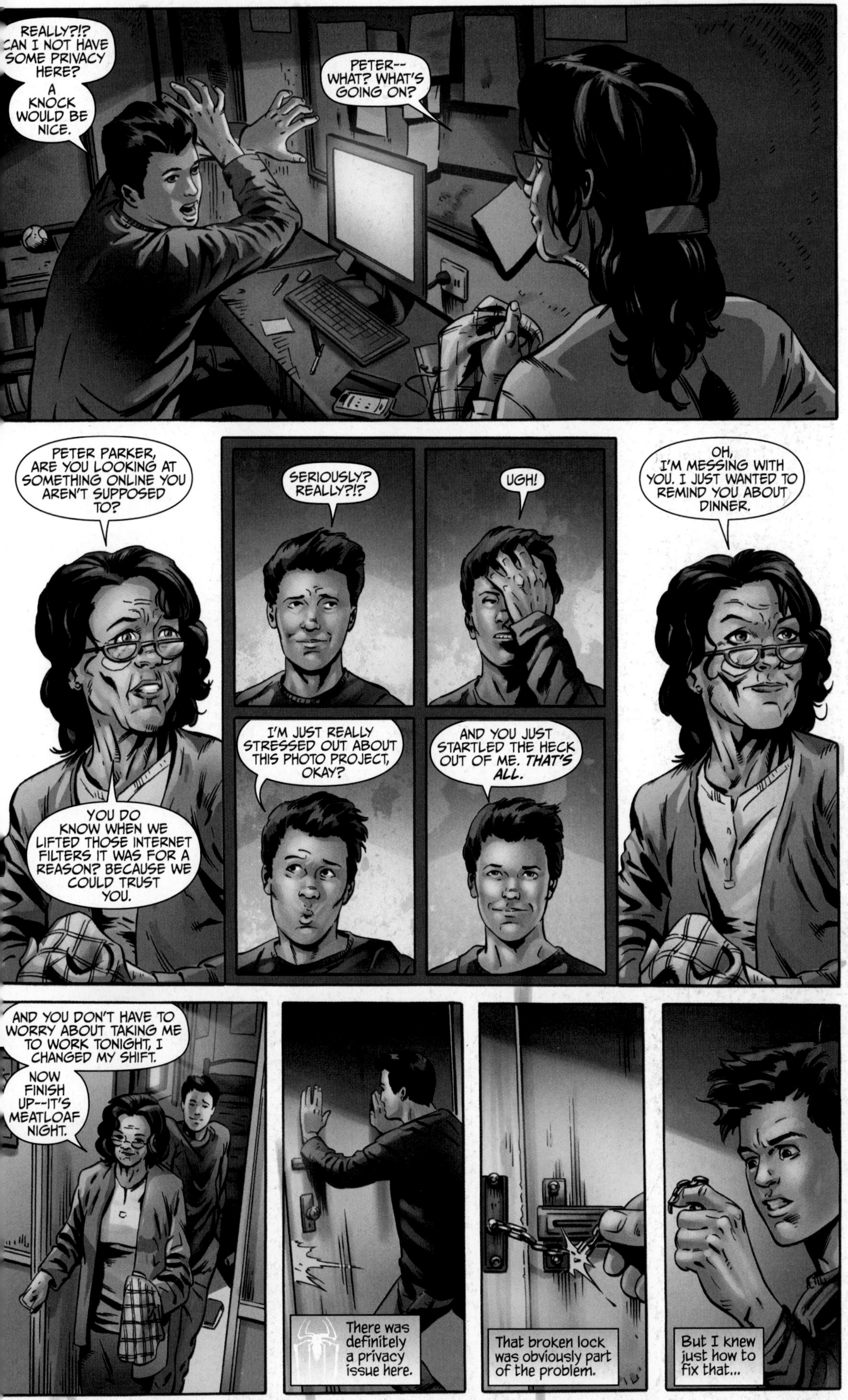
REALLY?!? CAN I NOT HAVE SOME PRIVACY HERE?
A KNOCK WOULD BE NICE.
PETER-- WHAT? WHAT'S GOING ON?
PETER PARKER, ARE YOU LOOKING AT SOMETHING ONLINE YOU AREN'T SUPPOSED TO?
YOU DO KNOW WHEN WE LIFTED THOSE INTERNET FILTERS IT WAS FOR A REASON? BECAUSE WE COULD TRUST YOU.
SERIOUSLY? REALLY?!?
UGH!
I'M JUST REALLY STRESSED OUT ABOUT THIS PHOTO PROJECT, OKAY?
AND YOU JUST STARTLED THE HECK OUT OF ME. *THAT'S ALL.*
OH, I'M MESSING WITH YOU. I JUST WANTED TO REMIND YOU ABOUT DINNER.
AND YOU DON'T HAVE TO WORRY ABOUT TAKING ME TO WORK TONIGHT, I CHANGED MY SHIFT.
NOW FINISH UP--IT'S MEATLOAF NIGHT.
There was definitely a privacy issue here.
That broken lock was obviously part of the problem.
But I knew just how to fix that...

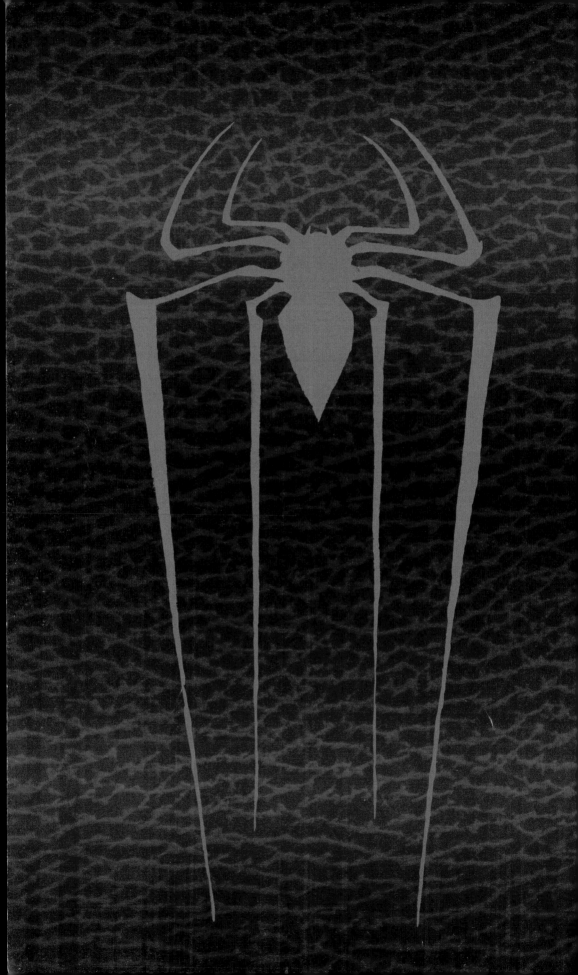

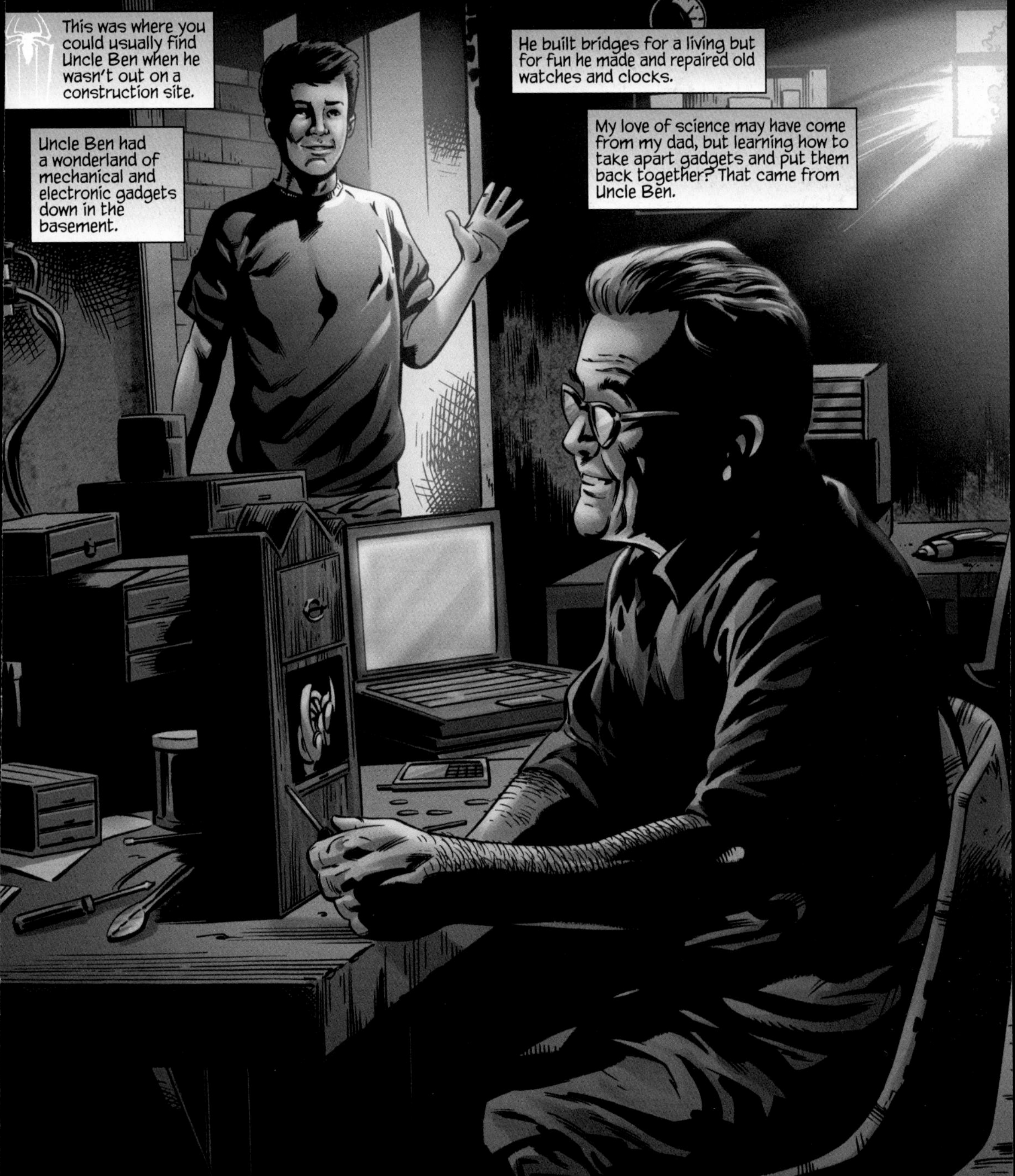
This was where you could usually find Uncle Ben when he wasn't out on a construction site.
Uncle Ben had a wonderland of mechanical and electronic gadgets down in the basement.
He built bridges for a living but for fun he made and repaired old watches and clocks.
My love of science may have come from my dad, but learning how to take apart gadgets and put them back together? That came from Uncle Ben.
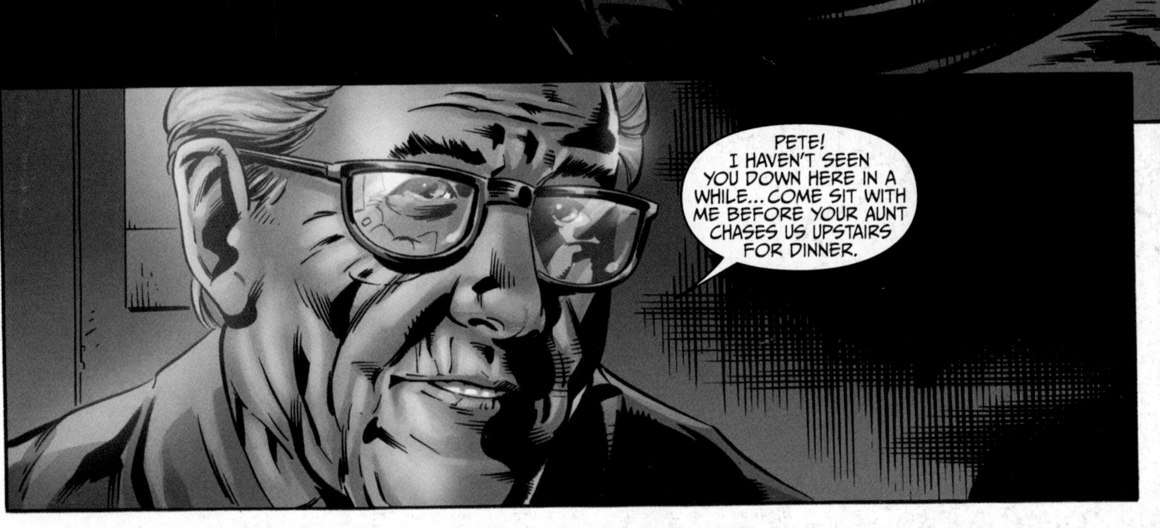
PETE! I HAVEN'T SEEN YOU DOWN HERE IN A WHILE... COME SIT WITH ME BEFORE YOUR AUNT CHASES US UPSTAIRS FOR DINNER.

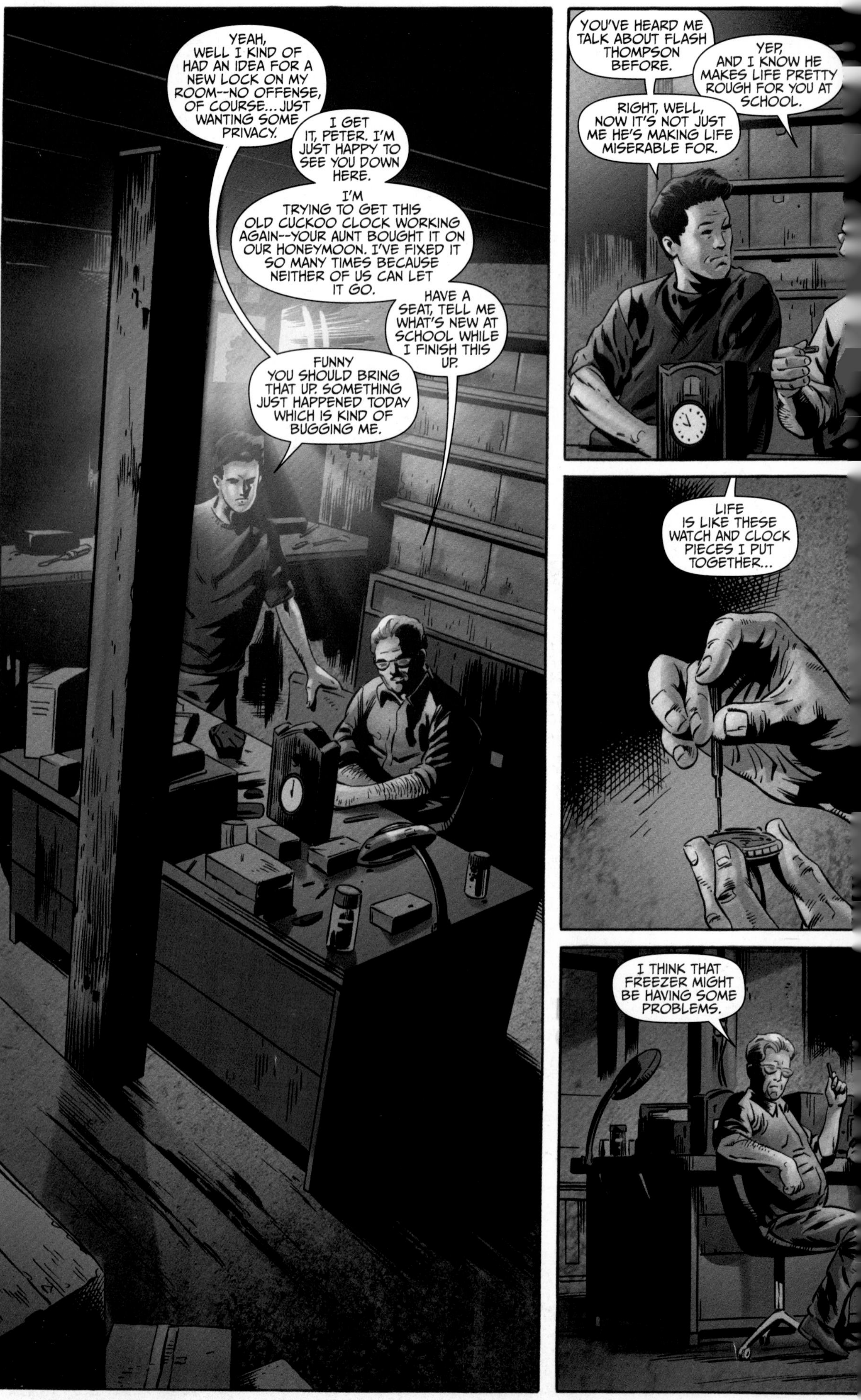
YEAH, WELL I KIND OF HAD AN IDEA FOR A NEW LOCK ON MY ROOM--NO OFFENSE, OF COURSE... JUST WANTING SOME PRIVACY.
I GET IT, PETER. I'M JUST HAPPY TO SEE YOU DOWN HERE.
I'M TRYING TO GET THIS OLD CUCKOO CLOCK WORKING AGAIN--YOUR AUNT BOUGHT IT ON OUR HONEYMOON. I'VE FIXED IT SO MANY TIMES BECAUSE NEITHER OF US CAN LET IT GO.
HAVE A SEAT, TELL ME WHAT'S NEW AT SCHOOL WHILE I FINISH THIS UP.
FUNNY YOU SHOULD BRING THAT UP. SOMETHING JUST HAPPENED TODAY WHICH IS KIND OF BUGGING ME.
YOU'VE HEARD ME TALK ABOUT FLASH THOMPSON BEFORE.
YEP, AND I KNOW HE MAKES LIFE PRETTY ROUGH FOR YOU AT SCHOOL.
RIGHT, WELL, NOW IT'S NOT JUST ME HE'S MAKING LIFE MISERABLE FOR.
LIFE IS LIKE THESE WATCH AND CLOCK PIECES I PUT TOGETHER...
I THINK THAT FREEZER MIGHT BE HAVING SOME PROBLEMS.

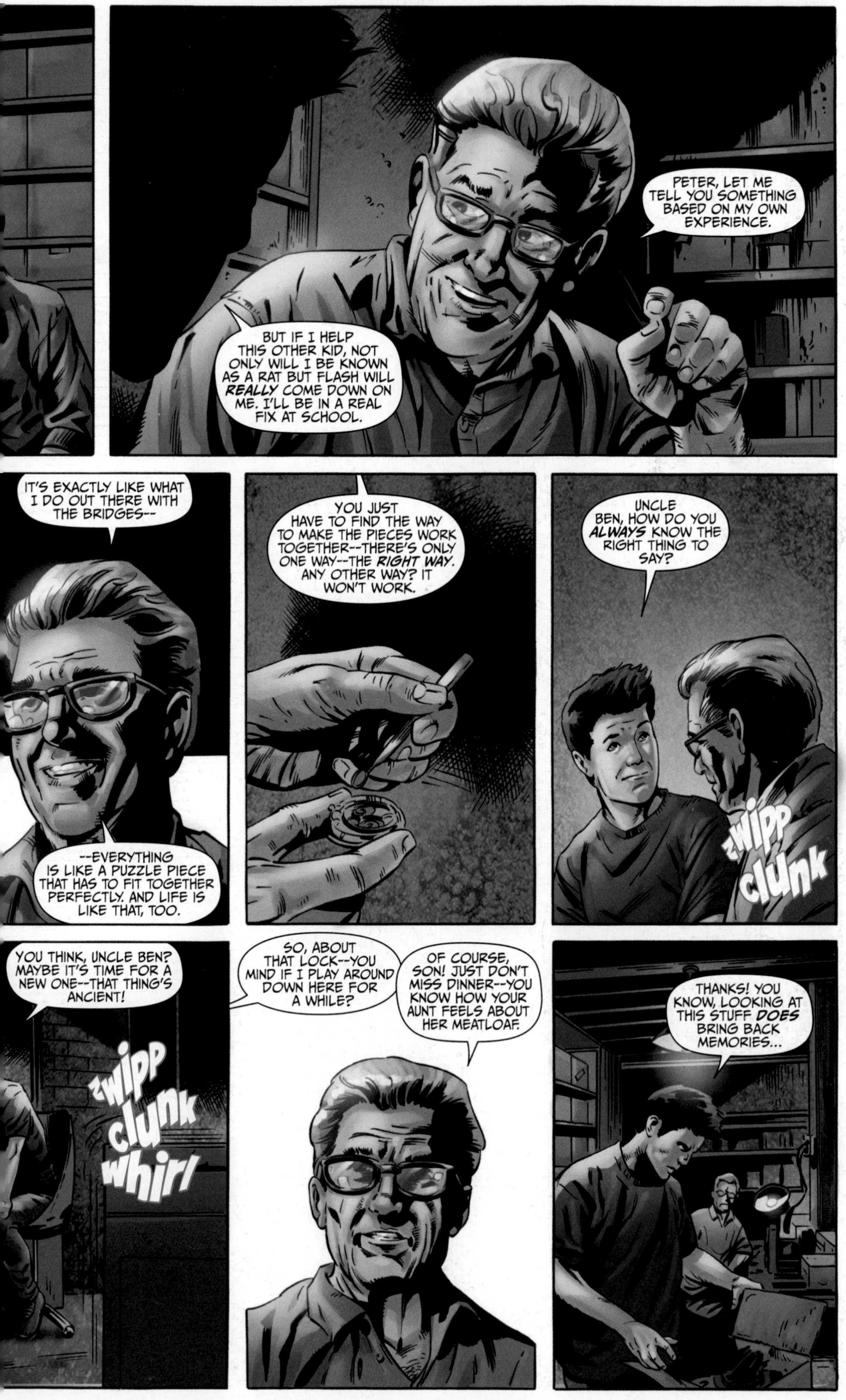
BUT IF I HELP THIS OTHER KID, NOT ONLY WILL I BE KNOWN AS A RAT BUT FLASH WILL REALLY COME DOWN ON ME. I'LL BE IN A REAL FIX AT SCHOOL.
PETER, LET ME TELL YOU SOMETHING BASED ON MY OWN EXPERIENCE.
IT'S EXACTLY LIKE WHAT I DO OUT THERE WITH THE BRIDGES--
--EVERYTHING IS LIKE A PUZZLE PIECE THAT HAS TO FIT TOGETHER PERFECTLY. AND LIFE IS LIKE THAT, TOO.
YOU JUST HAVE TO FIND THE WAY TO MAKE THE PIECES WORK TOGETHER--THERE'S ONLY ONE WAY--THE RIGHT WAY. ANY OTHER WAY? IT WON'T WORK.
UNCLE BEN, HOW DO YOU ALWAYS KNOW THE RIGHT THING TO SAY?
zWIPP
CLUNK
YOU THINK, UNCLE BEN? MAYBE IT'S TIME FOR A NEW ONE--THAT THING'S ANCIENT!
zWIPP
CLUNK
WHIRL
SO, ABOUT THAT LOCK--YOU MIND IF I PLAY AROUND DOWN HERE FOR A WHILE?
OF COURSE, SON! JUST DON'T MISS DINNER--YOU KNOW HOW YOUR AUNT FEELS ABOUT HER MEATLOAF.
THANKS! YOU KNOW, LOOKING AT THIS STUFF DOES BRING BACK MEMORIES...

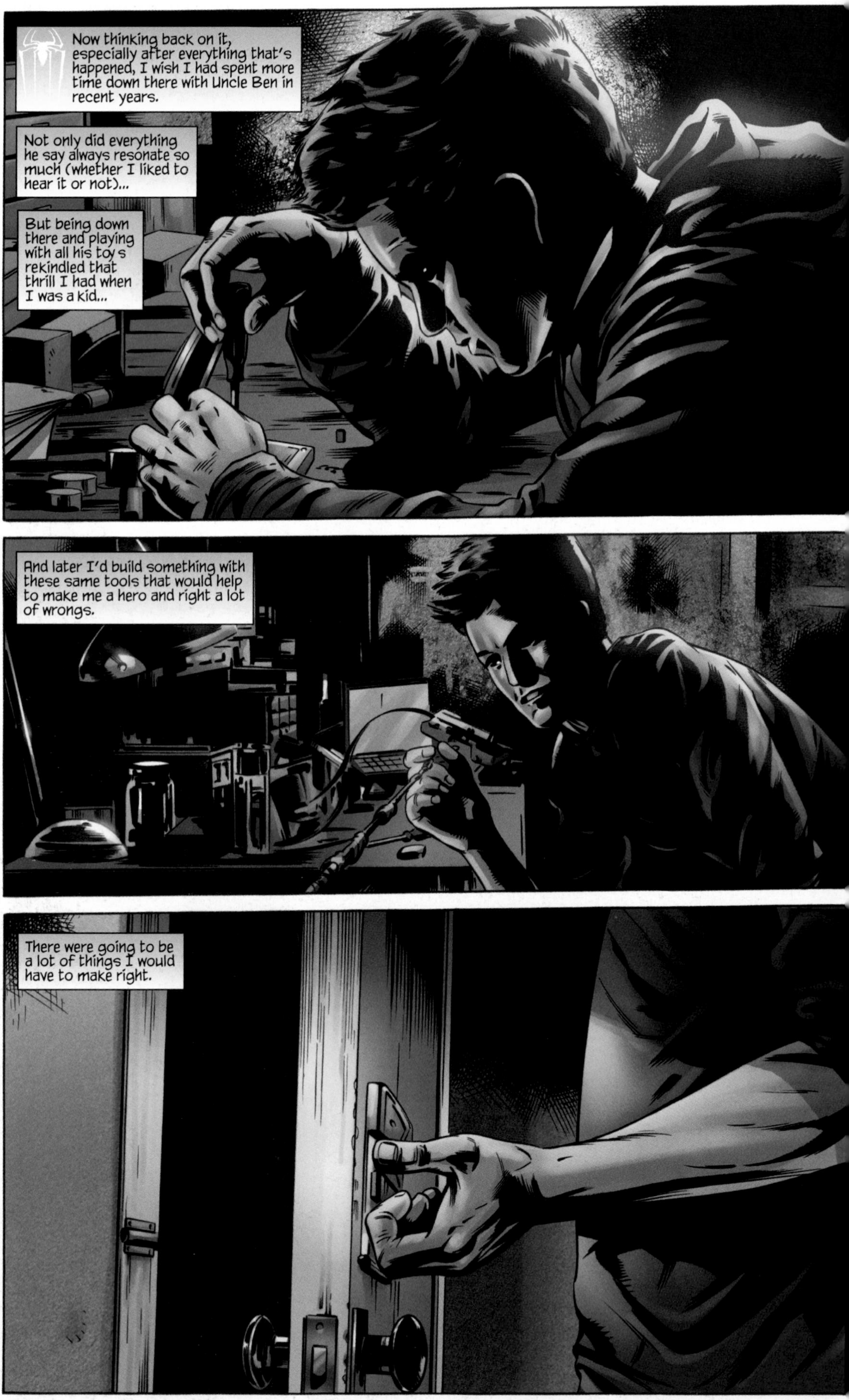
Now thinking back on it, especially after everything that's happened, I wish I had spent more time down there with Uncle Ben in recent years.
Not only did everything he say always resonate so much (whether I liked to hear it or not)...
But being down there and playing with all his toys rekindled that thrill I had when I was a kid...
And later I'd build something with these same tools that would help to make me a hero and right a lot of wrongs.
There were going to be a lot of things I would have to make right.

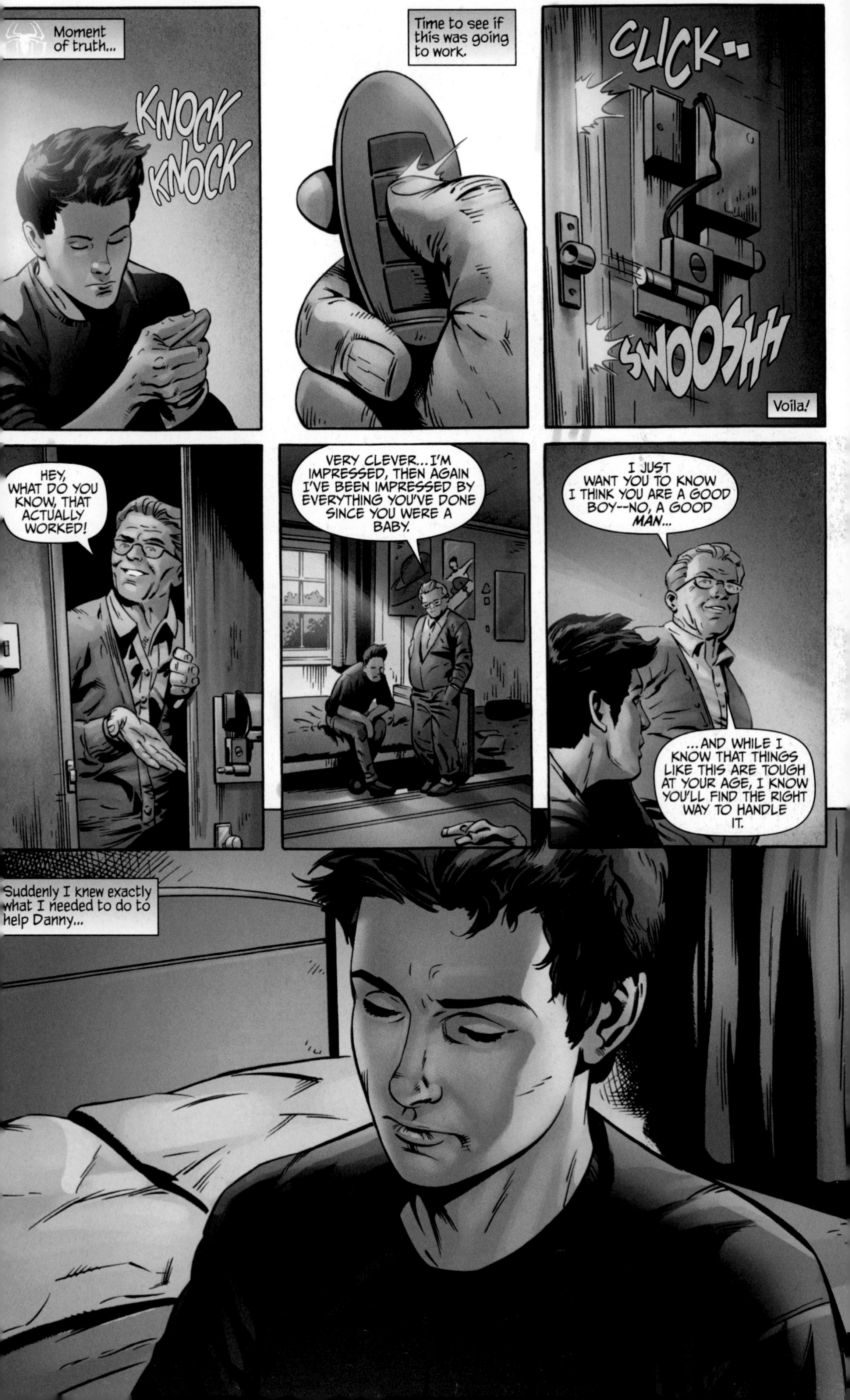
Moment of truth...
KNOCK KNOCK
Time to see if this was going to work.
CLICK..
SWOOSHH
Voila!
HEY, WHAT DO YOU KNOW, THAT ACTUALLY WORKED!
VERY CLEVER...I'M IMPRESSED, THEN AGAIN I'VE BEEN IMPRESSED BY EVERYTHING YOU'VE DONE SINCE YOU WERE A BABY.
I JUST WANT YOU TO KNOW I THINK YOU ARE A GOOD BOY--NO, A GOOD MAN...
...AND WHILE I KNOW THAT THINGS LIKE THIS ARE TOUGH AT YOUR AGE, I KNOW YOU'LL FIND THE RIGHT WAY TO HANDLE IT.
Suddenly I knew exactly what I needed to do to help Danny...

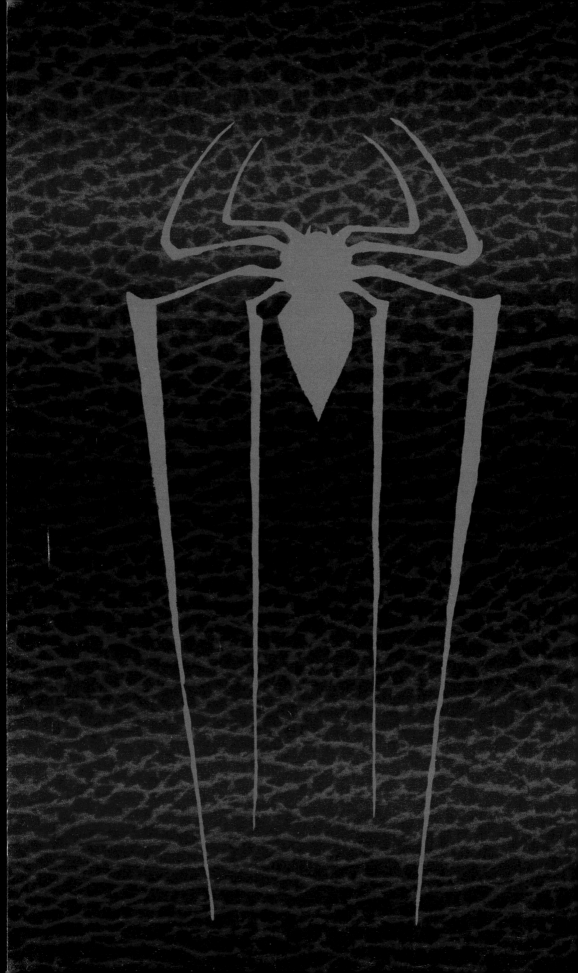

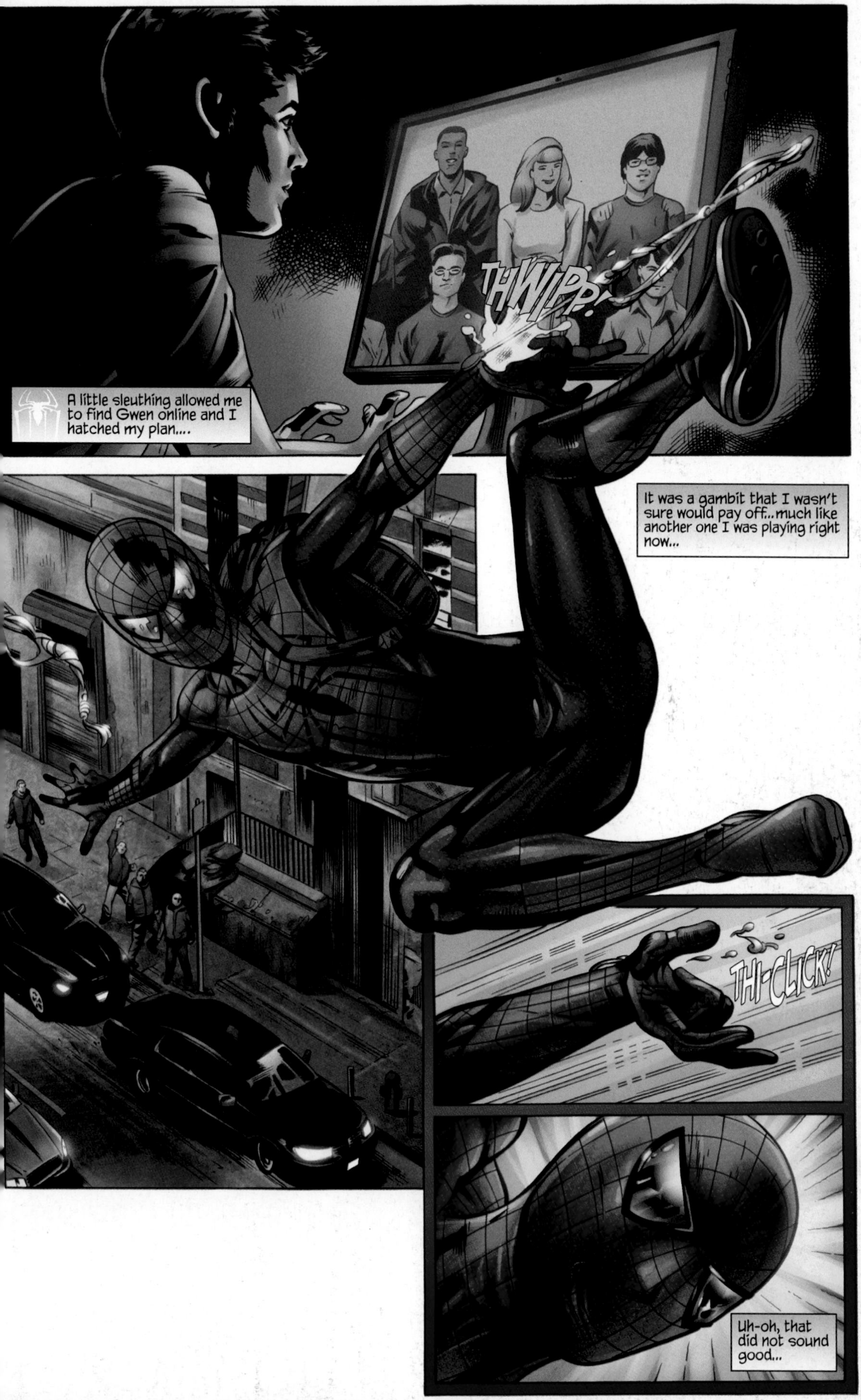
A little sleuthing allowed me to find Gwen online and I hatched my plan....
THWIPP!
It was a gambit that I wasn't sure would pay off...much like another one I was playing right now...
THI-CLICK!
Uh-oh, that did not sound good...

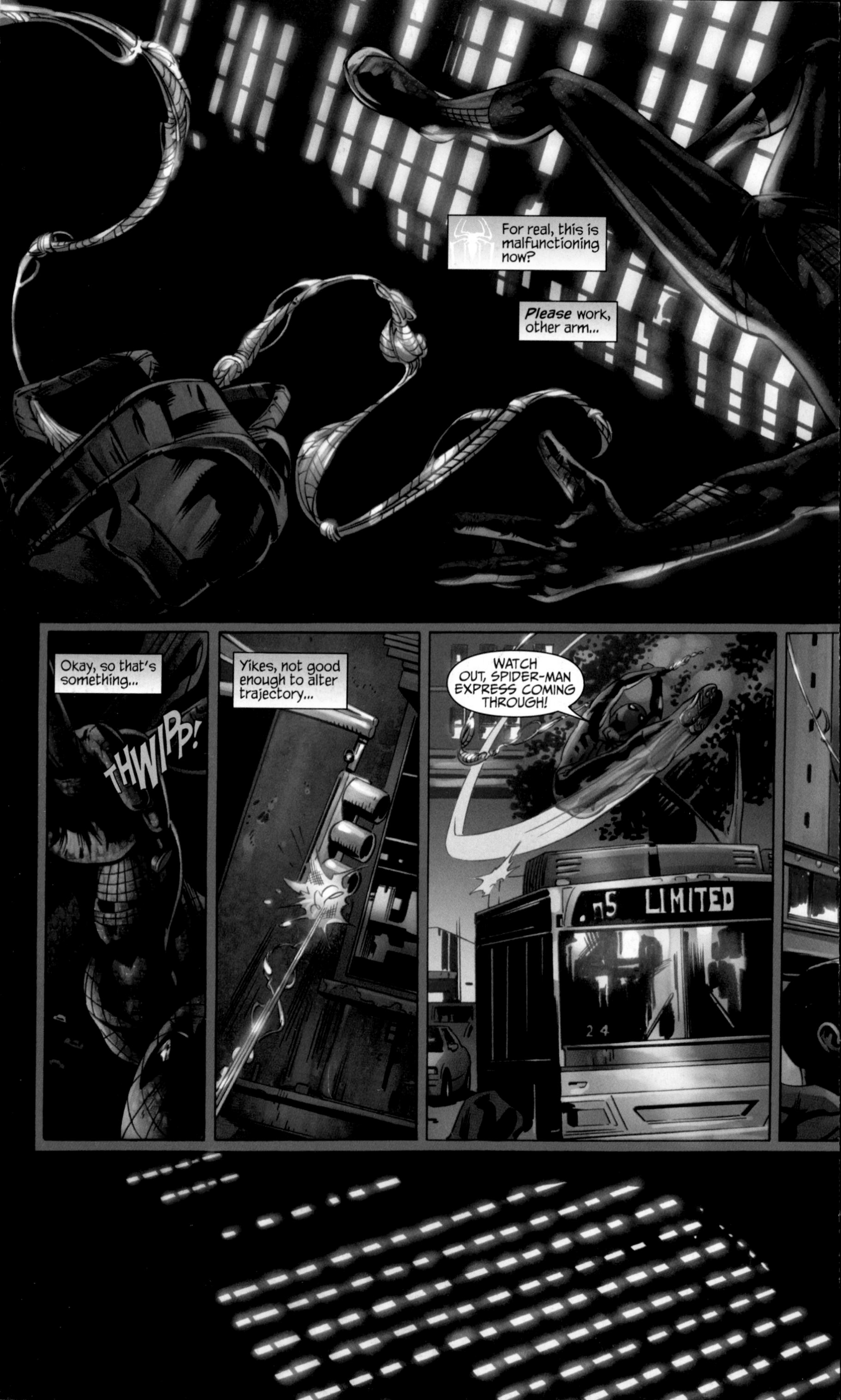

For real, this is malfunctioning now?
Please work, other arm...
Okay, so that's something...
THWIPP!
Yikes, not good enough to alter trajectory...
WATCH OUT, SPIDER-MAN EXPRESS COMING THROUGH!
M5 LIMITED
24

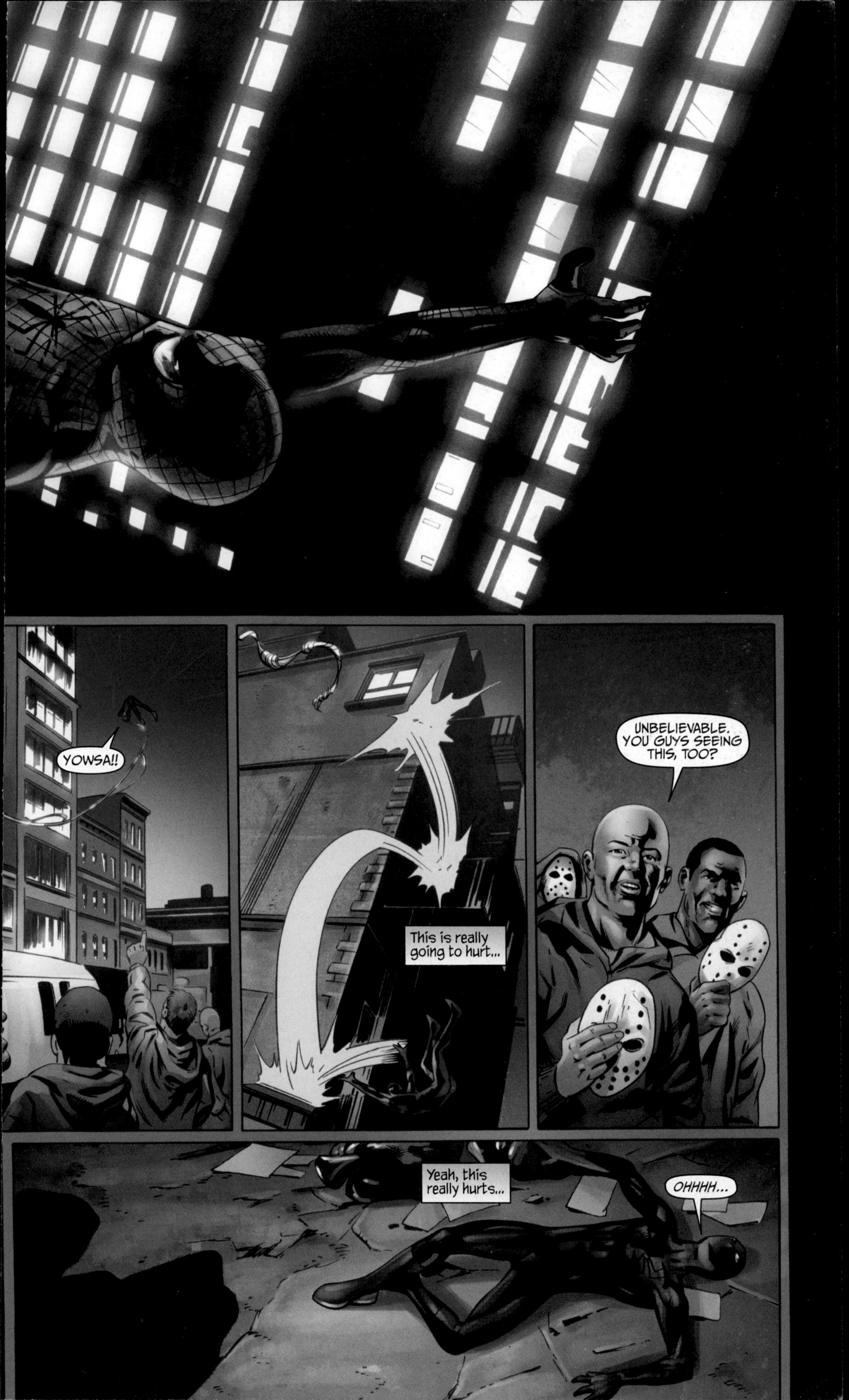
YOWSA!!
This is really going to hurt...
UNBELIEVABLE. YOU GUYS SEEING THIS, TOO?
Yeah, this really hurts...
OHHHH...

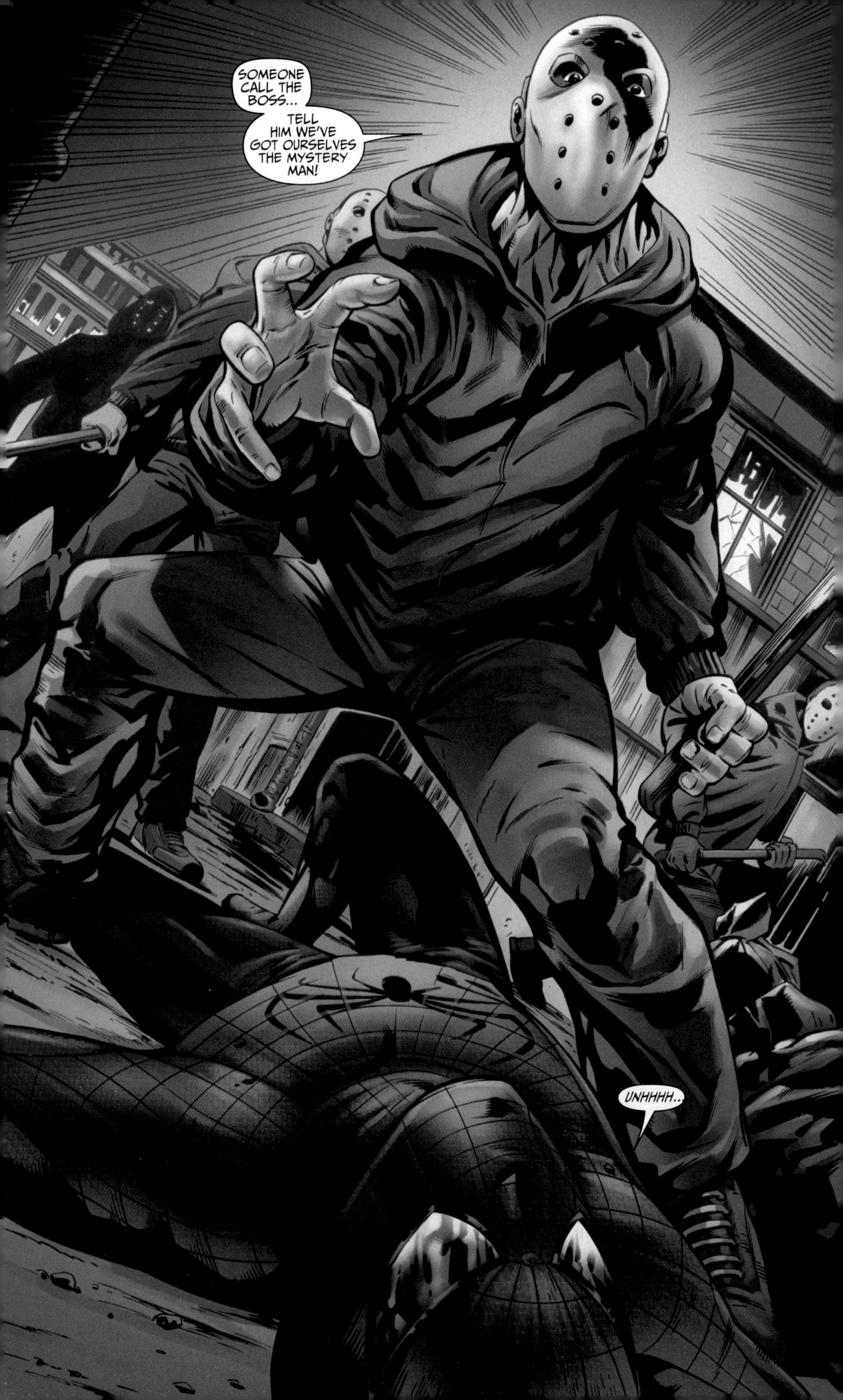
SOMEONE CALL THE BOSS...
TELL HIM WE'VE GOT OURSELVES THE MYSTERY MAN!
UNHHHH...

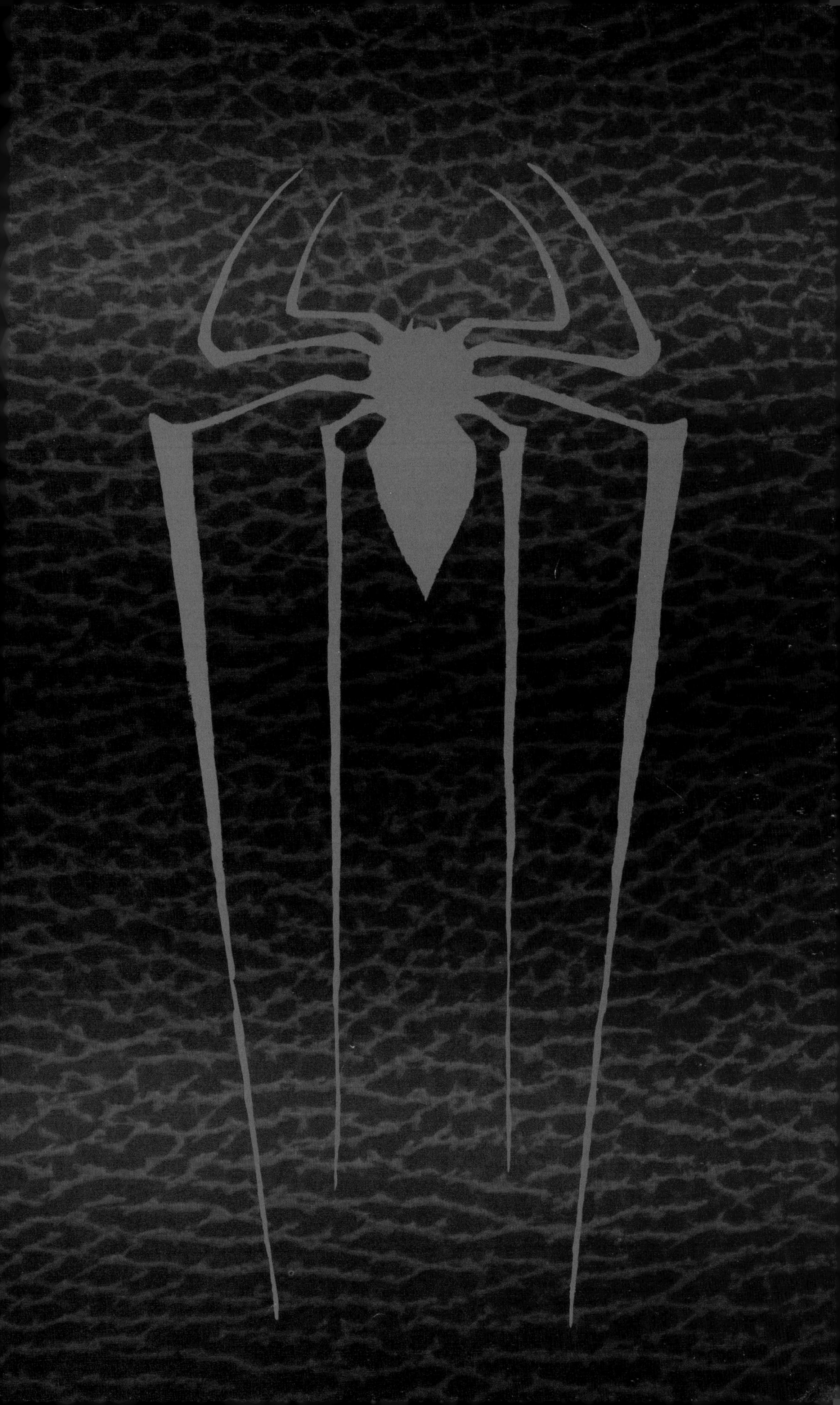

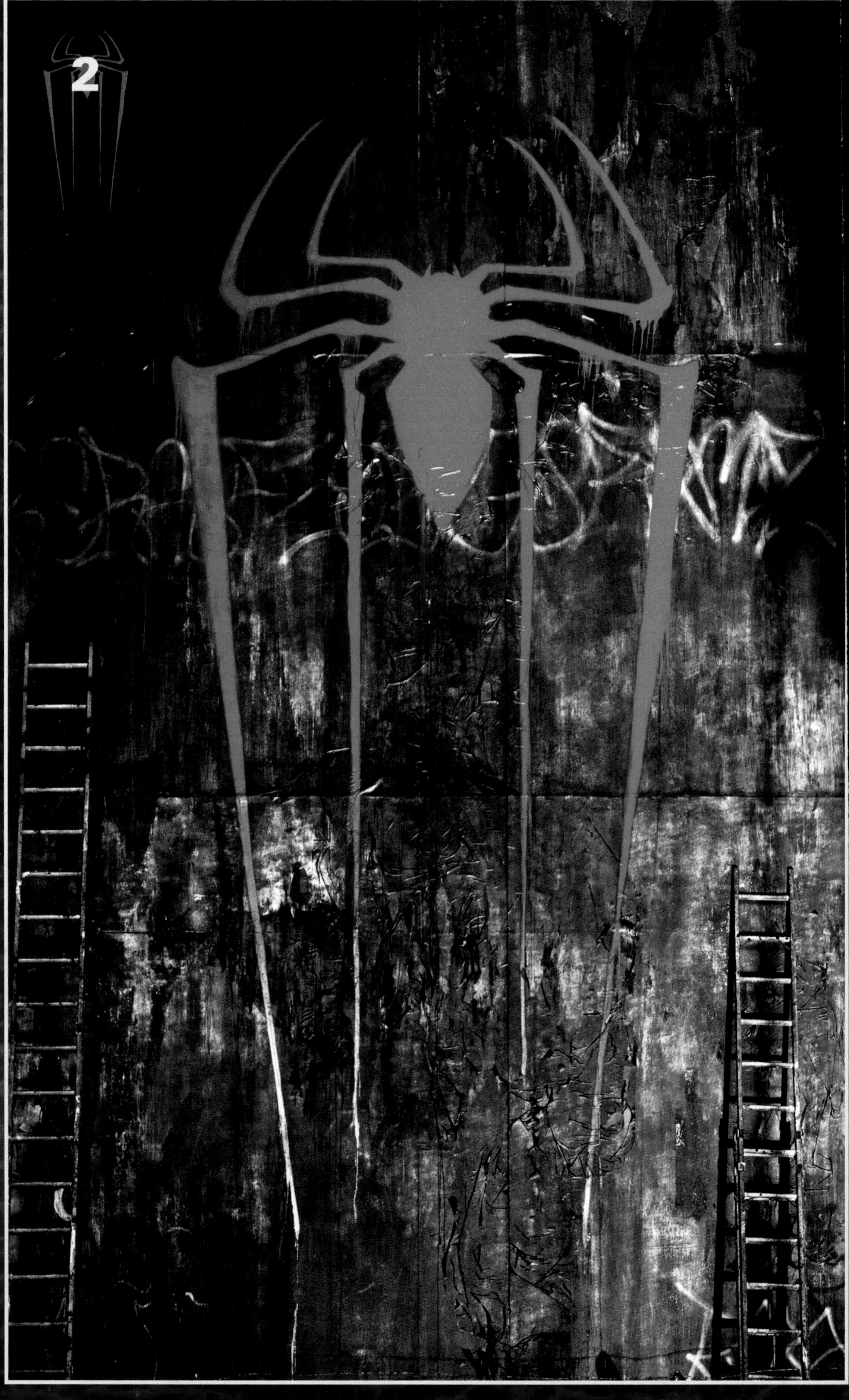
2

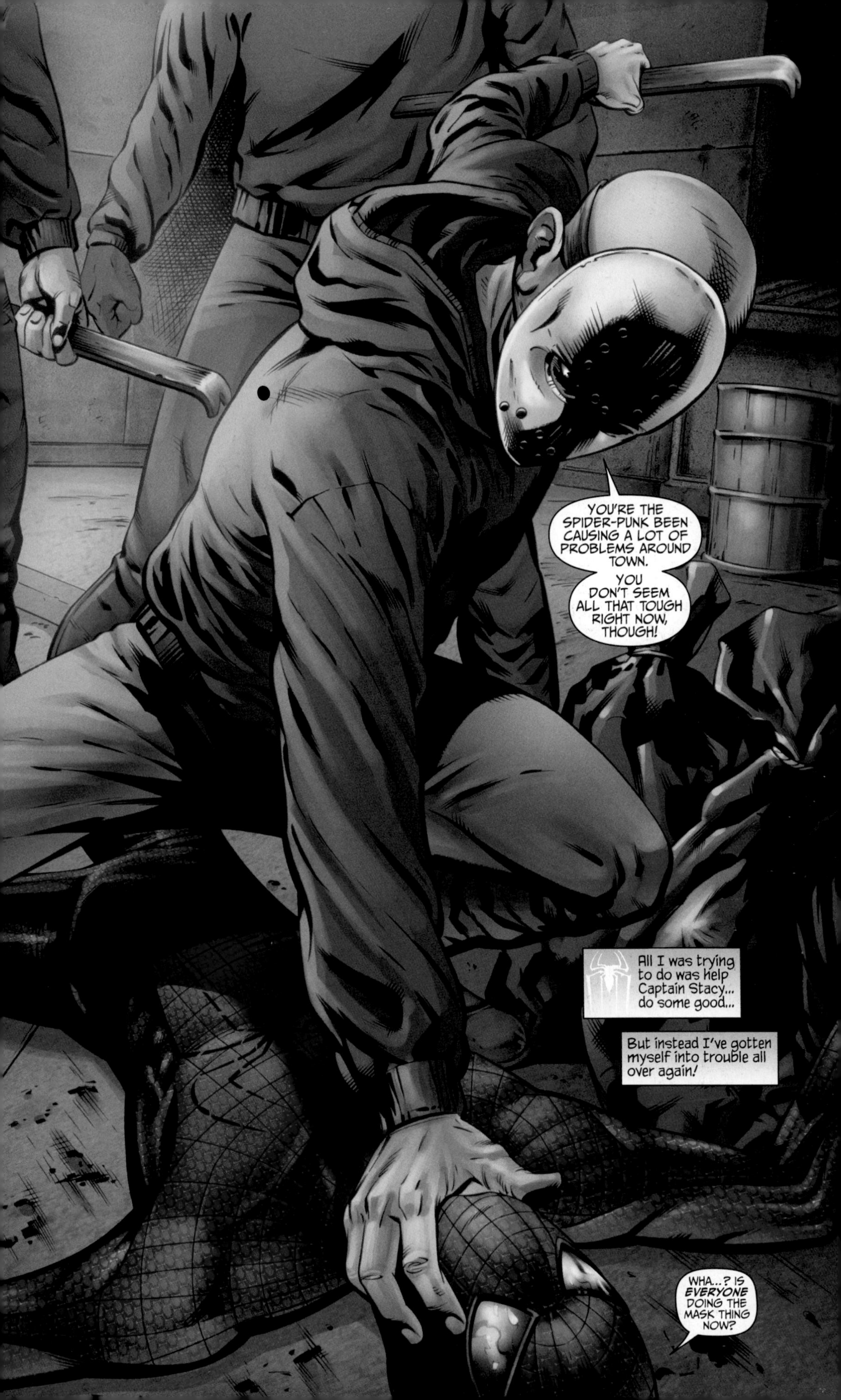
YOU'RE THE SPIDER-PUNK BEEN CAUSING A LOT OF PROBLEMS AROUND TOWN.
YOU DON'T SEEM ALL THAT TOUGH RIGHT NOW, THOUGH!
All I was trying to do was help Captain Stacy... do some good...
But instead I've gotten myself into trouble all over again!
WHA...? IS EVERYONE DOING THE MASK THING NOW?

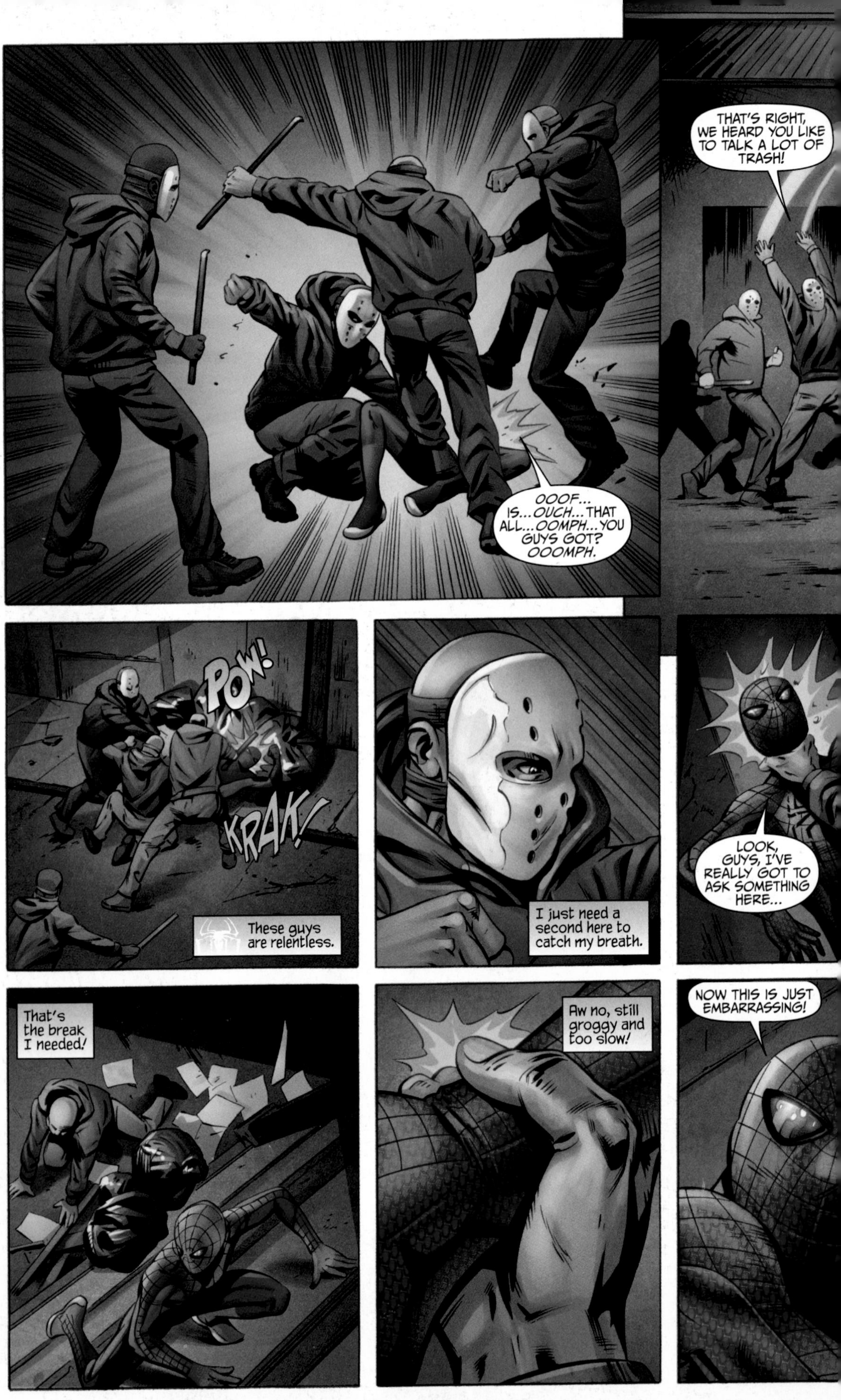
OOOF... IS...OUCH...THAT ALL...OOMPH...YOU GUYS GOT? OOOMPH.
THAT'S RIGHT, WE HEARD YOU LIKE TO TALK A LOT OF TRASH!
POW!
KRAK!
These guys are relentless.
I just need a second here to catch my breath.
LOOK, GUYS, I'VE REALLY GOT TO ASK SOMETHING HERE...
That's the break I needed!
Aw no, still groggy and too slow!
NOW THIS IS JUST EMBARRASSING!

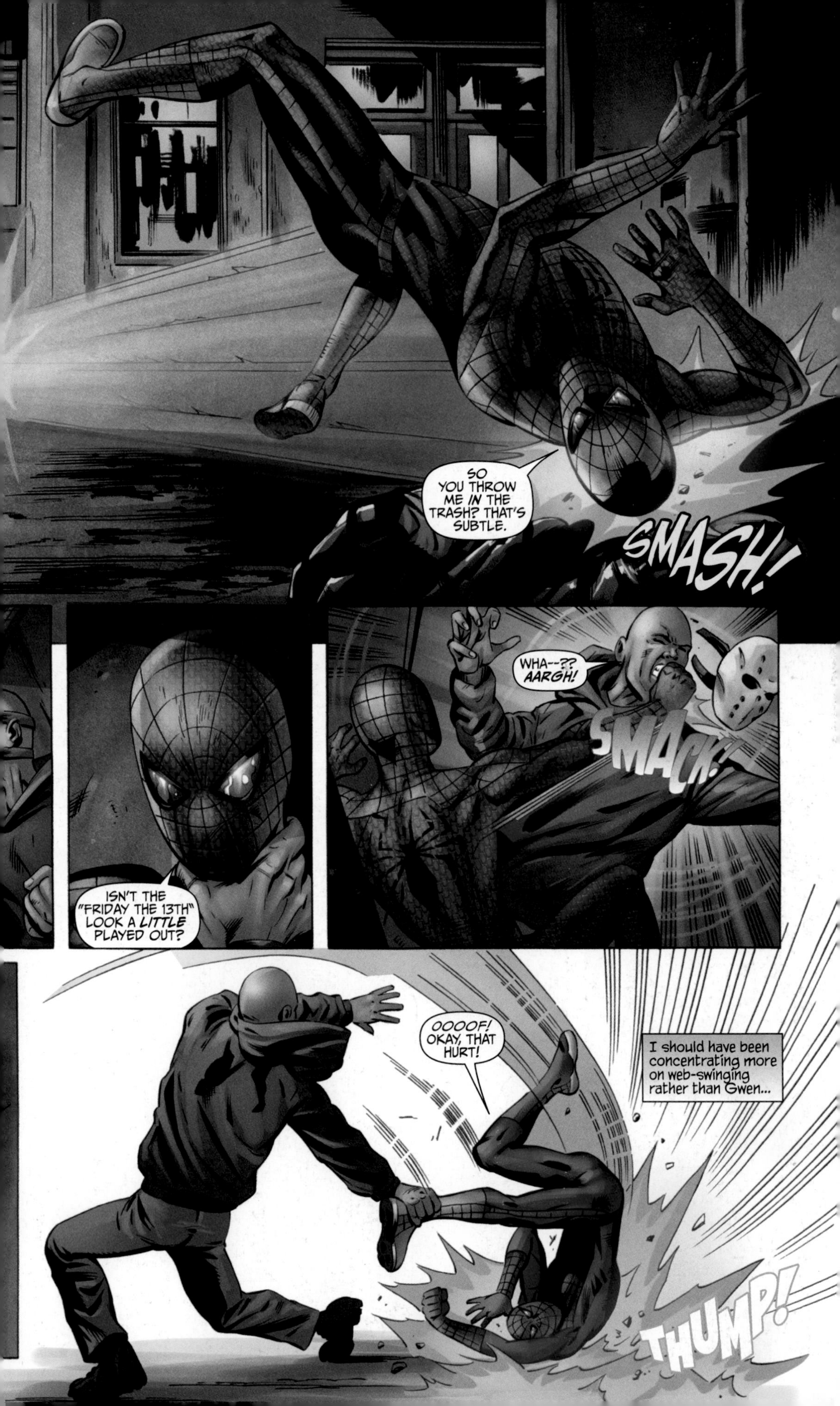

SO YOU THROW ME *IN* THE TRASH? THAT'S SUBTLE.
SMASH!
ISN'T THE "FRIDAY THE 13TH" LOOK A *LITTLE* PLAYED OUT?
WHA--?? *AARGH!*
SMACK!
OOOOF! OKAY, THAT HURT!
I should have been concentrating more on web-swinging rather than Gwen...
THUMP!

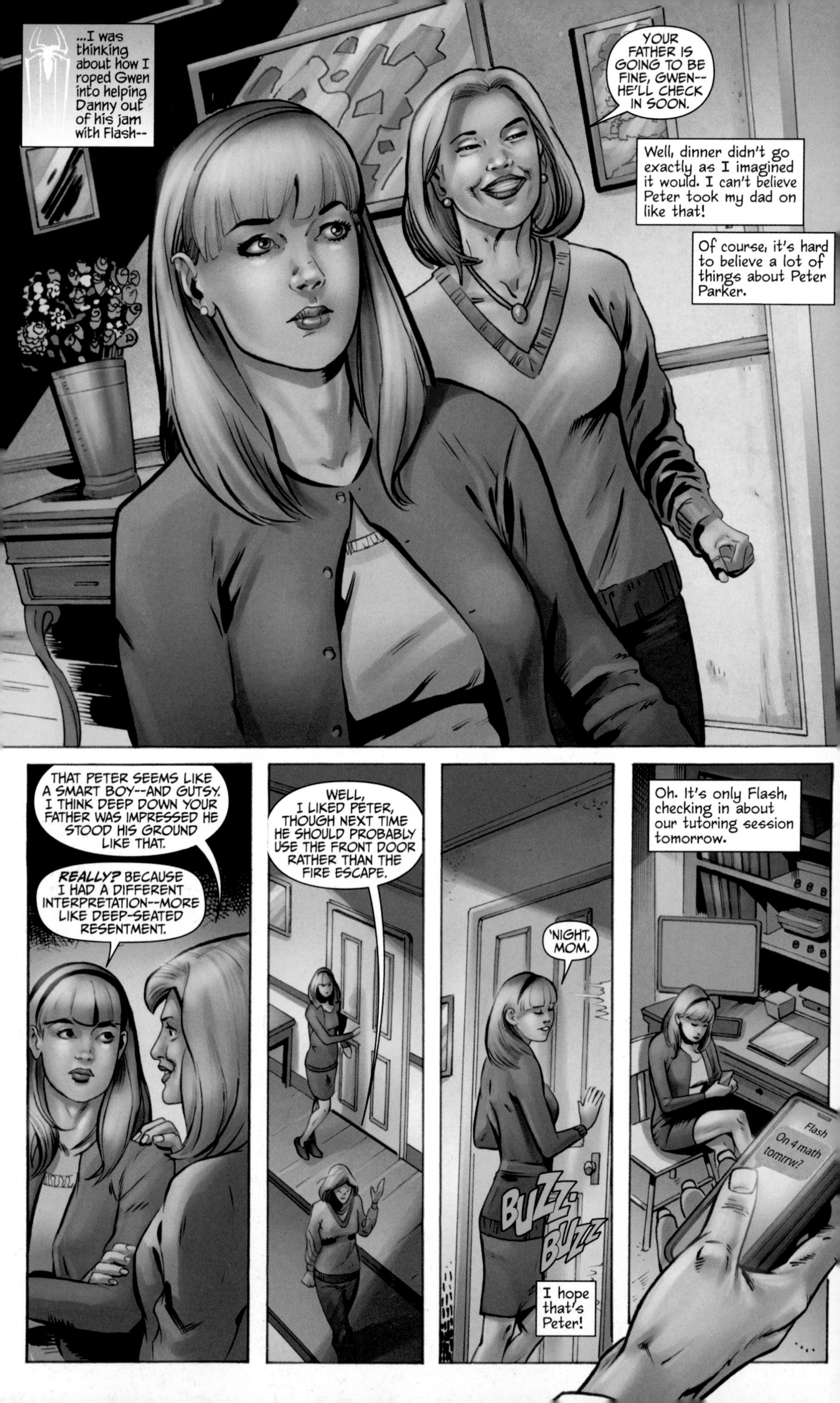
...I was thinking about how I roped Gwen into helping Danny out of his jam with Flash--
YOUR FATHER IS GOING TO BE FINE, GWEN-- HE'LL CHECK IN SOON.
Well, dinner didn't go exactly as I imagined it would. I can't believe Peter took my dad on like that!
Of course, it's hard to believe a lot of things about Peter Parker.
THAT PETER SEEMS LIKE A SMART BOY--AND GUTSY. I THINK DEEP DOWN YOUR FATHER WAS IMPRESSED HE STOOD HIS GROUND LIKE THAT.
REALLY? BECAUSE I HAD A DIFFERENT INTERPRETATION--MORE LIKE DEEP-SEATED RESENTMENT.
WELL, I LIKED PETER, THOUGH NEXT TIME HE SHOULD PROBABLY USE THE FRONT DOOR RATHER THAN THE FIRE ESCAPE.
'NIGHT, MOM.
BUZZ-BUZZ
I hope that's Peter!
Oh. It's only Flash, checking in about our tutoring session tomorrow.
Flash
On 4 math tomrrw?
...

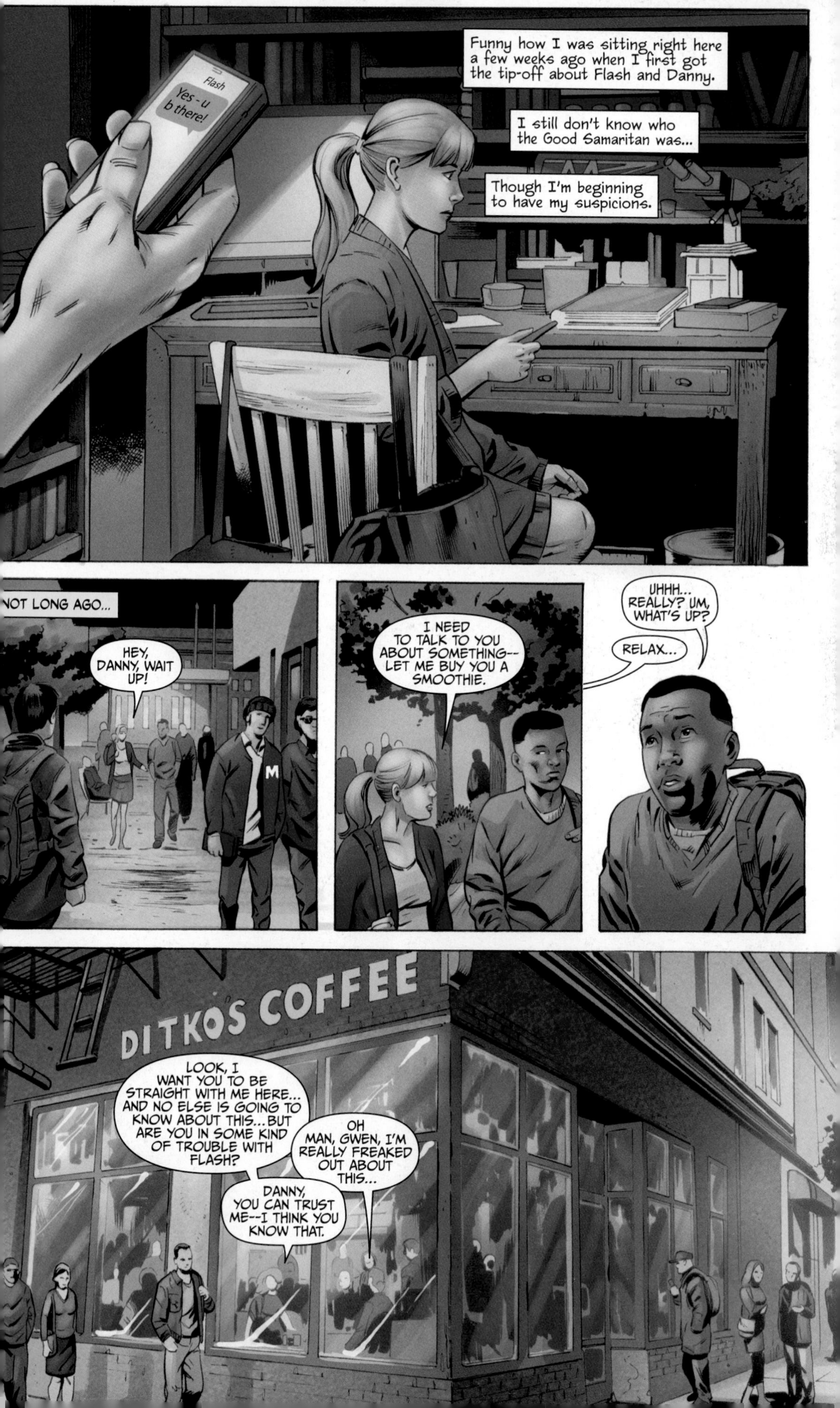
Flash
Yes - u b there!
Funny how I was sitting right here a few weeks ago when I first got the tip-off about Flash and Danny.
I still don't know who the Good Samaritan was...
Though I'm beginning to have my suspicions.
NOT LONG AGO...
HEY, DANNY, WAIT UP!
I NEED TO TALK TO YOU ABOUT SOMETHING-- LET ME BUY YOU A SMOOTHIE.
UHHH... REALLY? UM, WHAT'S UP?
RELAX...
DITKO'S COFFEE
LOOK, I WANT YOU TO BE STRAIGHT WITH ME HERE... AND NO ELSE IS GOING TO KNOW ABOUT THIS... BUT ARE YOU IN SOME KIND OF TROUBLE WITH FLASH?
OH MAN, GWEN, I'M REALLY FREAKED OUT ABOUT THIS...
DANNY, YOU CAN TRUST ME--I THINK YOU KNOW THAT.

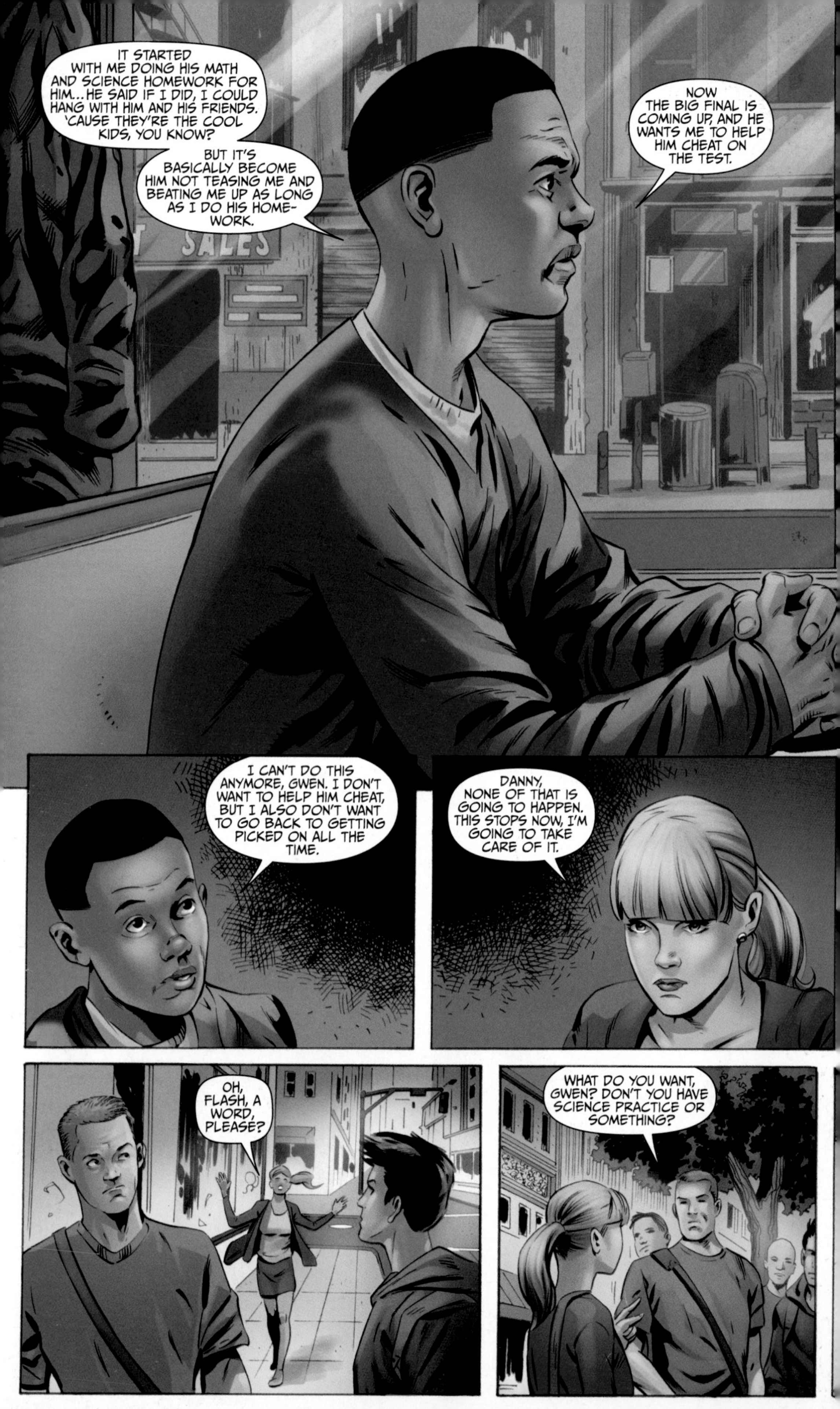
IT STARTED WITH ME DOING HIS MATH AND SCIENCE HOMEWORK FOR HIM...HE SAID IF I DID, I COULD HANG WITH HIM AND HIS FRIENDS. 'CAUSE THEY'RE THE COOL KIDS, YOU KNOW?
BUT IT'S BASICALLY BECOME HIM NOT TEASING ME AND BEATING ME UP AS LONG AS I DO HIS HOME-WORK.
NOW THE BIG FINAL IS COMING UP, AND HE WANTS ME TO HELP HIM CHEAT ON THE TEST.
SALES
I CAN'T DO THIS ANYMORE, GWEN. I DON'T WANT TO HELP HIM CHEAT, BUT I ALSO DON'T WANT TO GO BACK TO GETTING PICKED ON ALL THE TIME.
DANNY, NONE OF THAT IS GOING TO HAPPEN. THIS STOPS NOW, I'M GOING TO TAKE CARE OF IT.
OH, FLASH, A WORD, PLEASE?
WHAT DO YOU WANT, GWEN? DON'T YOU HAVE SCIENCE PRACTICE OR SOMETHING?

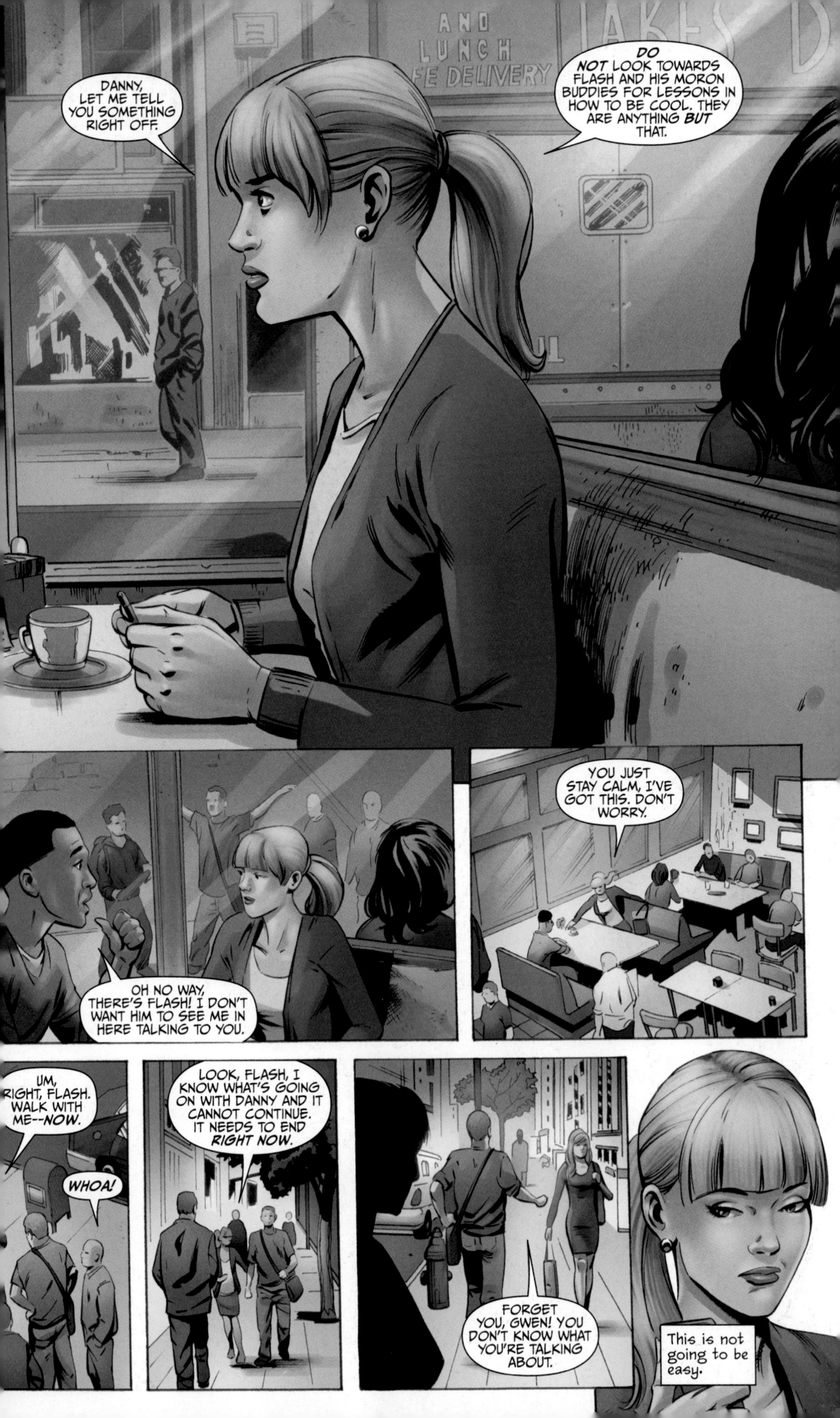

AND LUNCH
FE DELIVERY
DANNY, LET ME TELL YOU SOMETHING RIGHT OFF.
DO NOT LOOK TOWARDS FLASH AND HIS MORON BUDDIES FOR LESSONS IN HOW TO BE COOL. THEY ARE ANYTHING BUT THAT.
OH NO WAY, THERE'S FLASH! I DON'T WANT HIM TO SEE ME IN HERE TALKING TO YOU.
YOU JUST STAY CALM, I'VE GOT THIS. DON'T WORRY.
UM, RIGHT, FLASH. WALK WITH ME--NOW.
WHOA!
LOOK, FLASH, I KNOW WHAT'S GOING ON WITH DANNY AND IT CANNOT CONTINUE. IT NEEDS TO END RIGHT NOW.
FORGET YOU, GWEN! YOU DON'T KNOW WHAT YOU'RE TALKING ABOUT.
This is not going to be easy.

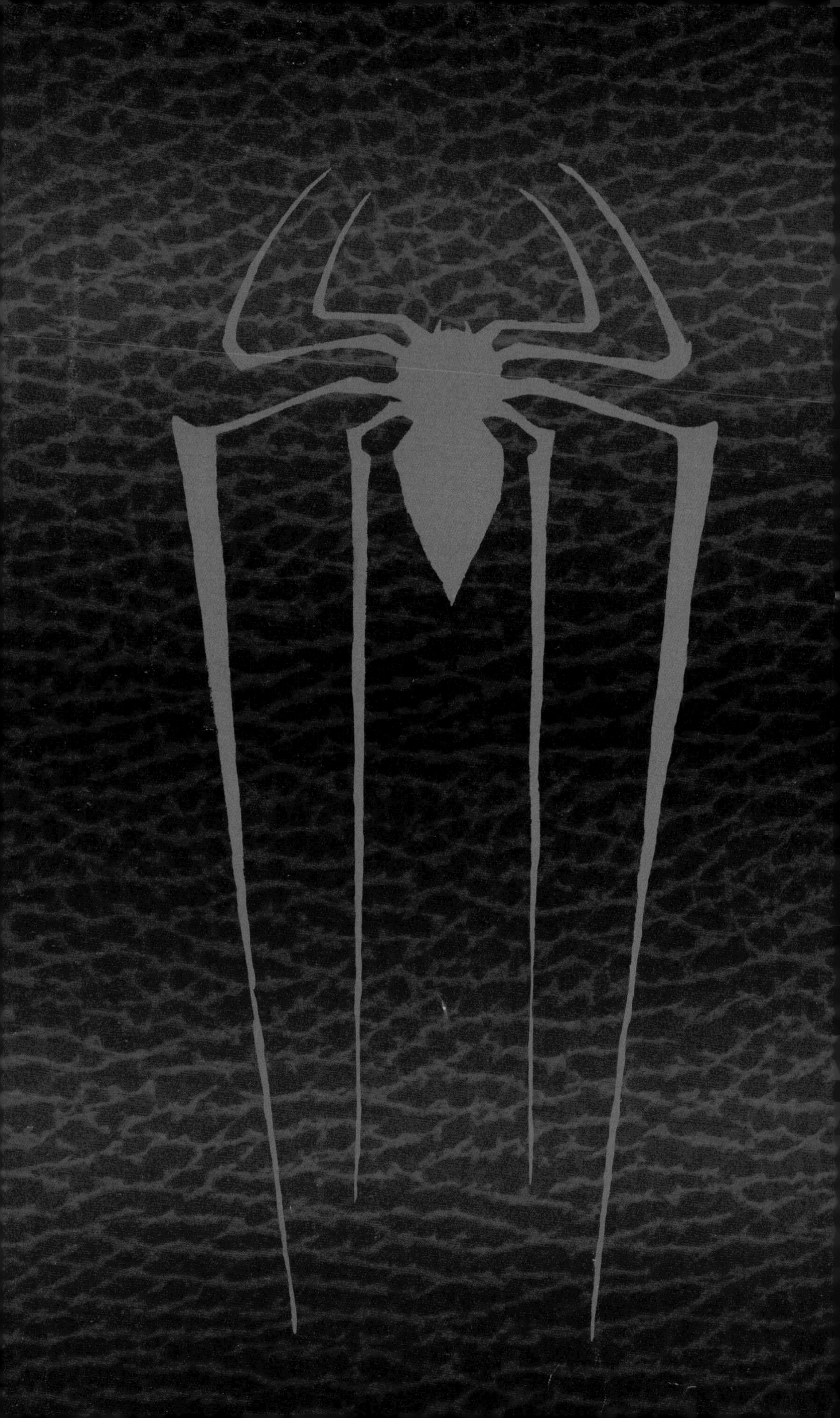

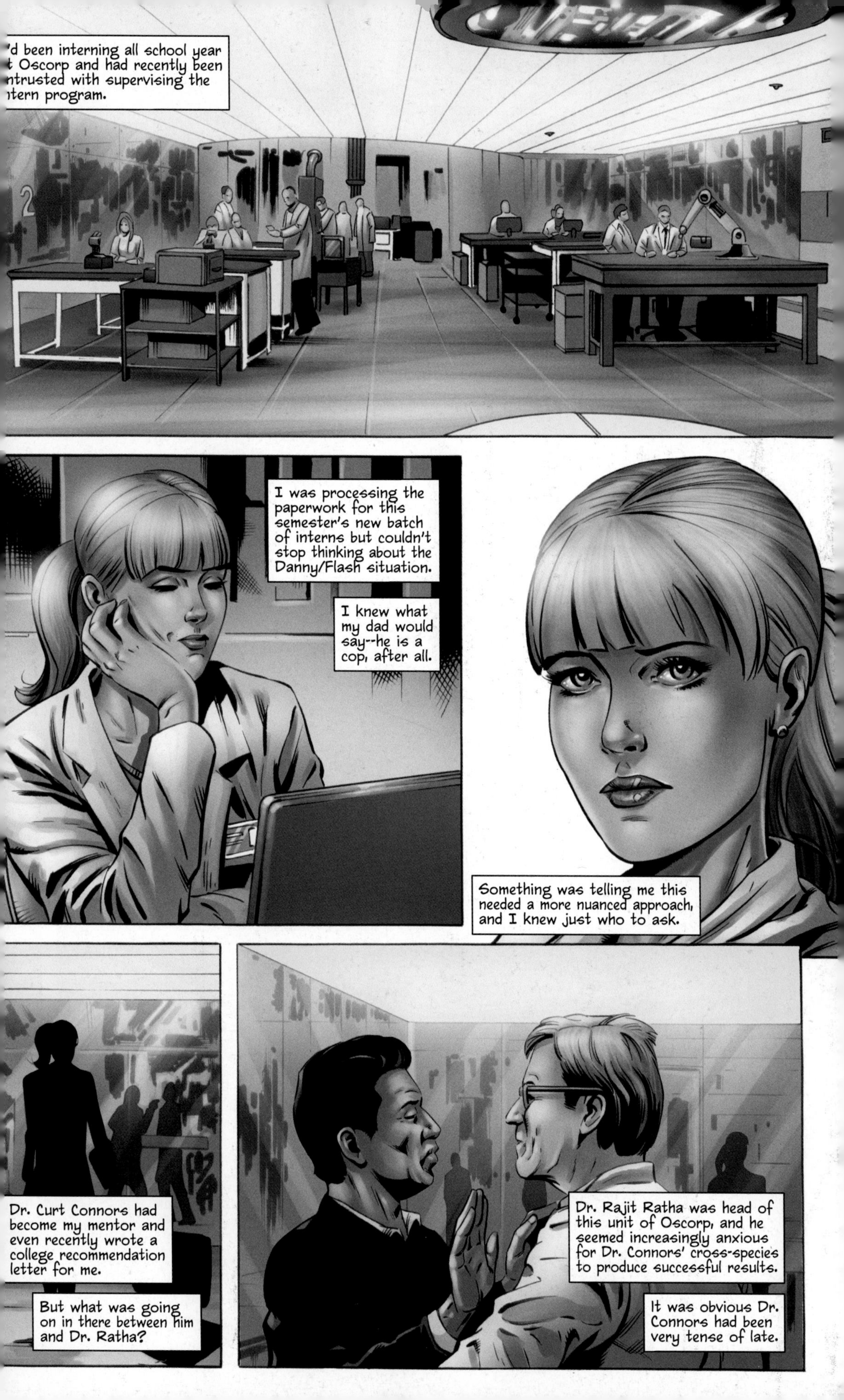
'd been interning all school year t Oscorp and had recently been ntrusted with supervising the tern program.
I was processing the paperwork for this semester's new batch of interns but couldn't stop thinking about the Danny/Flash situation.
I knew what my dad would say--he is a cop, after all.
Something was telling me this needed a more nuanced approach, and I knew just who to ask.
Dr. Curt Connors had become my mentor and even recently wrote a college recommendation letter for me.
But what was going on in there between him and Dr. Ratha?
Dr. Rajit Ratha was head of this unit of Oscorp, and he seemed increasingly anxious for Dr. Connors' cross-species to produce successful results.
It was obvious Dr. Connors had been very tense of late.

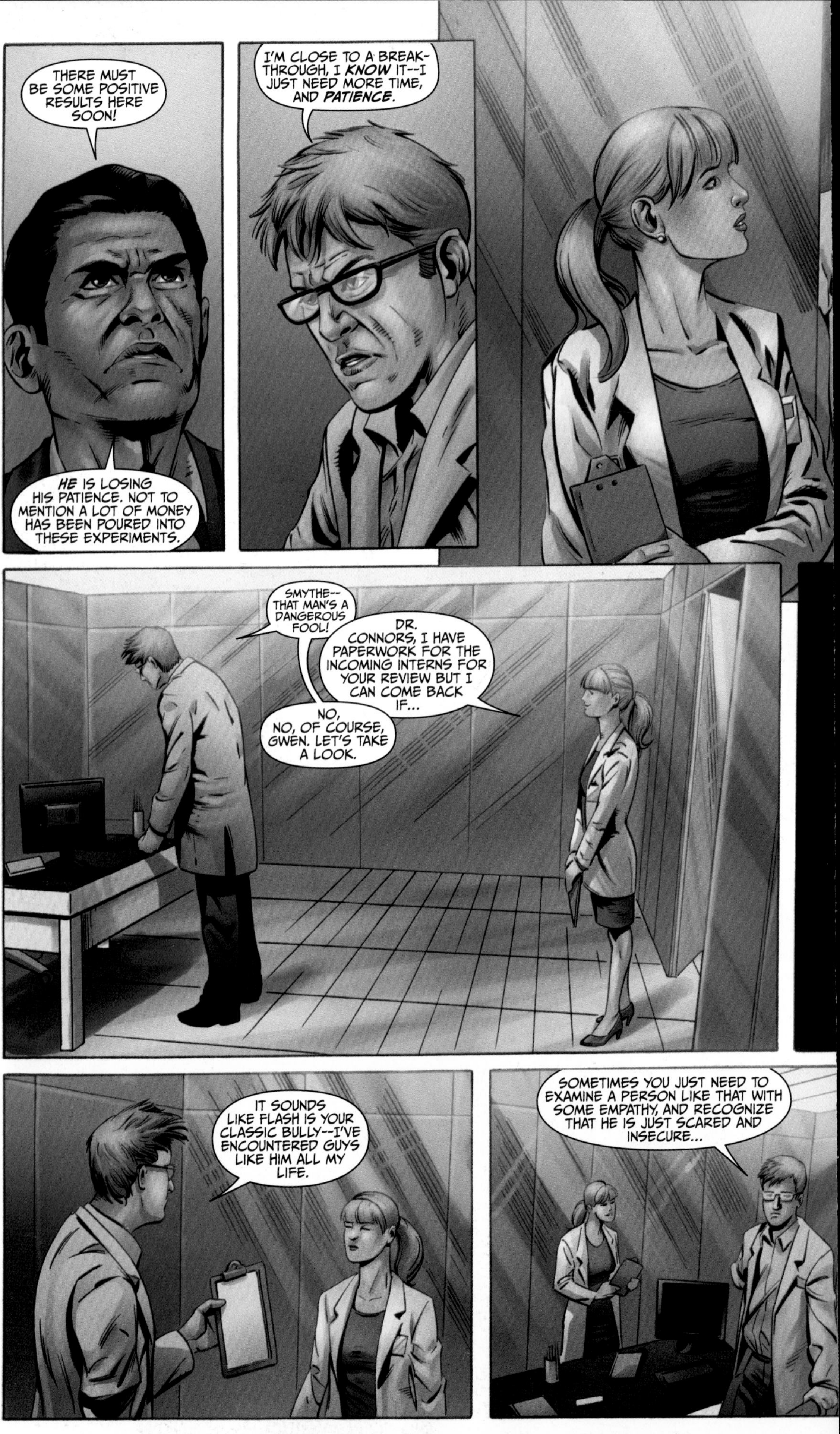

THERE MUST BE SOME POSITIVE RESULTS HERE SOON!
HE IS LOSING HIS PATIENCE. NOT TO MENTION A LOT OF MONEY HAS BEEN POURED INTO THESE EXPERIMENTS.
I'M CLOSE TO A BREAK-THROUGH, I KNOW IT--I JUST NEED MORE TIME, AND PATIENCE.
SMYTHE-- THAT MAN'S A DANGEROUS FOOL!
DR. CONNORS, I HAVE PAPERWORK FOR THE INCOMING INTERNS FOR YOUR REVIEW BUT I CAN COME BACK IF...
NO, NO, OF COURSE, GWEN. LET'S TAKE A LOOK.
IT SOUNDS LIKE FLASH IS YOUR CLASSIC BULLY--I'VE ENCOUNTERED GUYS LIKE HIM ALL MY LIFE.
SOMETIMES YOU JUST NEED TO EXAMINE A PERSON LIKE THAT WITH SOME EMPATHY, AND RECOGNIZE THAT HE IS JUST SCARED AND INSECURE...

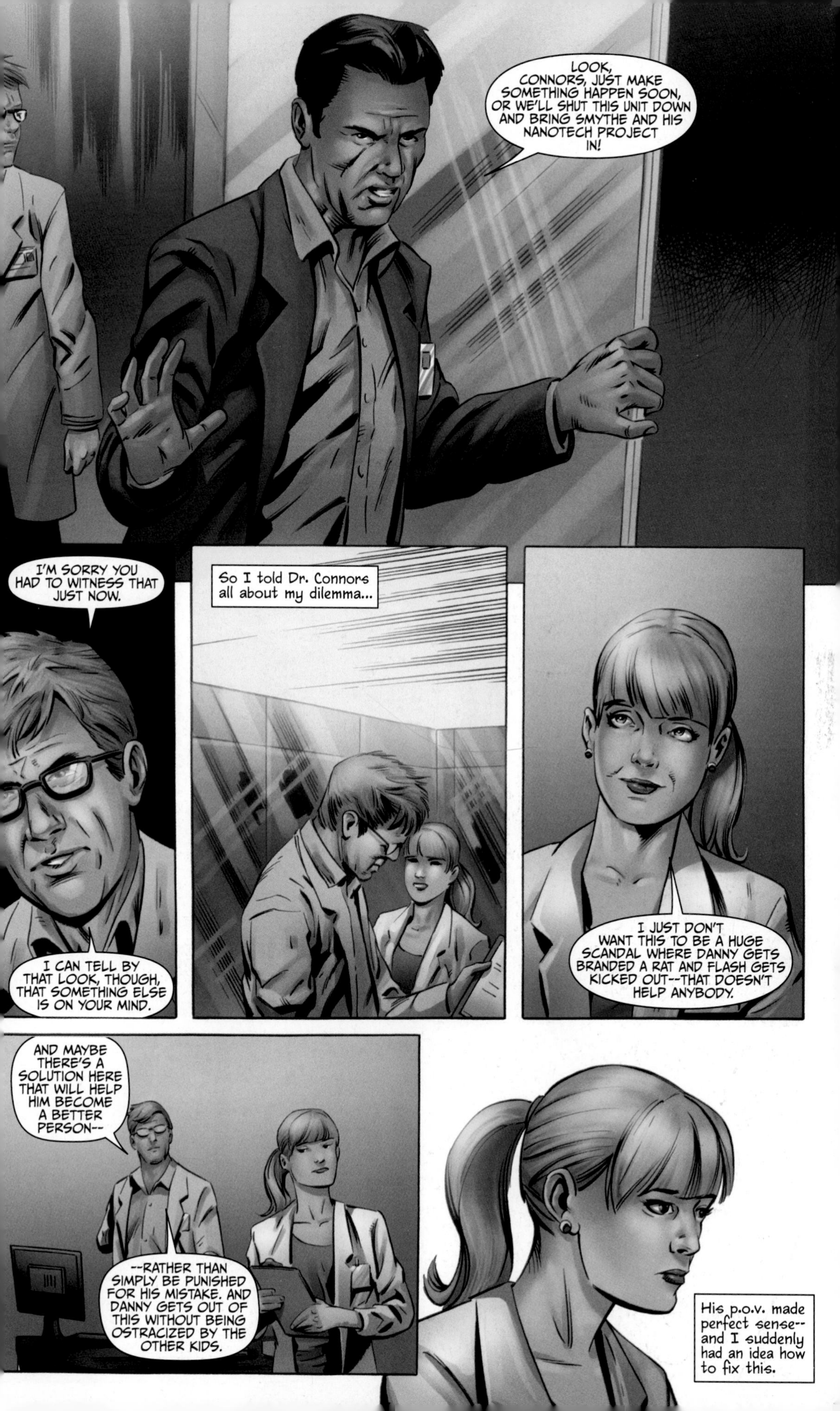
LOOK, CONNORS, JUST MAKE SOMETHING HAPPEN SOON, OR WE'LL SHUT THIS UNIT DOWN AND BRING SMYTHE AND HIS NANOTECH PROJECT IN!
I'M SORRY YOU HAD TO WITNESS THAT JUST NOW.
I CAN TELL BY THAT LOOK, THOUGH, THAT SOMETHING ELSE IS ON YOUR MIND.
So I told Dr. Connors all about my dilemma...
I JUST DON'T WANT THIS TO BE A HUGE SCANDAL WHERE DANNY GETS BRANDED A RAT AND FLASH GETS KICKED OUT--THAT DOESN'T HELP ANYBODY.
AND MAYBE THERE'S A SOLUTION HERE THAT WILL HELP HIM BECOME A BETTER PERSON--
--RATHER THAN SIMPLY BE PUNISHED FOR HIS MISTAKE. AND DANNY GETS OUT OF THIS WITHOUT BEING OSTRACIZED BY THE OTHER KIDS.
His p.o.v. made perfect sense--and I suddenly had an idea how to fix this.

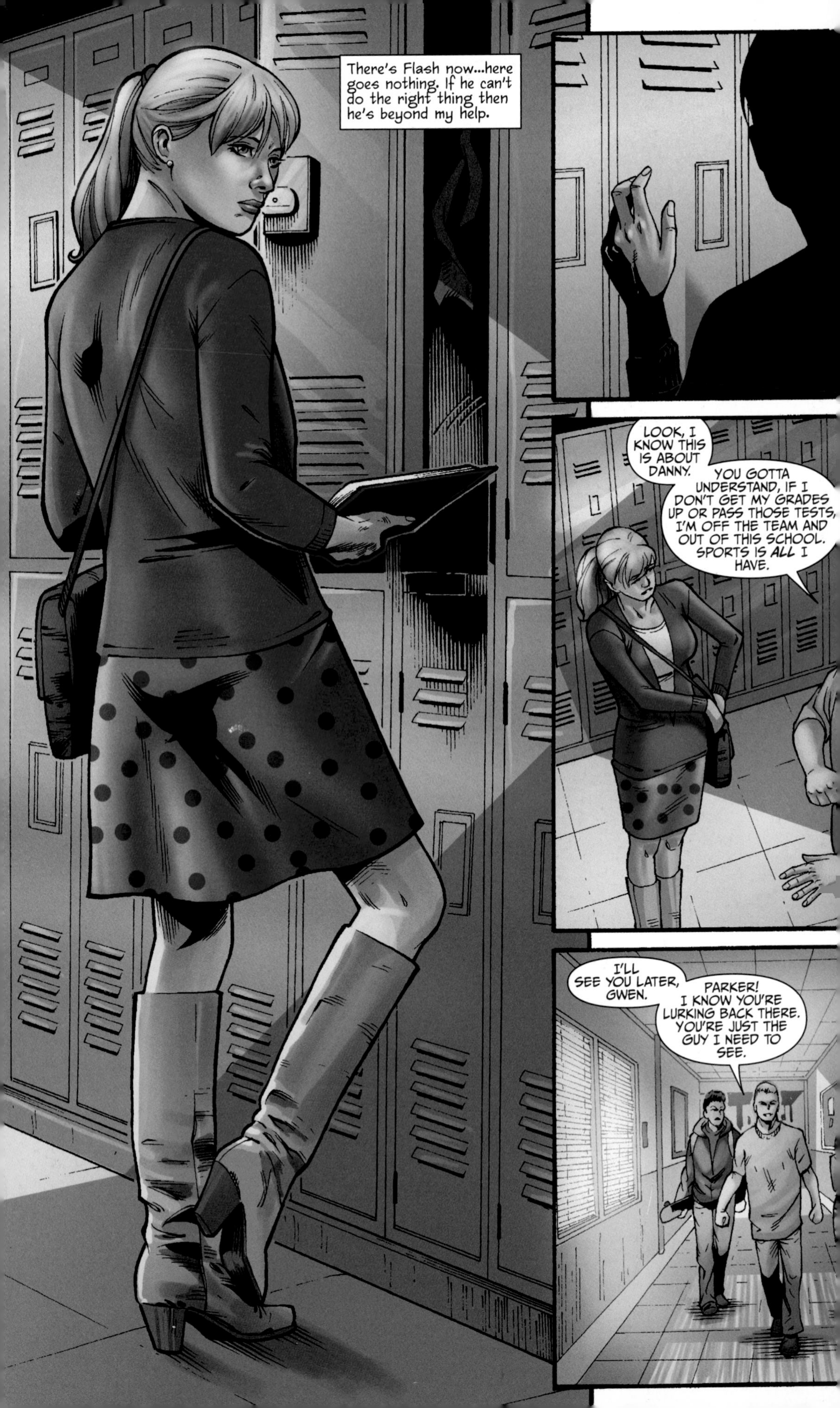
There's Flash now...here goes nothing. If he can't do the right thing then he's beyond my help.
LOOK, I KNOW THIS IS ABOUT DANNY.
YOU GOTTA UNDERSTAND, IF I DON'T GET MY GRADES UP OR PASS THOSE TESTS, I'M OFF THE TEAM AND OUT OF THIS SCHOOL. SPORTS IS ALL I HAVE.
I'LL SEE YOU LATER, GWEN.
PARKER! I KNOW YOU'RE LURKING BACK THERE. YOU'RE JUST THE GUY I NEED TO SEE.

HEY, FLASH! YOU GOT A MINUTE? I *REALLY* NEED TO TALK YOU.

YEAH... OKAY, OKAY.

BESIDES, IT'S NOT LIKE I'M *HURTING* DANNY...

JUST STOP IT THERE, FLASH-- *THIS IS HOW IT'S GOING TO BE.*

WE'RE GOING TO MEET EVERY SINGLE DAY AND YOU ARE GOING TO STUDY. HARD. YOU'RE GOING TO PASS EVERYTHING, AND YOU ARE GOING TO *EARN* IT.

IF NOT, I'M DONE, AND *YOU'RE* DONE. SAVVY?

UGH...OKAY. I'LL DO IT. BUT *NO ONE FINDS OUT* HOW THIS WENT DOWN.

DEAL. AND WE'RE STARTING TODAY. I'LL SEE YOU IN THE LIBRARY AFTER SCHOOL.

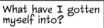

What have I gotten myself into?

YOU BETTER GET MY NAME RIGHT UNDER THE TEAM YEARBOOK PHOTO THIS TIME!

DUNNO WHAT TO TELL YOU, FLASH. CAPTIONS ARE NOT MY DEPARTMENT.

Yep, Flash is going to be a project.

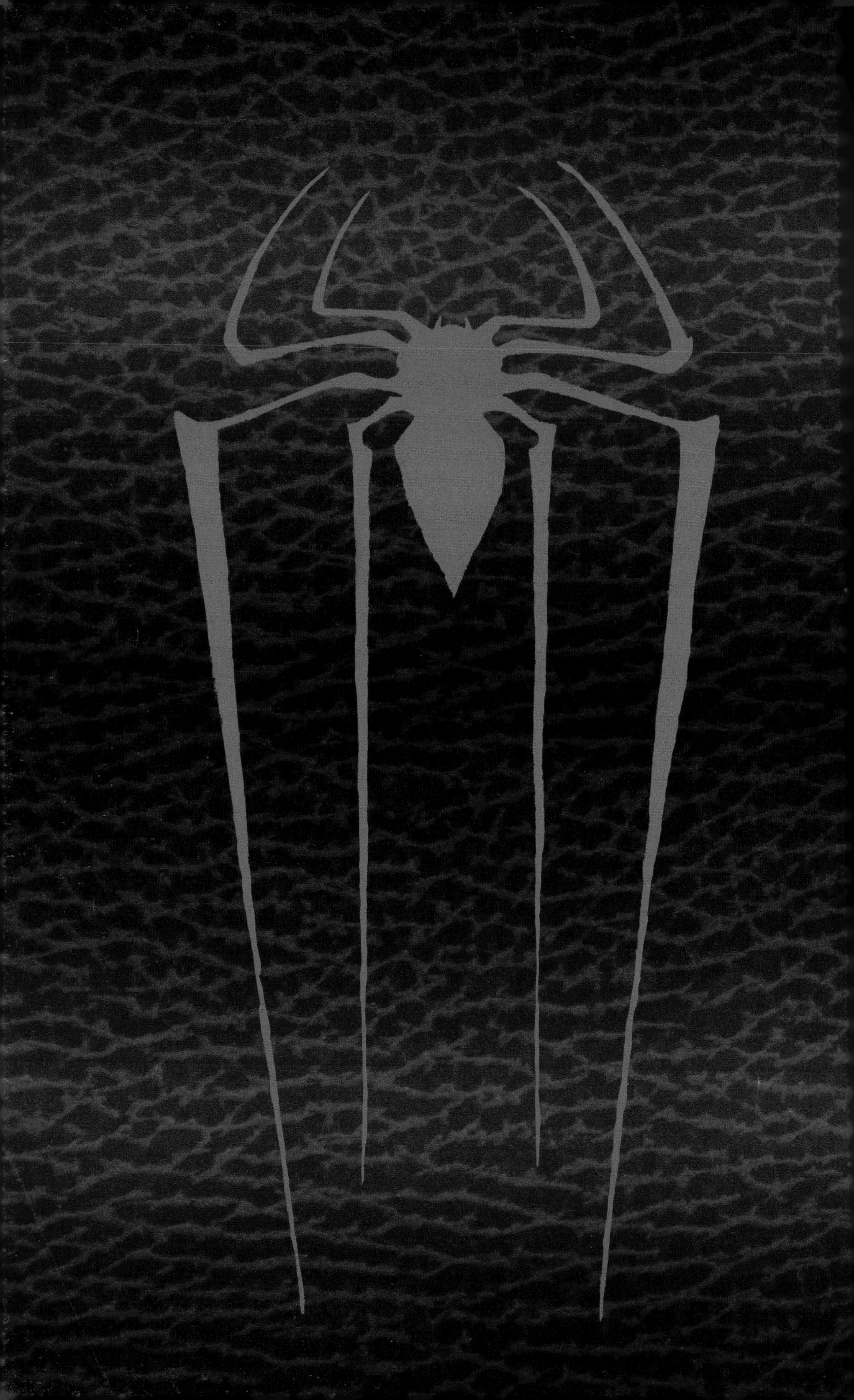

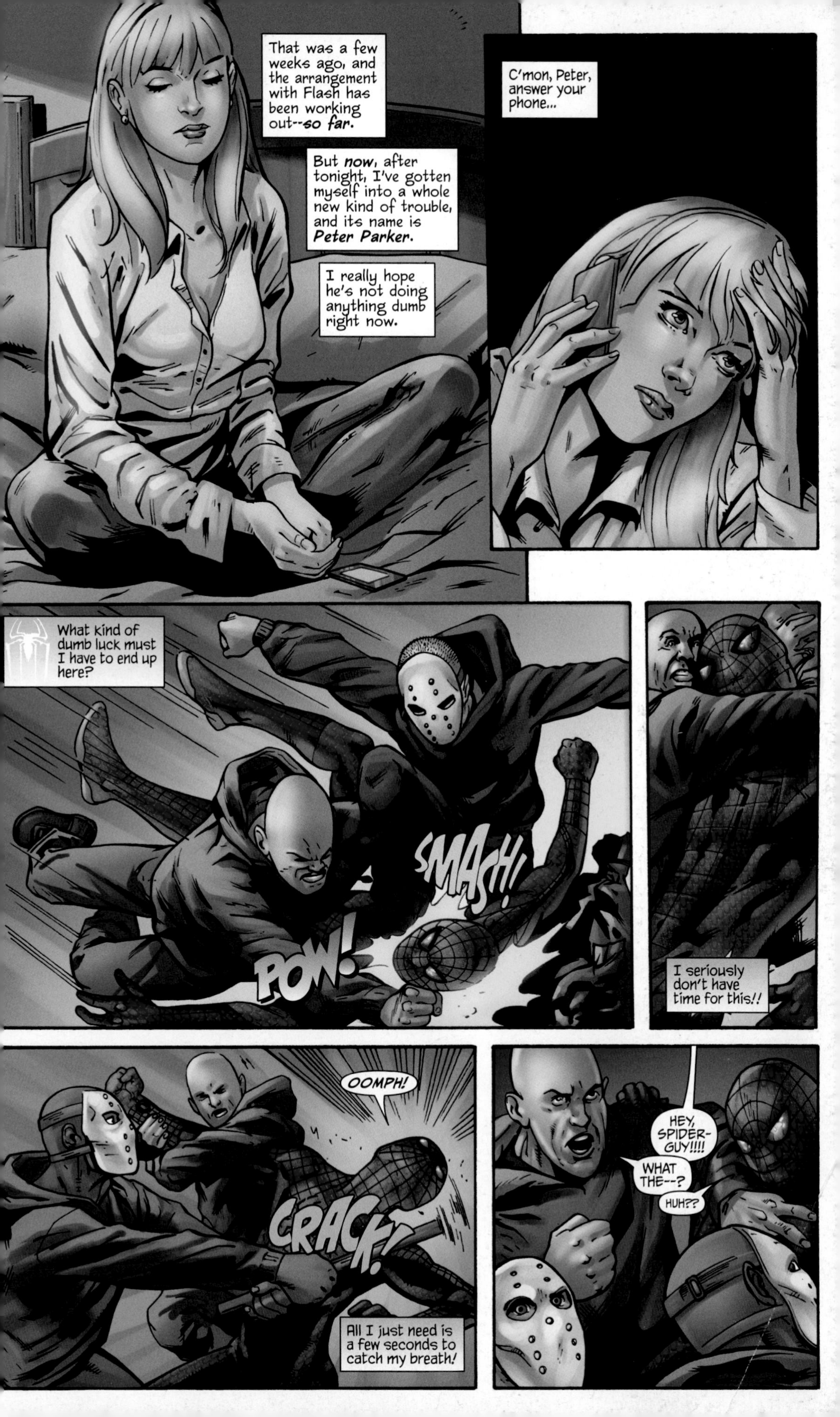
That was a few weeks ago, and the arrangement with Flash has been working out--*so far.*
But *now*, after tonight, I've gotten myself into a whole new kind of trouble, and its name is *Peter Parker.*
I really hope he's not doing anything dumb right now.
C'mon, Peter, answer your phone...
What kind of dumb luck must I have to end up here?
SMASH!
POW!
I seriously don't have time for this!!
OOMPH!
CRACK!
All I just need is a few seconds to catch my breath!
HEY, SPIDER-GUY!!!!
WHAT THE--?
HUH??

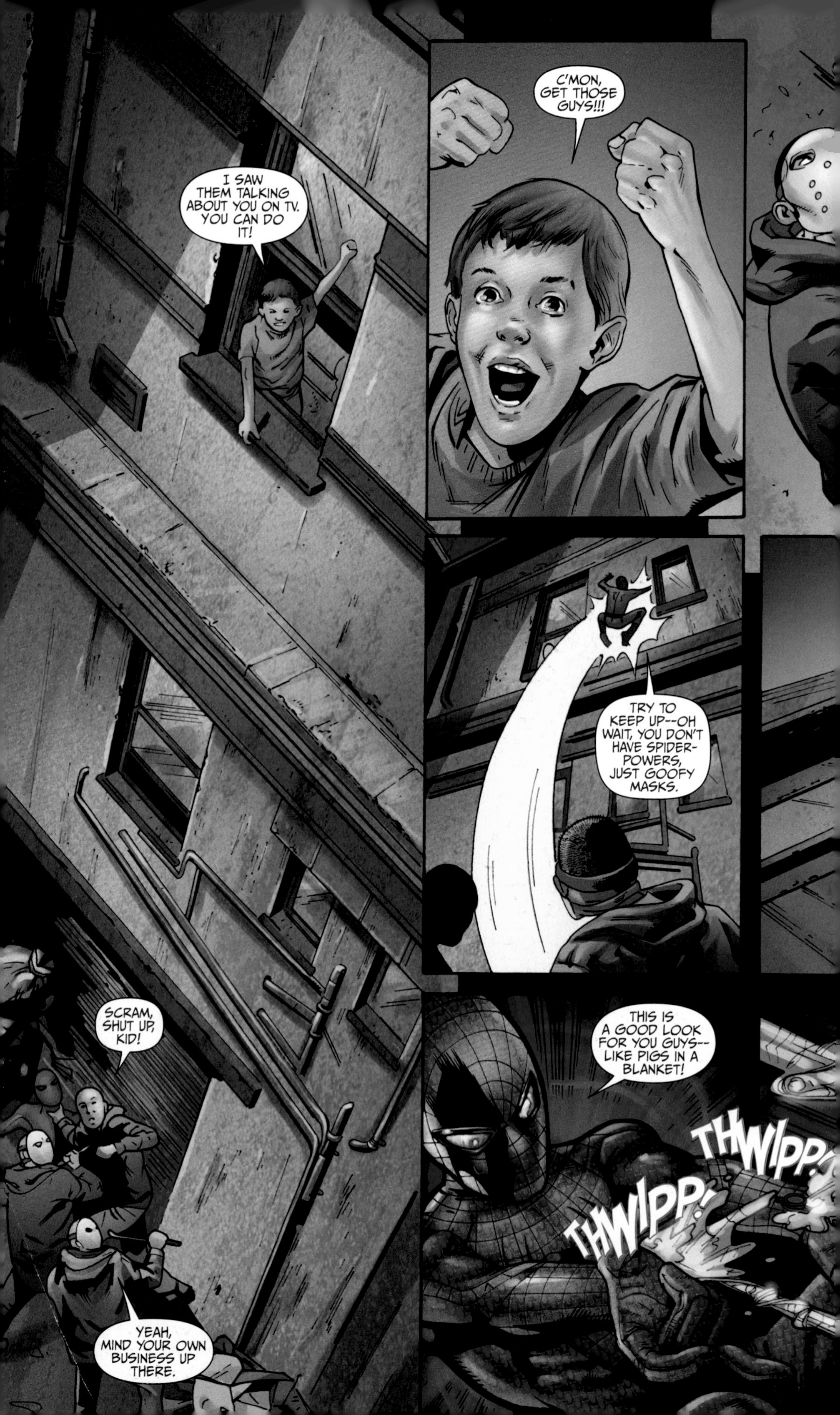
I SAW THEM TALKING ABOUT YOU ON TV. YOU CAN DO IT!
C'MON, GET THOSE GUYS!!!
SCRAM, SHUT UP, KID!
YEAH, MIND YOUR OWN BUSINESS UP THERE.
TRY TO KEEP UP--OH WAIT, YOU DON'T HAVE SPIDER-POWERS, JUST GOOFY MASKS.
THIS IS A GOOD LOOK FOR YOU GUYS--LIKE PIGS IN A BLANKET!
THWIPP!
THWIPP!

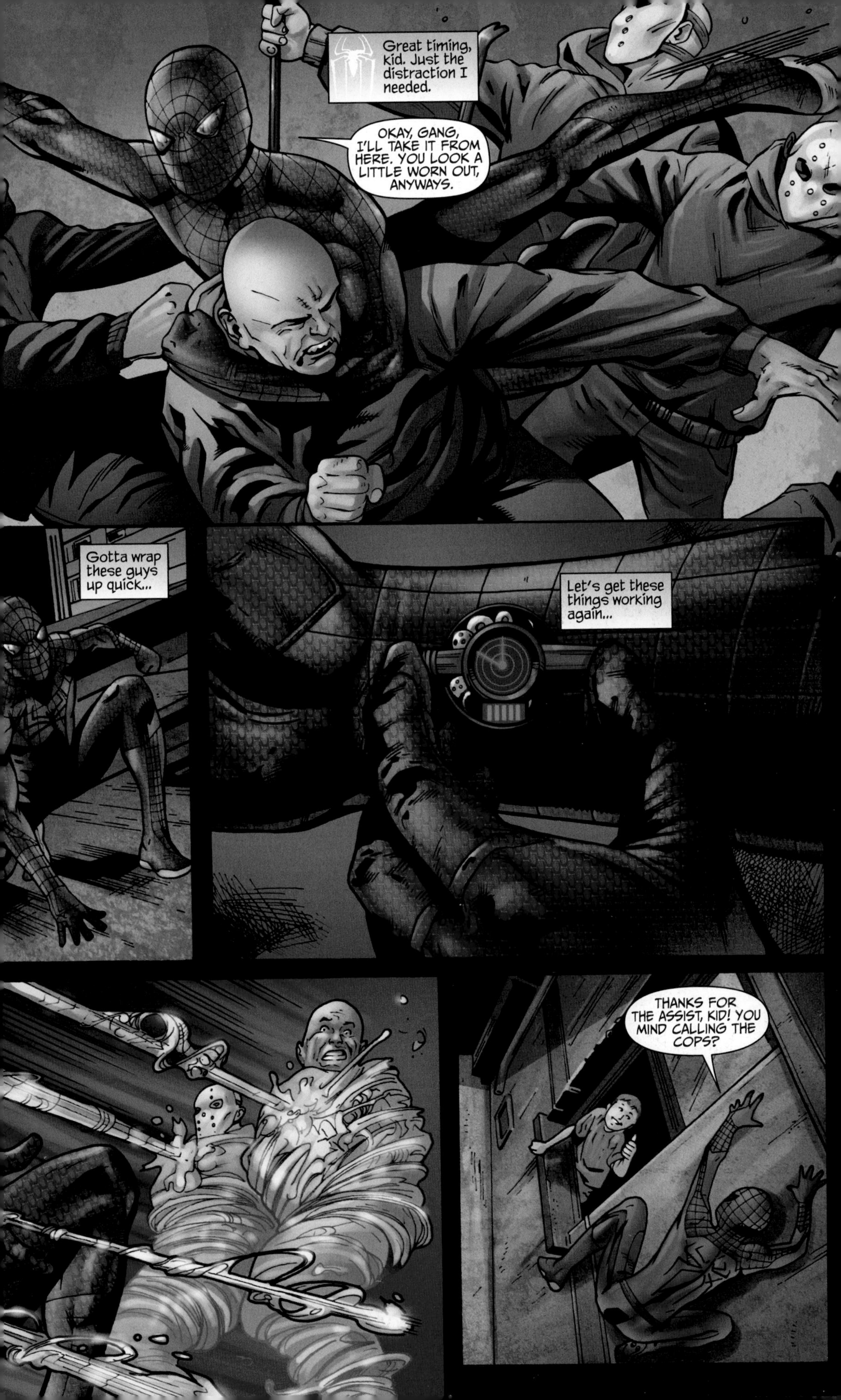
Great timing, kid. Just the distraction I needed.
OKAY, GANG, I'LL TAKE IT FROM HERE. YOU LOOK A LITTLE WORN OUT, ANYWAYS.
Gotta wrap these guys up quick...
Let's get these things working again...
THANKS FOR THE ASSIST, KID! YOU MIND CALLING THE COPS?

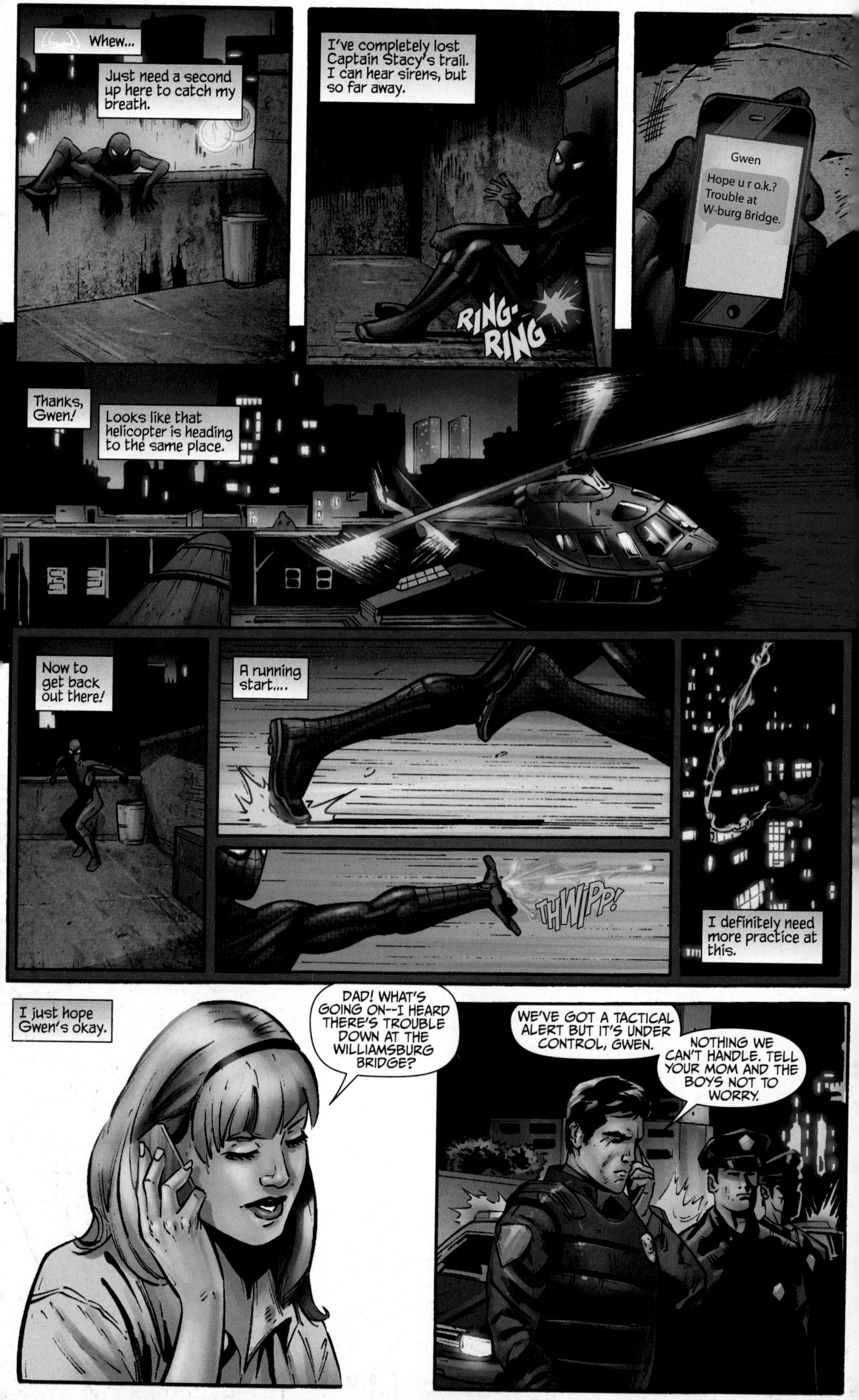

Whew...
Just need a second up here to catch my breath.
I've completely lost Captain Stacy's trail. I can hear sirens, but so far away.
RING-RING
Gwen
Hope u r o.k.? Trouble at W-burg Bridge.
Thanks, Gwen!
Looks like that helicopter is heading to the same place.
Now to get back out there!
A running start....
THWIPP!
I definitely need more practice at this.
I just hope Gwen's okay.
DAD! WHAT'S GOING ON--I HEARD THERE'S TROUBLE DOWN AT THE WILLIAMSBURG BRIDGE?
WE'VE GOT A TACTICAL ALERT BUT IT'S UNDER CONTROL, GWEN.
NOTHING WE CAN'T HANDLE. TELL YOUR MOM AND THE BOYS NOT TO WORRY.

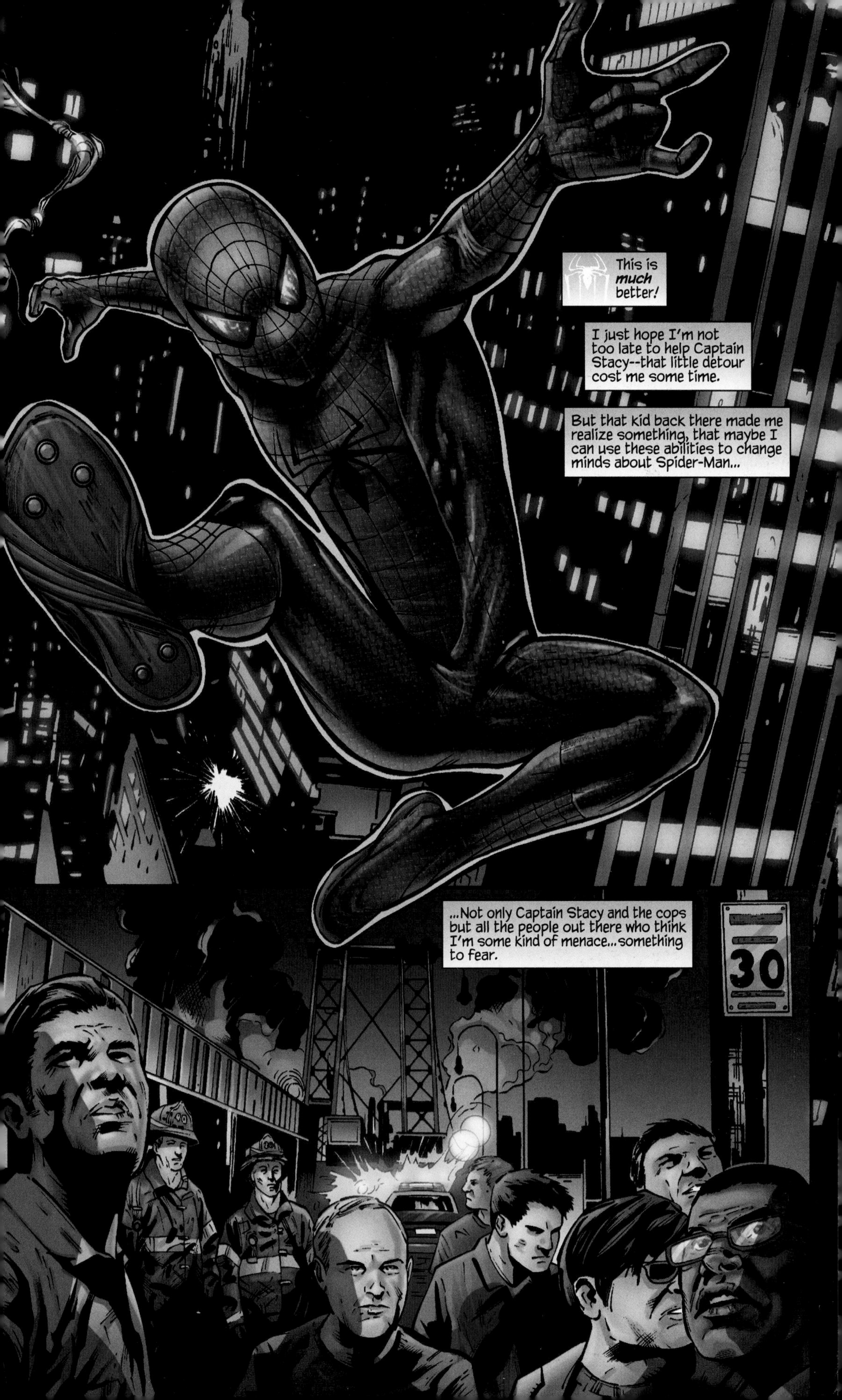
This is *much* better!
I just hope I'm not too late to help Captain Stacy--that little detour cost me some time.
But that kid back there made me realize something, that maybe I can use these abilities to change minds about Spider-Man...
...Not only Captain Stacy and the cops but all the people out there who think I'm some kind of menace...something to fear.
30

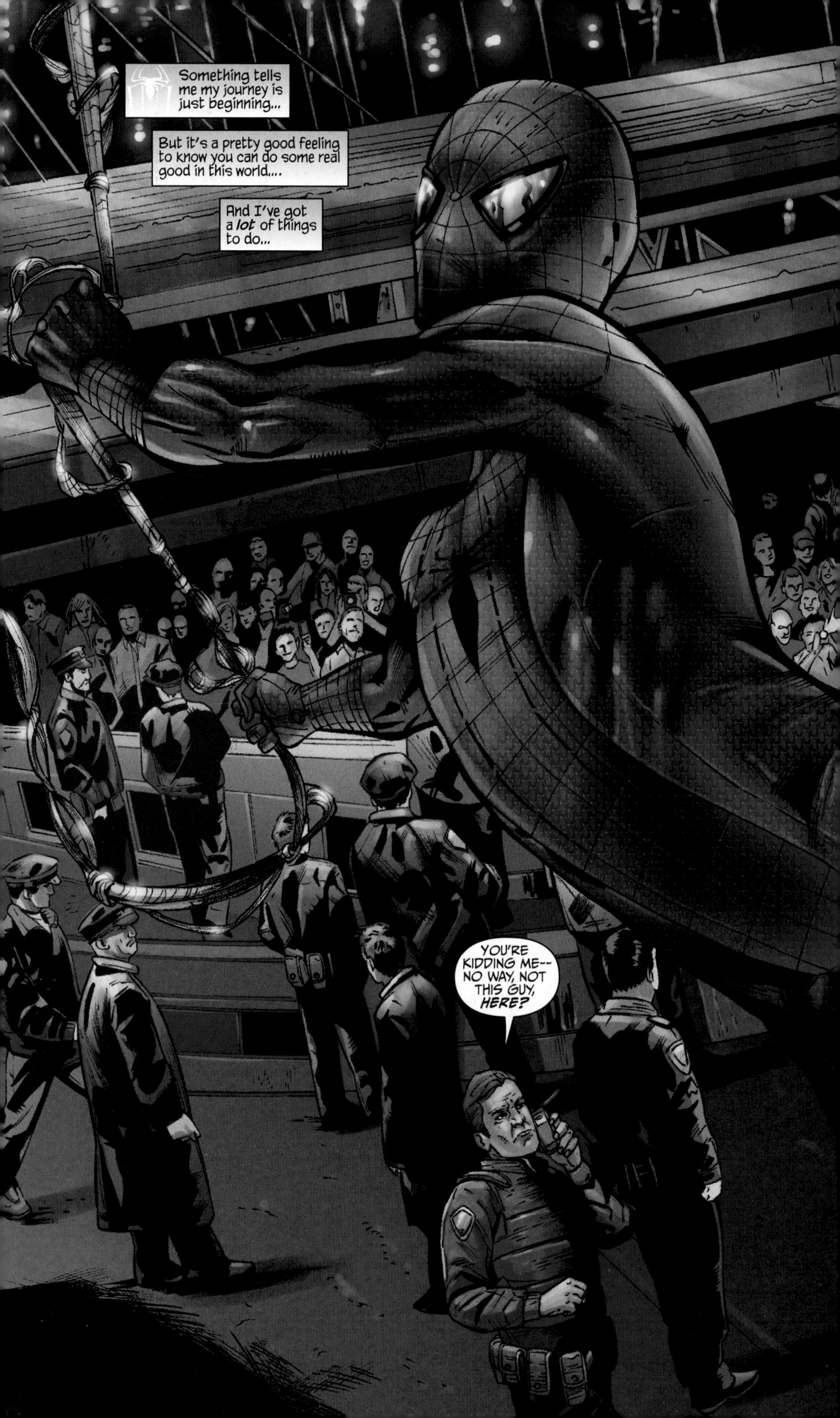
Something tells me my journey is just beginning...
But it's a pretty good feeling to know you can do some real good in this world....
And I've got a *lot* of things to do...
YOU'RE KIDDING ME-- NO WAY, NOT THIS GUY, *HERE?*

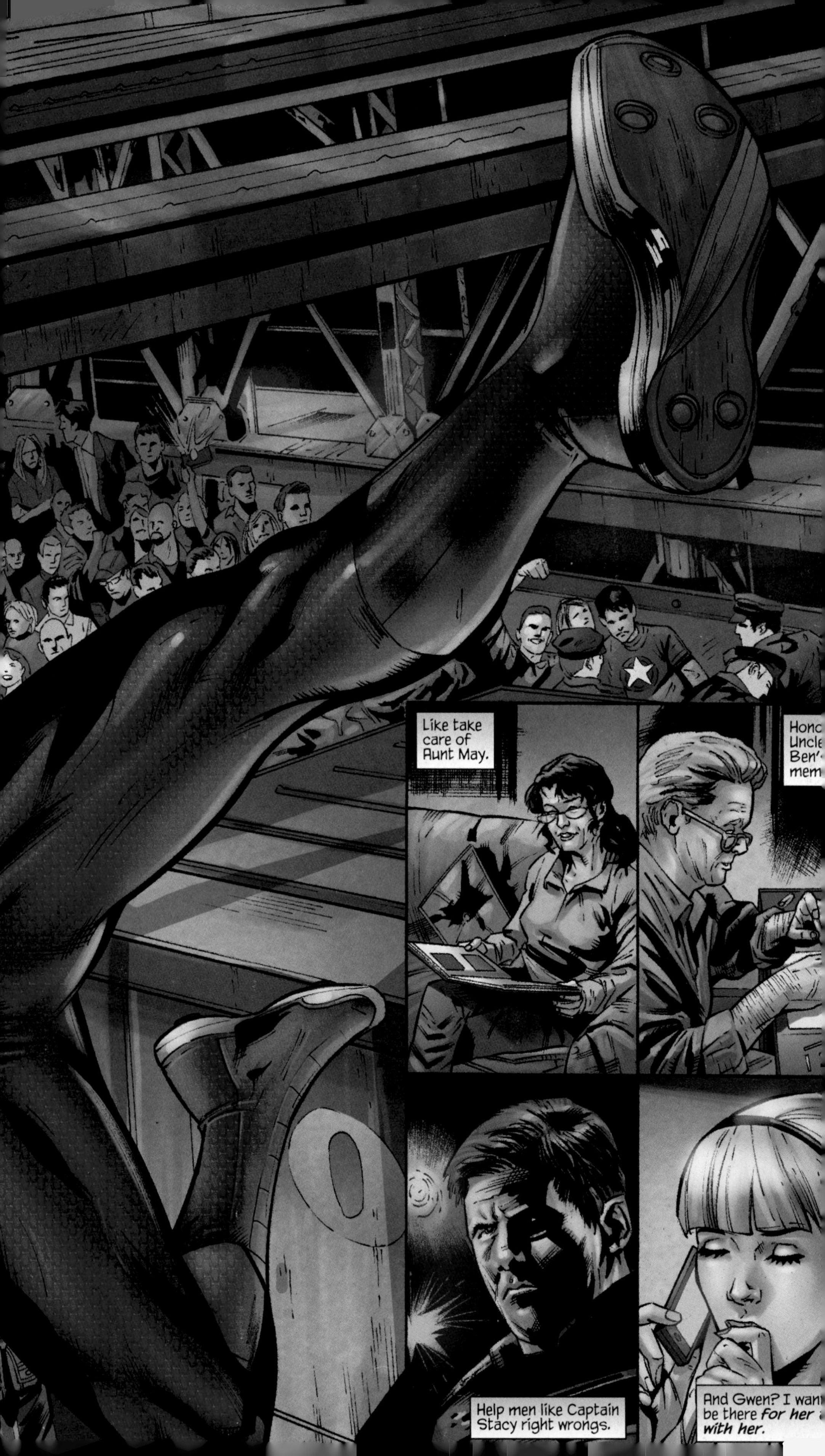
Like take care of Aunt May.
Honc Uncle Ben'- mem
Help men like Captain Stacy right wrongs.
And Gwen? I wan be there *for her* *with her.*

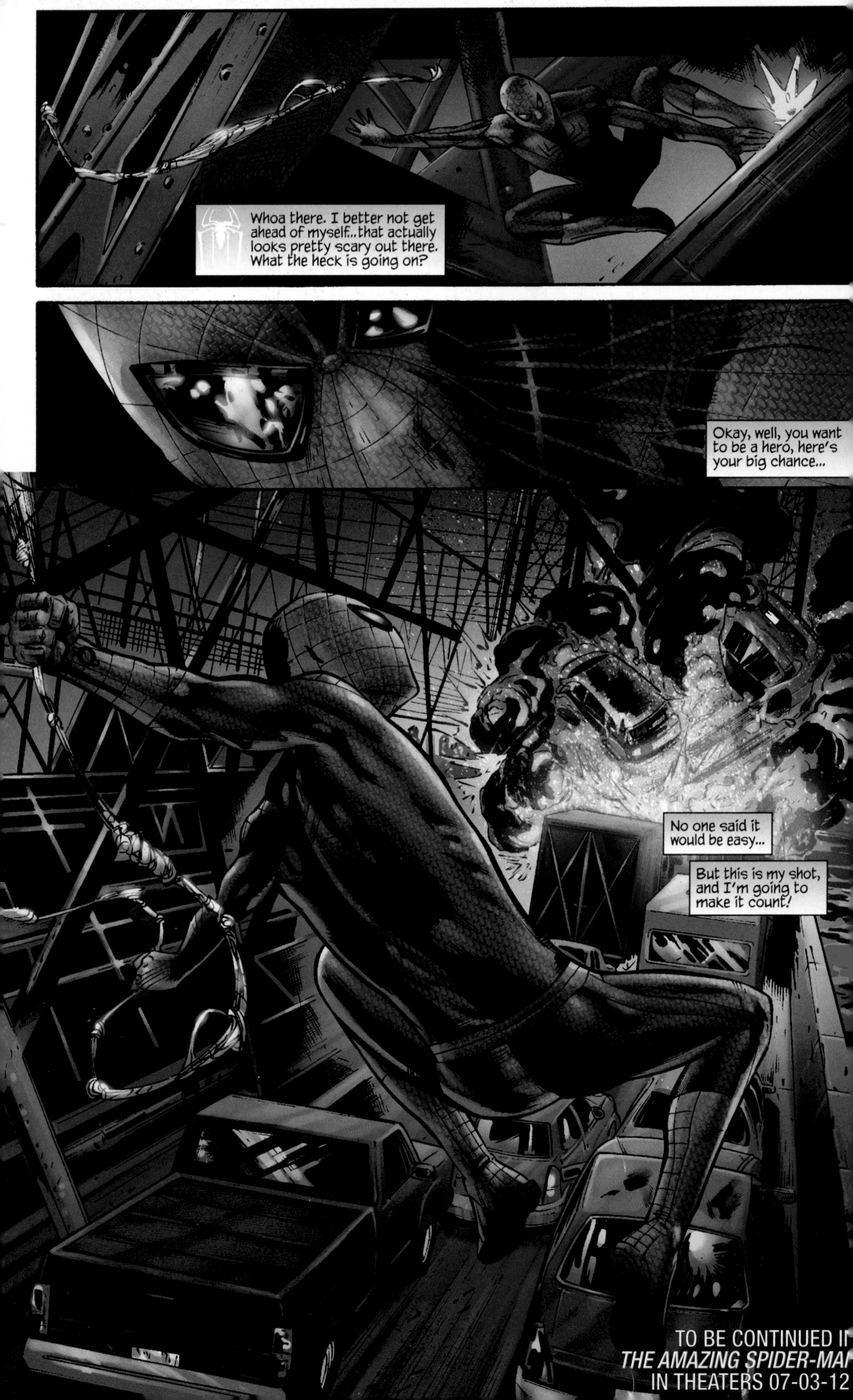
Whoa there. I better not get ahead of myself...that actually looks pretty scary out there. What the heck is going on?
Okay, well, you want to be a hero, here's your big chance...
No one said it would be easy...
But this is my shot, and I'm going to make it count!
TO BE CONTINUED I
THE AMAZING SPIDER-MA
IN THEATERS 07-03-12

THE STORY CONTINUES IN:

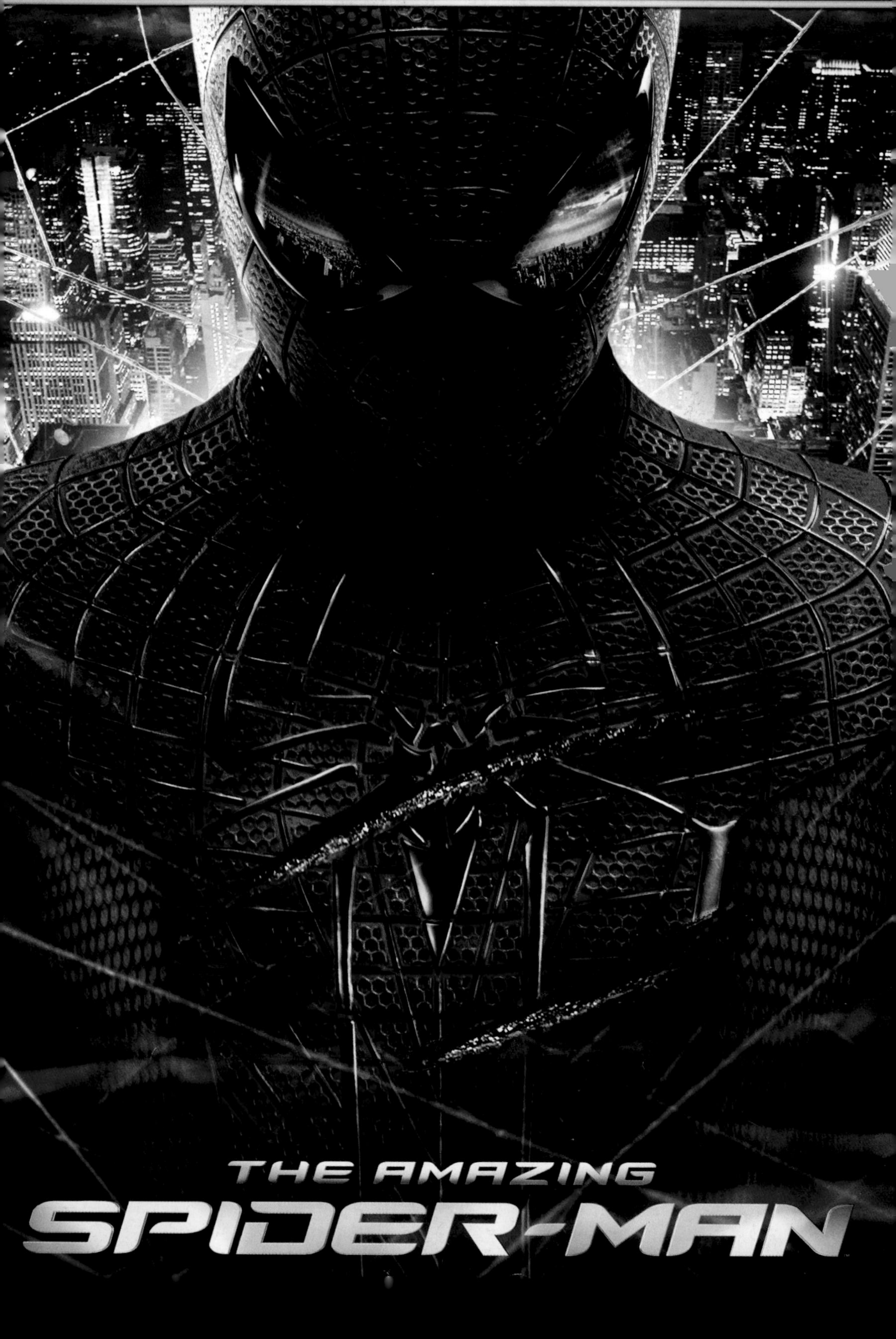
THE AMAZING
SPIDER-MAN

SPIDER-MAN
15¢ IND.
75 AUG
the AMAZING SPIDER-MAN
APPROVED BY THE COMICS CODE AUTHORITY
MARVEL COMICS GROUP
DEATH WITHOUT WARNING!
ROMITA

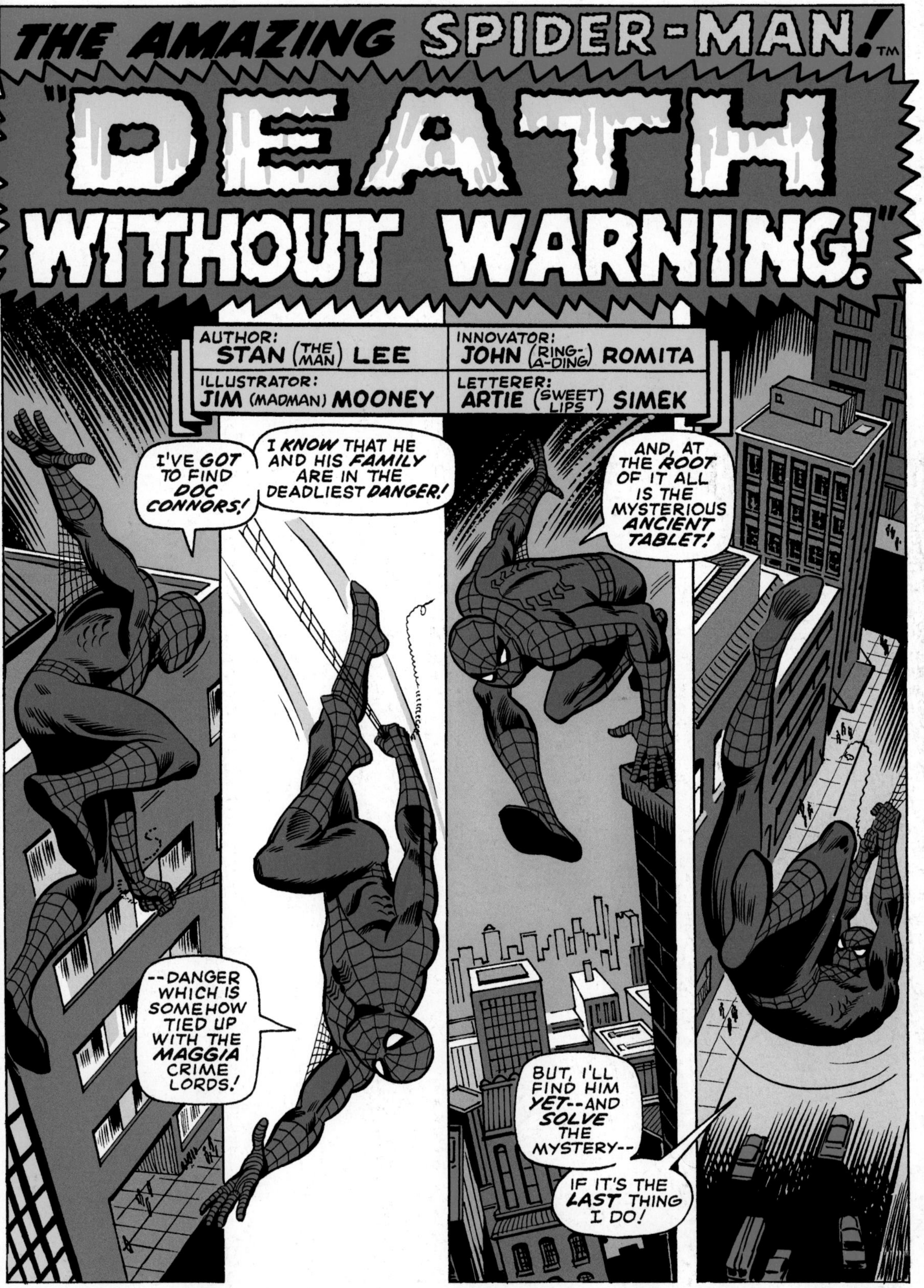
THE AMAZING SPIDER-MAN! ™
"DEATH WITHOUT WARNING!"
AUTHOR: STAN (THE MAN) LEE
INNOVATOR: JOHN (RING-A-DING) ROMITA
ILLUSTRATOR: JIM (MADMAN) MOONEY
LETTERER: ARTIE (SWEET LIPS) SIMEK
I'VE GOT TO FIND DOC CONNORS!
I KNOW THAT HE AND HIS FAMILY ARE IN THE DEADLIEST DANGER!
--DANGER WHICH IS SOMEHOW TIED UP WITH THE MAGGIA CRIME LORDS!
AND, AT THE ROOT OF IT ALL IS THE MYSTERIOUS ANCIENT TABLET!
BUT, I'LL FIND HIM YET--AND SOLVE THE MYSTERY--
IF IT'S THE LAST THING I DO!

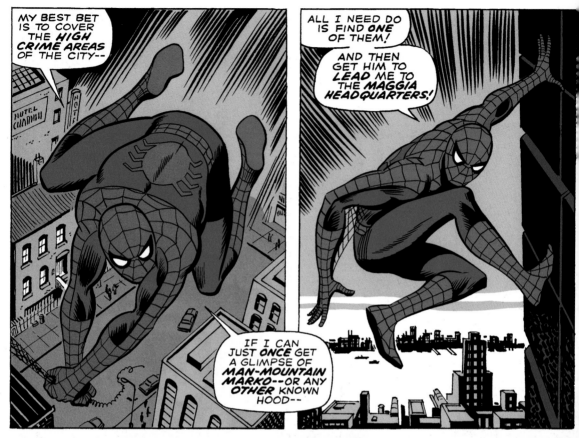

MY BEST BET IS TO COVER THE **HIGH CRIME AREAS** OF THE CITY--

ALL I NEED DO IS FIND **ONE** OF THEM!

AND THEN GET HIM TO **LEAD** ME TO THE **MAGGIA HEADQUARTERS!**

IF I CAN JUST **ONCE** GET A GLIMPSE OF **MAN-MOUNTAIN MARKO**--OR ANY **OTHER** KNOWN HOOD--

A COUPLE OF SMALL-TIMERS, MAKING **BOOK!** MAYBE **THEY** HAVE THE **INFO** THAT I NEED!

HOLD IT, BLACKIE! THERE'S SOMETHING OUT THE **WINDOW!**

YA SOUND LIKE A **NUT!** WE'RE **20 STORIES** HIGH!

I TELL YOU I SAW **SOMETHING!** BUT--

HOW'S **THIS** FOR STARTERS, GUYS?

YEAH! YEAH! WHAT **ELSE** IS NEW?

SPIDER-MAN!

LOOK OUT! WE--WE'LL **FALL!**

2

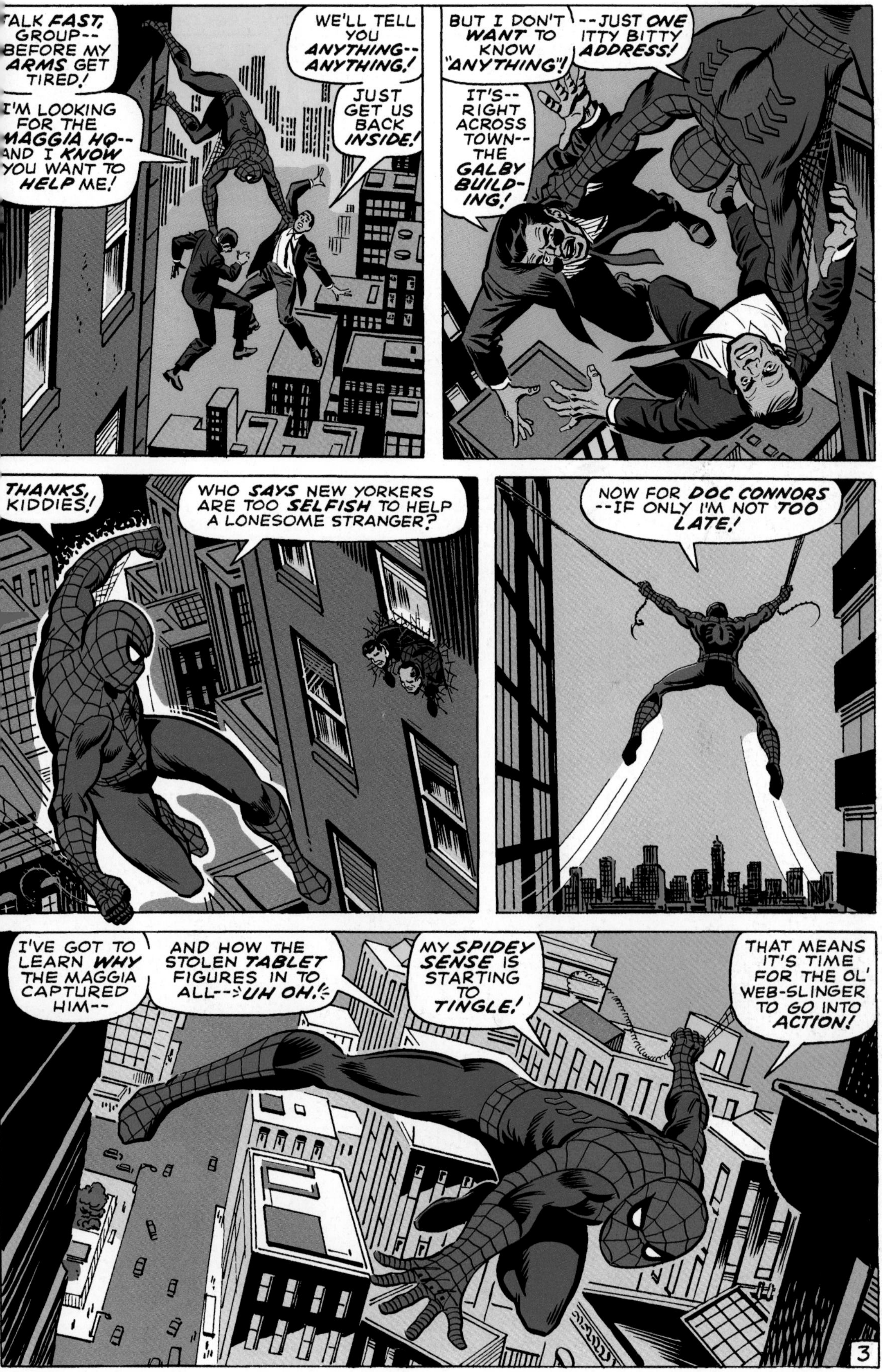

TALK FAST, GROUP-- BEFORE MY ARMS GET TIRED!
I'M LOOKING FOR THE MAGGIA HQ-- AND I KNOW YOU WANT TO HELP ME!
WE'LL TELL YOU ANYTHING-- ANYTHING!
JUST GET US BACK INSIDE!
BUT I DON'T WANT TO KNOW "ANYTHING"!
--JUST ONE ITTY BITTY ADDRESS!
IT'S-- RIGHT ACROSS TOWN-- THE GALBY BUILD-ING!
THANKS, KIDDIES!
WHO SAYS NEW YORKERS ARE TOO SELFISH TO HELP A LONESOME STRANGER?
NOW FOR DOC CONNORS --IF ONLY I'M NOT TOO LATE!
I'VE GOT TO LEARN WHY THE MAGGIA CAPTURED HIM--
AND HOW THE STOLEN TABLET FIGURES IN TO ALL-- UH OH!
MY SPIDEY SENSE IS STARTING TO TINGLE!
THAT MEANS IT'S TIME FOR THE OL' WEB-SLINGER TO GO INTO ACTION!

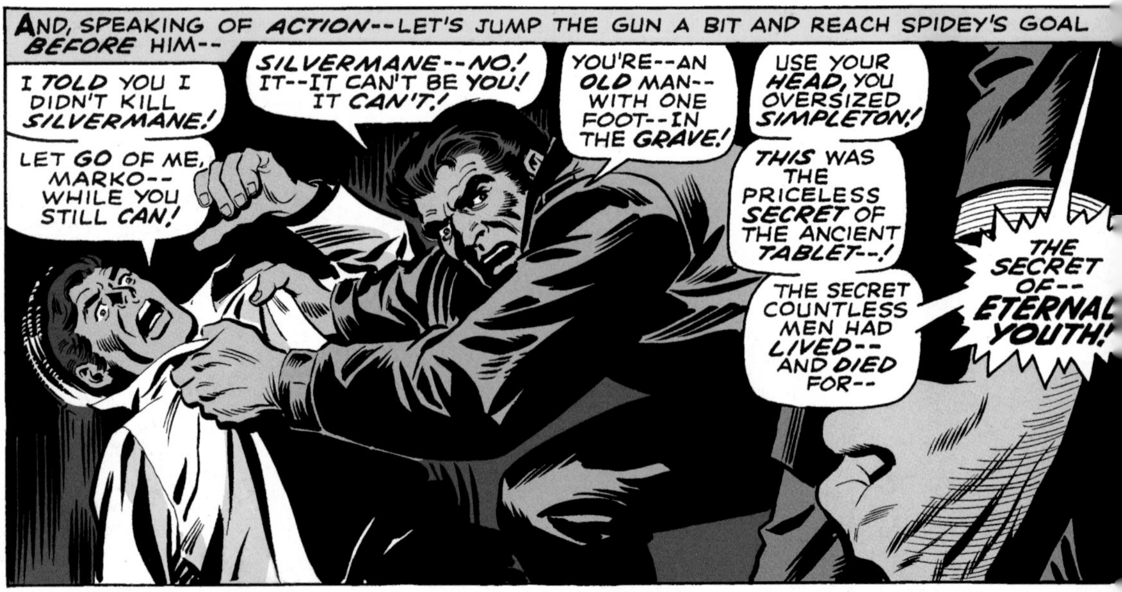
AND, SPEAKING OF ACTION--LET'S JUMP THE GUN A BIT AND REACH SPIDEY'S GOAL BEFORE HIM--
SILVERMANE--NO! IT--IT CAN'T BE YOU! IT CAN'T!
YOU'RE--AN OLD MAN--WITH ONE FOOT--IN THE GRAVE!
I TOLD YOU I DIDN'T KILL SILVERMANE!
LET GO OF ME, MARKO--WHILE YOU STILL CAN!
USE YOUR HEAD, YOU OVERSIZED SIMPLETON!
THIS WAS THE PRICELESS SECRET OF THE ANCIENT TABLET--!
THE SECRET COUNTLESS MEN HAD LIVED--AND DIED FOR--
THE SECRET OF--ETERNAL YOUTH!
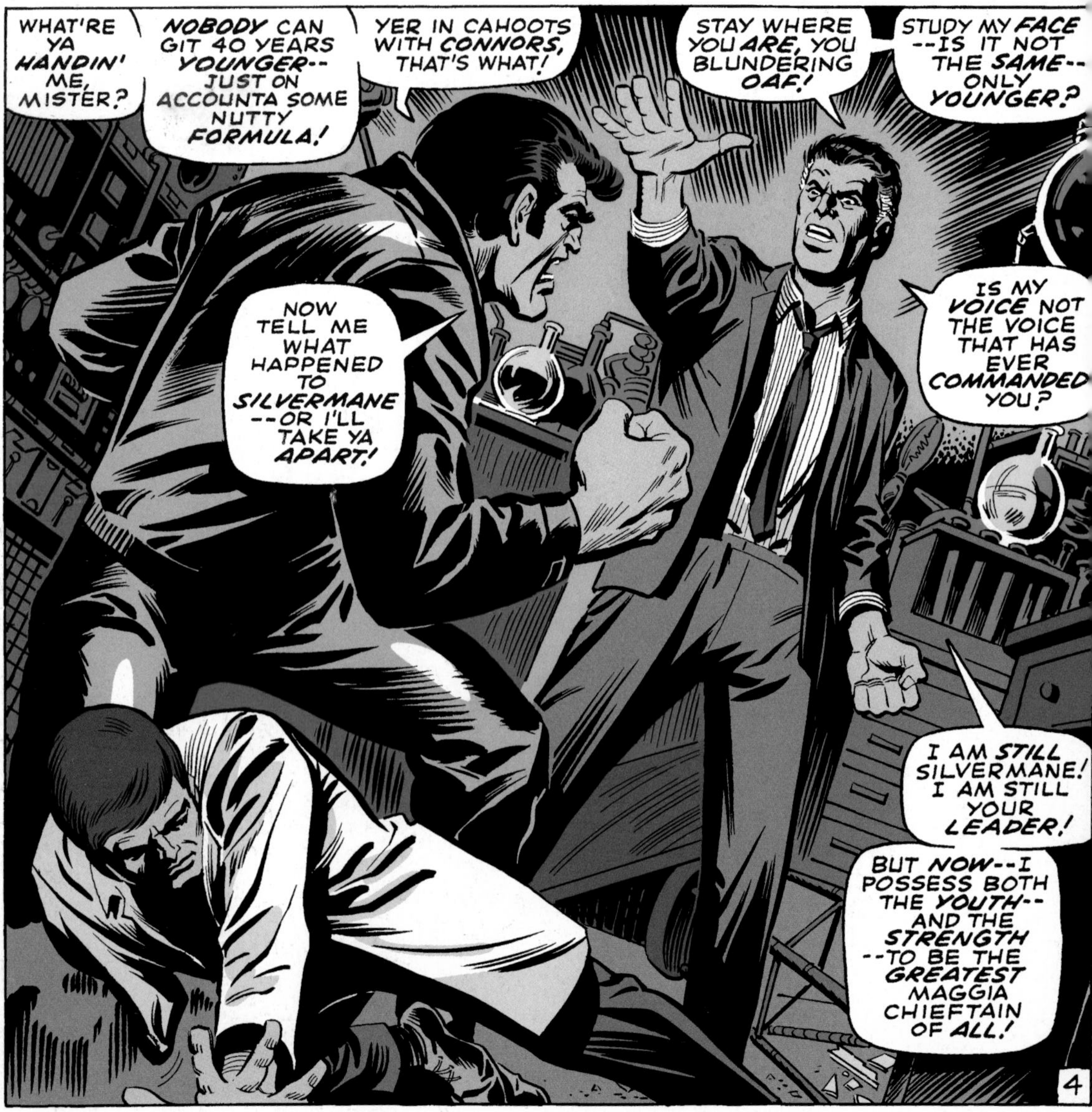
WHAT'RE YA HANDIN' ME, MISTER?
NOBODY CAN GIT 40 YEARS YOUNGER--JUST ON ACCOUNTA SOME NUTTY FORMULA!
YER IN CAHOOTS WITH CONNORS, THAT'S WHAT!
STAY WHERE YOU ARE, YOU BLUNDERING OAF!
STUDY MY FACE--IS IT NOT THE SAME--ONLY YOUNGER?
NOW TELL ME WHAT HAPPENED TO SILVERMANE--OR I'LL TAKE YA APART!
IS MY VOICE NOT THE VOICE THAT HAS EVER COMMANDED YOU?
I AM STILL SILVERMANE! I AM STILL YOUR LEADER!
BUT NOW--I POSSESS BOTH THE YOUTH--AND THE STRENGTH--TO BE THE GREATEST MAGGIA CHIEFTAIN OF ALL!

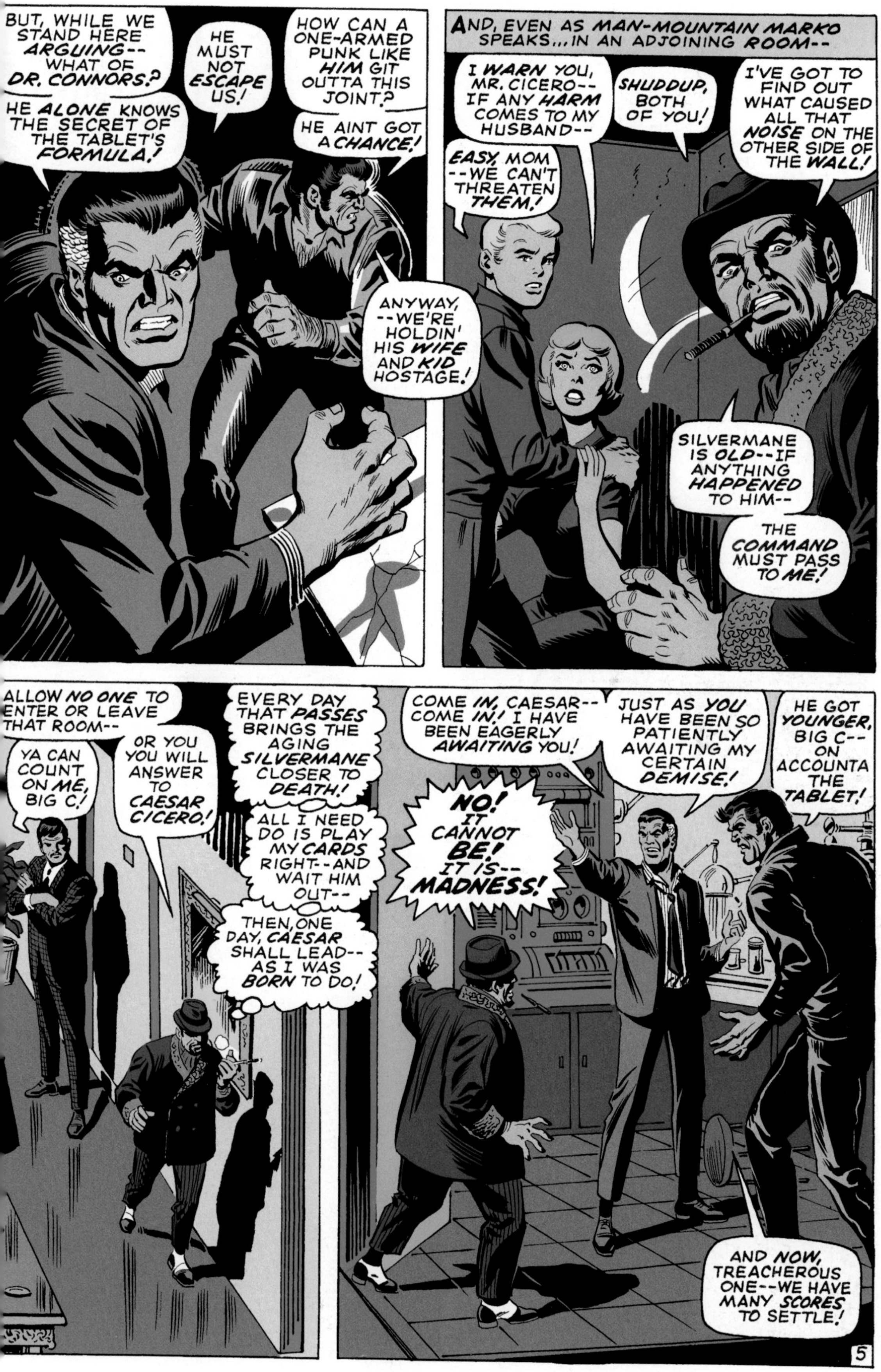
BUT, WHILE WE STAND HERE ARGUING-- WHAT OF DR. CONNORS?
HE ALONE KNOWS THE SECRET OF THE TABLET'S FORMULA!
HE MUST NOT ESCAPE US!
HOW CAN A ONE-ARMED PUNK LIKE HIM GIT OUTTA THIS JOINT?
HE AINT GOT A CHANCE!
ANYWAY, --WE'RE HOLDIN' HIS WIFE AND KID HOSTAGE!
AND, EVEN AS MAN-MOUNTAIN MARKO SPEAKS... IN AN ADJOINING ROOM--
I WARN YOU, MR. CICERO-- IF ANY HARM COMES TO MY HUSBAND--
EASY, MOM --WE CAN'T THREATEN THEM!
SHUDDUP, BOTH OF YOU!
I'VE GOT TO FIND OUT WHAT CAUSED ALL THAT NOISE ON THE OTHER SIDE OF THE WALL!
SILVERMANE IS OLD--IF ANYTHING HAPPENED TO HIM--
THE COMMAND MUST PASS TO ME!
ALLOW NO ONE TO ENTER OR LEAVE THAT ROOM--
YA CAN COUNT ON ME, BIG C!
OR YOU YOU WILL ANSWER TO CAESAR CICERO!
EVERY DAY THAT PASSES BRINGS THE AGING SILVERMANE CLOSER TO DEATH!
ALL I NEED DO IS PLAY MY CARDS RIGHT--AND WAIT HIM OUT--
THEN, ONE DAY, CAESAR SHALL LEAD-- AS I WAS BORN TO DO!
COME IN, CAESAR-- COME IN! I HAVE BEEN EAGERLY AWAITING YOU!
NO! IT CANNOT BE! IT IS-- MADNESS!
JUST AS YOU HAVE BEEN SO PATIENTLY AWAITING MY CERTAIN DEMISE!
HE GOT YOUNGER, BIG C-- ON ACCOUNTA THE TABLET!
AND NOW, TREACHEROUS ONE--WE HAVE MANY SCORES TO SETTLE!

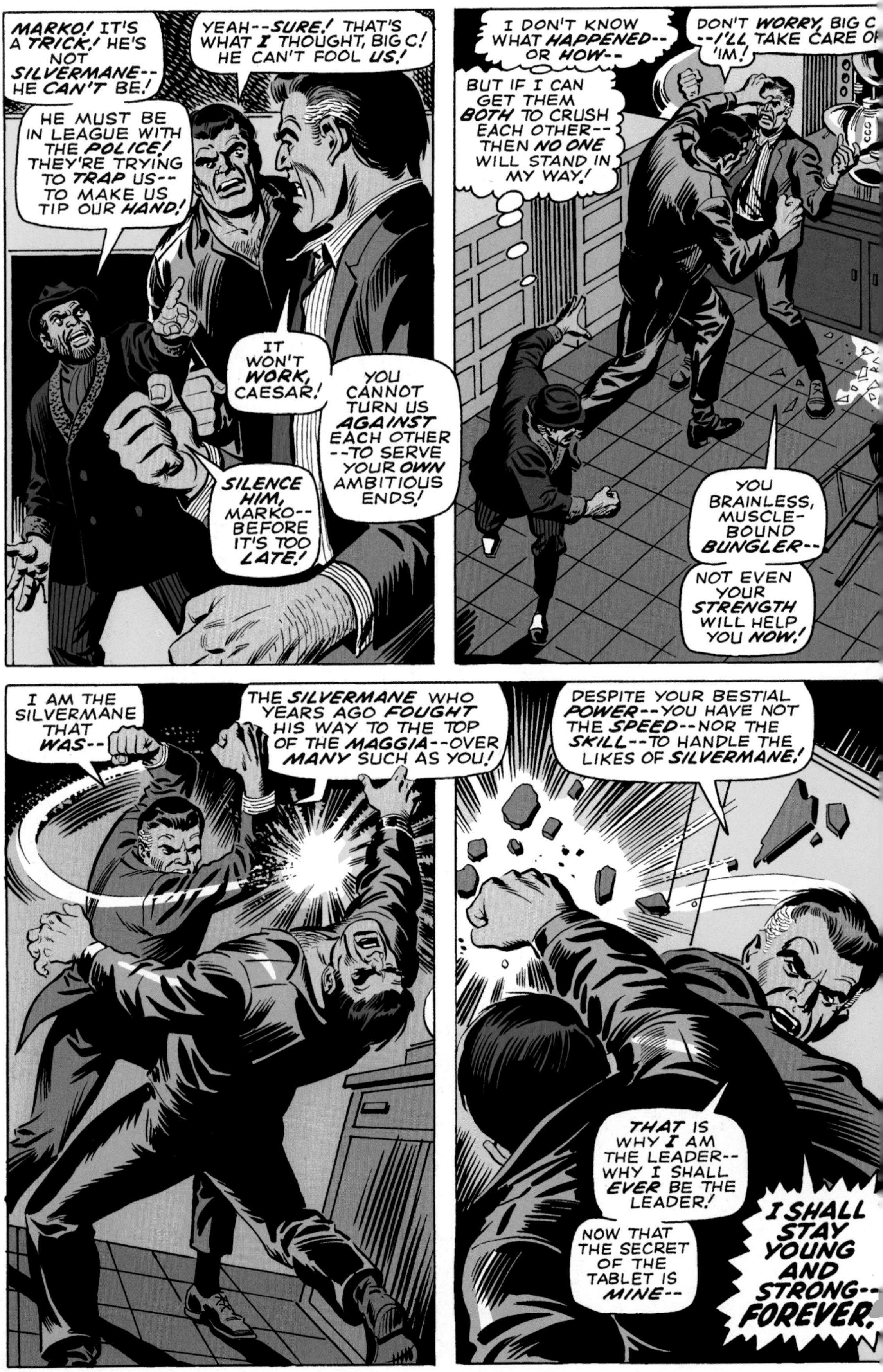
MARKO! IT'S A TRICK! HE'S NOT SILVERMANE--HE CAN'T BE!
YEAH--SURE! THAT'S WHAT I THOUGHT, BIG C! HE CAN'T FOOL US!
HE MUST BE IN LEAGUE WITH THE POLICE! THEY'RE TRYING TO TRAP US--TO MAKE US TIP OUR HAND!
IT WON'T WORK, CAESAR!
YOU CANNOT TURN US AGAINST EACH OTHER--TO SERVE YOUR OWN AMBITIOUS ENDS!
SILENCE HIM, MARKO--BEFORE IT'S TOO LATE!
I DON'T KNOW WHAT HAPPENED--OR HOW--
BUT IF I CAN GET THEM BOTH TO CRUSH EACH OTHER--THEN NO ONE WILL STAND IN MY WAY!
DON'T WORRY, BIG C--I'LL TAKE CARE OF 'IM!
YOU BRAINLESS, MUSCLE-BOUND BUNGLER--
NOT EVEN YOUR STRENGTH WILL HELP YOU NOW!
I AM THE SILVERMANE THAT WAS--
THE SILVERMANE WHO YEARS AGO FOUGHT HIS WAY TO THE TOP OF THE MAGGIA--OVER MANY SUCH AS YOU!
DESPITE YOUR BESTIAL POWER--YOU HAVE NOT THE SPEED--NOR THE SKILL--TO HANDLE THE LIKES OF SILVERMANE!
THAT IS WHY I AM THE LEADER--WHY I SHALL EVER BE THE LEADER!
NOW THAT THE SECRET OF THE TABLET IS MINE--
I SHALL STAY YOUNG AND STRONG--FOREVER!

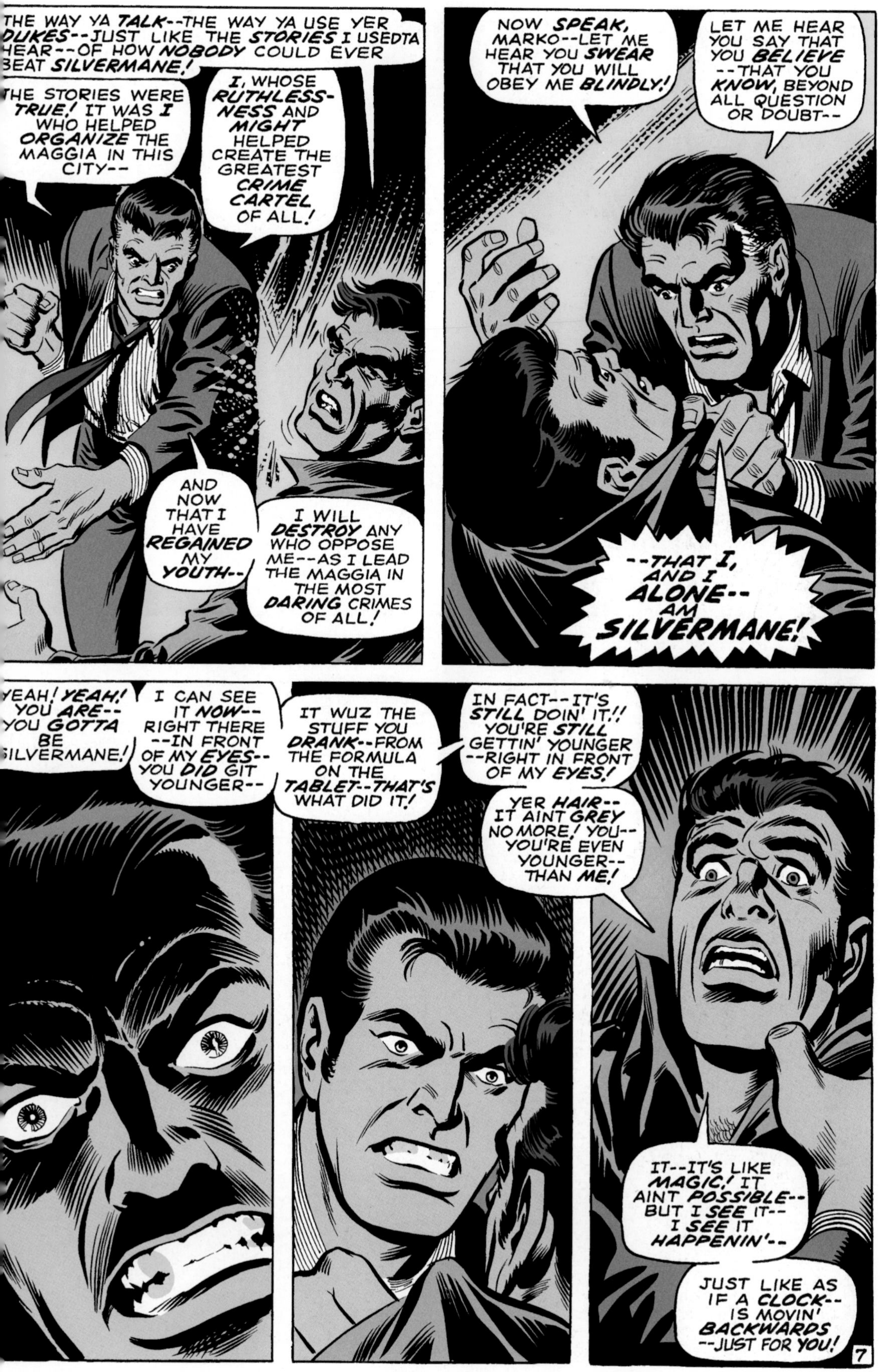
THE WAY YA TALK--THE WAY YA USE YER DUKES--JUST LIKE THE STORIES I USEDTA HEAR--OF HOW NOBODY COULD EVER BEAT SILVERMANE!
THE STORIES WERE TRUE! IT WAS I WHO HELPED ORGANIZE THE MAGGIA IN THIS CITY--
I, WHOSE RUTHLESS-NESS AND MIGHT HELPED CREATE THE GREATEST CRIME CARTEL OF ALL!
AND NOW THAT I HAVE REGAINED MY YOUTH--
I WILL DESTROY ANY WHO OPPOSE ME--AS I LEAD THE MAGGIA IN THE MOST DARING CRIMES OF ALL!
NOW SPEAK, MARKO--LET ME HEAR YOU SWEAR THAT YOU WILL OBEY ME BLINDLY!
LET ME HEAR YOU SAY THAT YOU BELIEVE --THAT YOU KNOW, BEYOND ALL QUESTION OR DOUBT--
--THAT I, AND I ALONE-- AM SILVERMANE!
YEAH! YEAH! YOU ARE-- YOU GOTTA BE SILVERMANE!
I CAN SEE IT NOW-- RIGHT THERE --IN FRONT OF MY EYES-- YOU DID GIT YOUNGER--
IT WUZ THE STUFF YOU DRANK--FROM THE FORMULA ON THE TABLET--THAT'S WHAT DID IT!
IN FACT--IT'S STILL DOIN' IT!! YOU'RE STILL GETTIN' YOUNGER --RIGHT IN FRONT OF MY EYES!
YER HAIR-- IT AINT GREY NO MORE! YOU-- YOU'RE EVEN YOUNGER-- THAN ME!
IT--IT'S LIKE MAGIC! IT AINT POSSIBLE-- BUT I SEE IT-- I SEE IT HAPPENIN'--
JUST LIKE AS IF A CLOCK-- IS MOVIN' BACKWARDS --JUST FOR YOU!
7

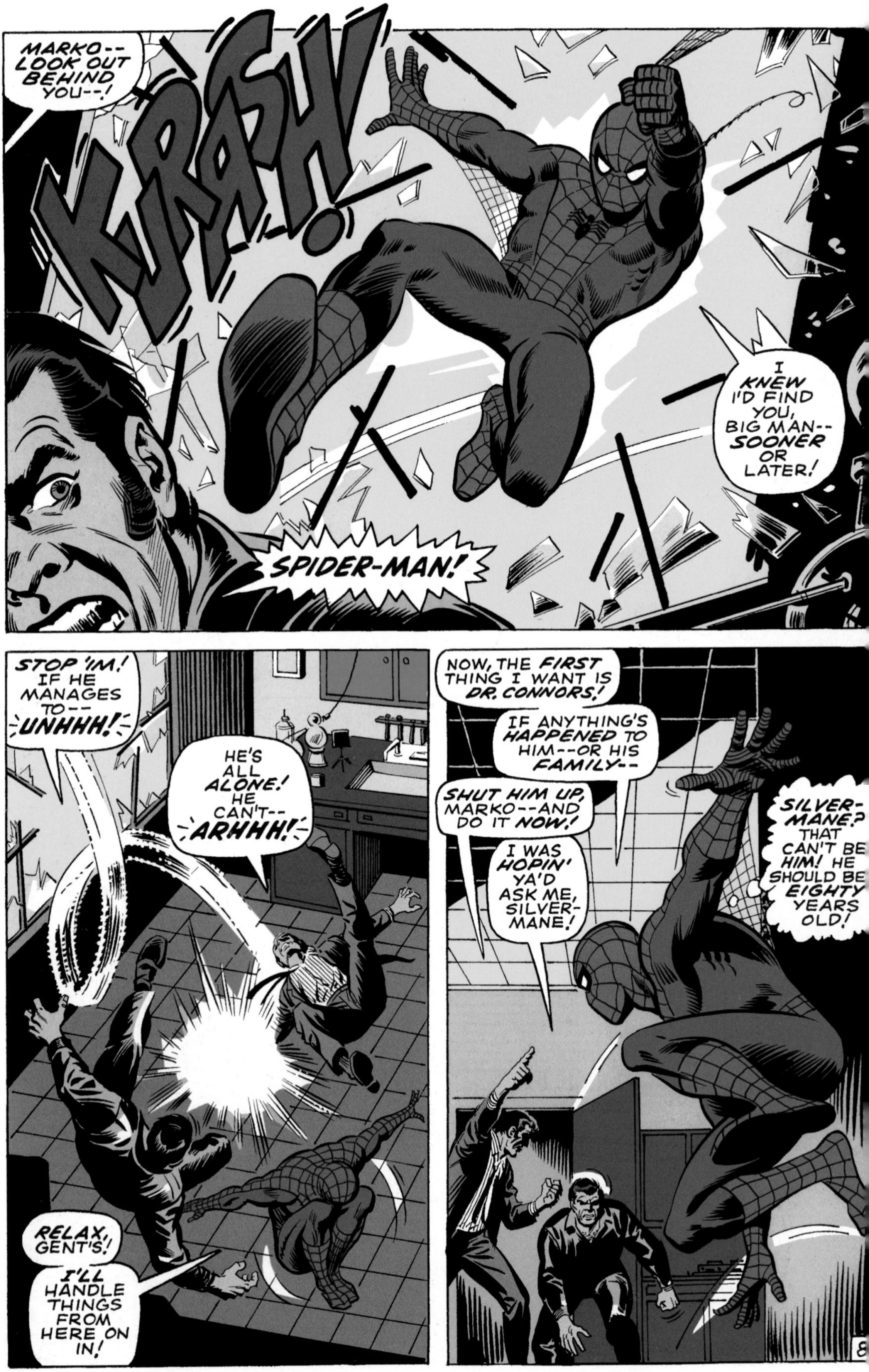
MARKO-- LOOK OUT BEHIND YOU--!
KRASH!
I KNEW I'D FIND YOU, BIG MAN-- SOONER OR LATER!
SPIDER-MAN!
STOP 'IM! IF HE MANAGES TO-- UNHHH!
HE'S ALL ALONE! HE CAN'T-- ARHHH!
RELAX, GENT'S!
I'LL HANDLE THINGS FROM HERE ON IN!
NOW, THE FIRST THING I WANT IS DR. CONNORS!
IF ANYTHING'S HAPPENED TO HIM--OR HIS FAMILY--
SHUT HIM UP, MARKO--AND DO IT NOW!
I WAS HOPIN' YA'D ASK ME, SILVERMANE!
SILVERMANE? THAT CAN'T BE HIM! HE SHOULD BE EIGHTY YEARS OLD!
8

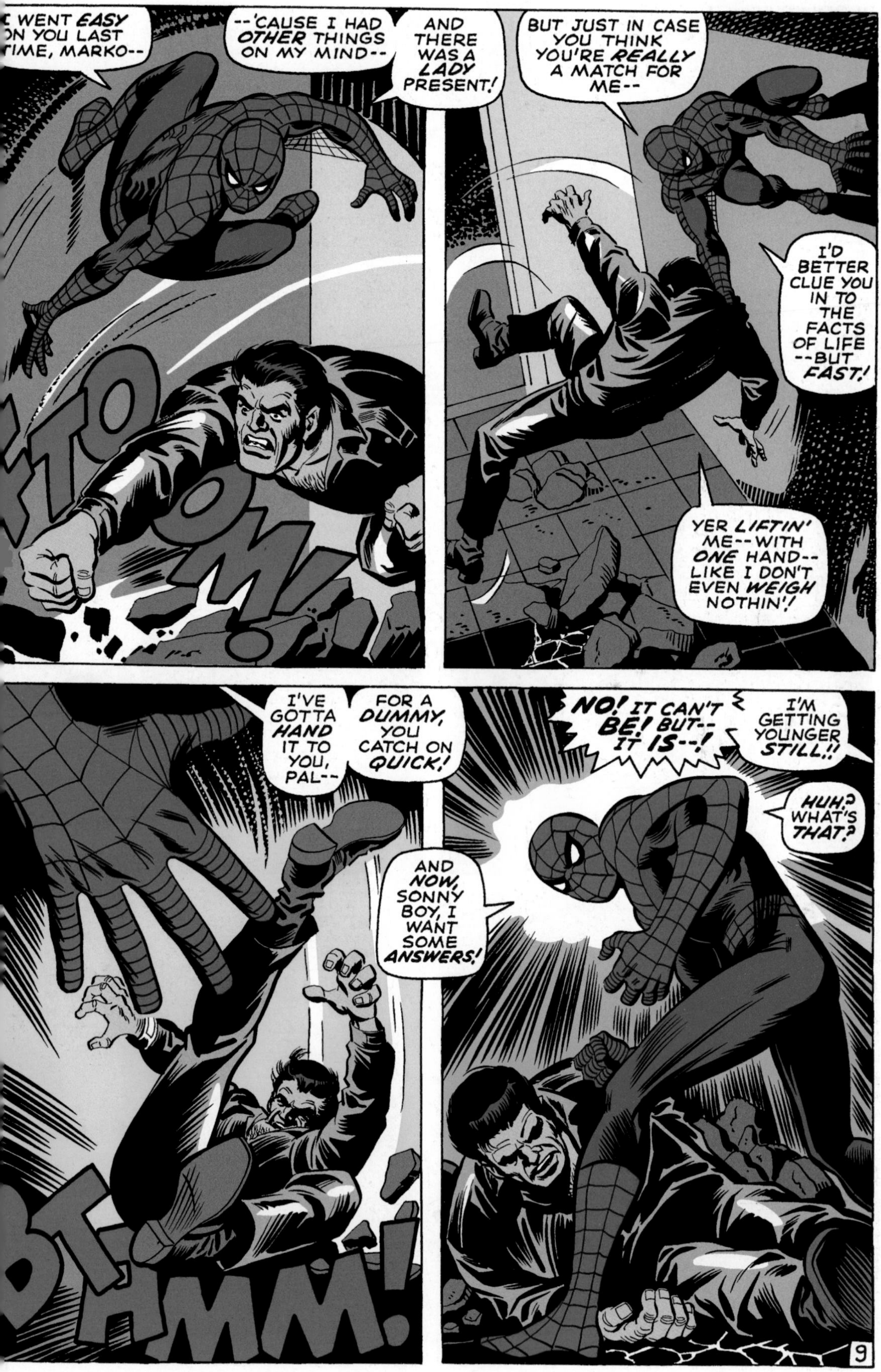
I WENT EASY ON YOU LAST TIME, MARKO--
--'CAUSE I HAD OTHER THINGS ON MY MIND--
AND THERE WAS A LADY PRESENT!
TOOM!
BUT JUST IN CASE YOU THINK YOU'RE REALLY A MATCH FOR ME--
I'D BETTER CLUE YOU IN TO THE FACTS OF LIFE --BUT FAST!
YER LIFTIN' ME--WITH ONE HAND--LIKE I DON'T EVEN WEIGH NOTHIN'!
I'VE GOTTA HAND IT TO YOU, PAL--
FOR A DUMMY, YOU CATCH ON QUICK!
AND NOW, SONNY BOY, I WANT SOME ANSWERS!
BTHAMM!
NO! IT CAN'T BE! BUT--IT IS--!
I'M GETTING YOUNGER STILL!!
HUH? WHAT'S THAT?
9

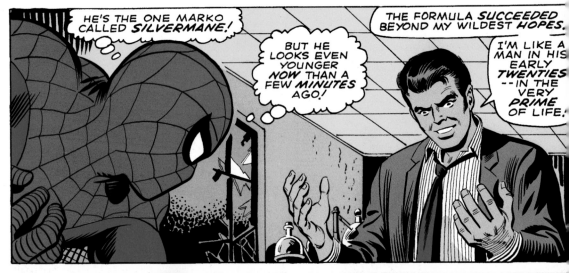

HE'S THE ONE MARKO CALLED **SILVERMANE!**

BUT HE LOOKS EVEN *YOUNGER* NOW THAN A FEW *MINUTES* AGO!

THE FORMULA *SUCCEEDED* BEYOND MY WILDEST *HOPES.*

I'M LIKE A MAN IN HIS EARLY *TWENTIES* -- IN THE VERY *PRIME* OF LIFE!

AND, THE *YOUNGER* I GET--THE *HEALTHIER* I GET-- THE MORE *ALIVE*-- THE MORE *POWERFUL* I BECOME!

THERE IS *NOTHING* I CANNOT DO-- *NO ONE* I CANNOT *DEFEAT!*

NOT EVEN *SPIDER-MAN* CAN HOPE TO OPPOSE ONE WHO HAS DRUNK FROM THE WATERS OF THE *FOUNTAIN OF YOUTH!*

HE--REALLY *MEANS* IT

MEANWHILE--

I DON'T KNOW WHERE *SPIDER-MAN* CAME FROM--BUT THIS IS MY CHANCE TO *ESCAPE!*

ALL RIGHT, WALL-CRAWLER --LET'S SEE WHAT YOU'RE *MADE OF!*

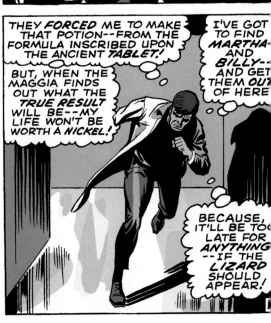

THEY *FORCED* ME TO MAKE THAT POTION--FROM THE FORMULA INSCRIBED UPON THE ANCIENT *TABLET!*

BUT, WHEN THE MAGGIA FINDS OUT WHAT THE *TRUE RESULT* WILL BE--MY LIFE WON'T BE WORTH A *NICKEL!*

I'VE GOT TO FIND *MARTHA* AND *BILLY*-- AND GET THEM *OUT* OF HERE

BECAUSE, IT'LL BE TOO LATE FOR *ANYTHING* --IF THE *LIZARD* SHOULD APPEAR!

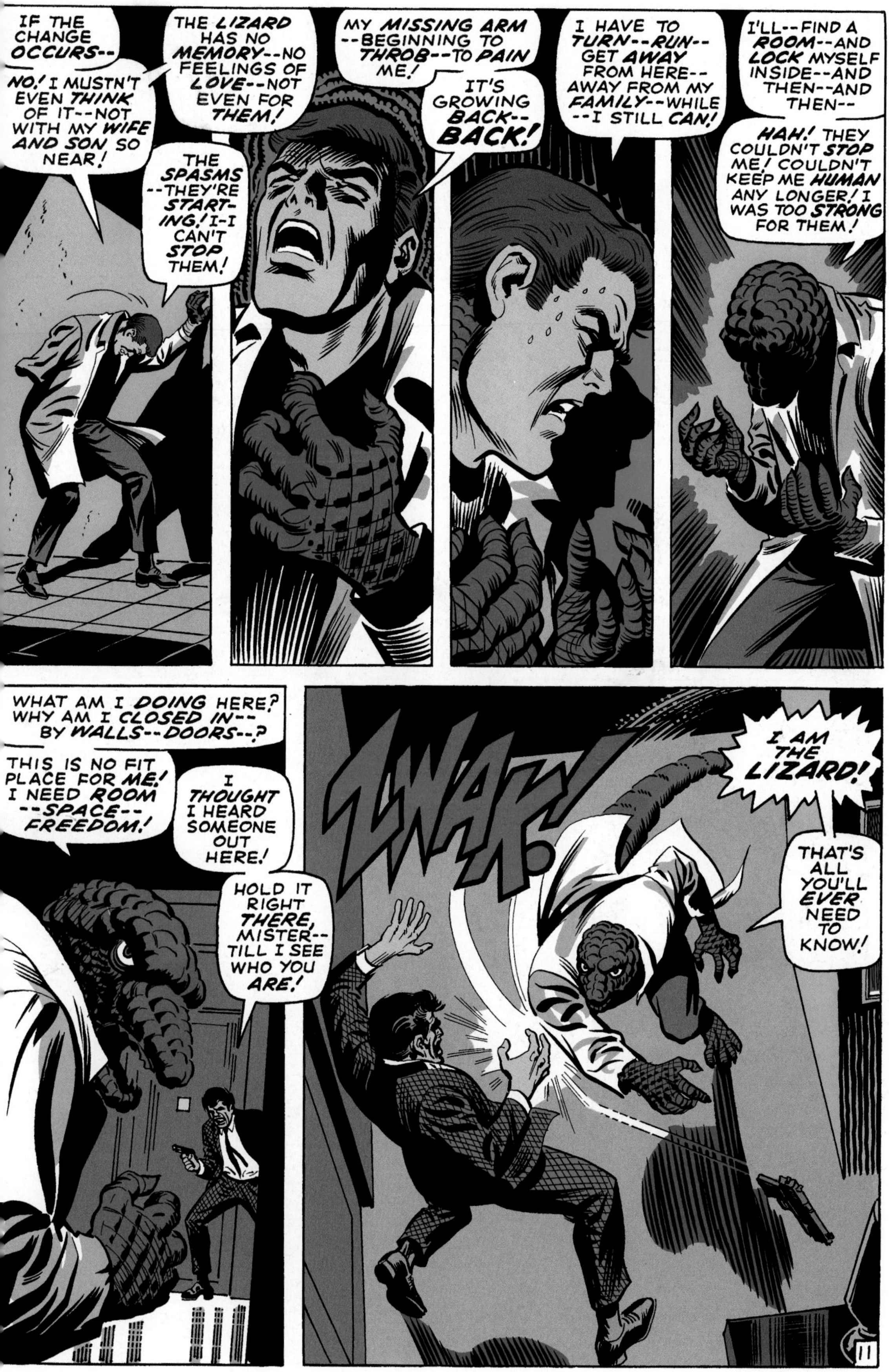
IF THE CHANGE OCCURS--
NO! I MUSTN'T EVEN THINK OF IT--NOT WITH MY WIFE AND SON SO NEAR!
THE LIZARD HAS NO MEMORY--NO FEELINGS OF LOVE--NOT EVEN FOR THEM!
THE SPASMS--THEY'RE STARTING! I-I CAN'T STOP THEM!
MY MISSING ARM--BEGINNING TO THROB--TO PAIN ME!
IT'S GROWING BACK--BACK!
I HAVE TO TURN--RUN--GET AWAY FROM HERE--AWAY FROM MY FAMILY--WHILE--I STILL CAN!
I'LL--FIND A ROOM--AND LOCK MYSELF INSIDE--AND THEN--AND THEN--
HAH! THEY COULDN'T STOP ME! COULDN'T KEEP ME HUMAN ANY LONGER! I WAS TOO STRONG FOR THEM!
WHAT AM I DOING HERE? WHY AM I CLOSED IN--BY WALLS--DOORS--?
THIS IS NO FIT PLACE FOR ME! I NEED ROOM--SPACE--FREEDOM!
I THOUGHT I HEARD SOMEONE OUT HERE!
HOLD IT RIGHT THERE, MISTER--TILL I SEE WHO YOU ARE!
ZWAK!
I AM THE LIZARD!
THAT'S ALL YOU'LL EVER NEED TO KNOW!

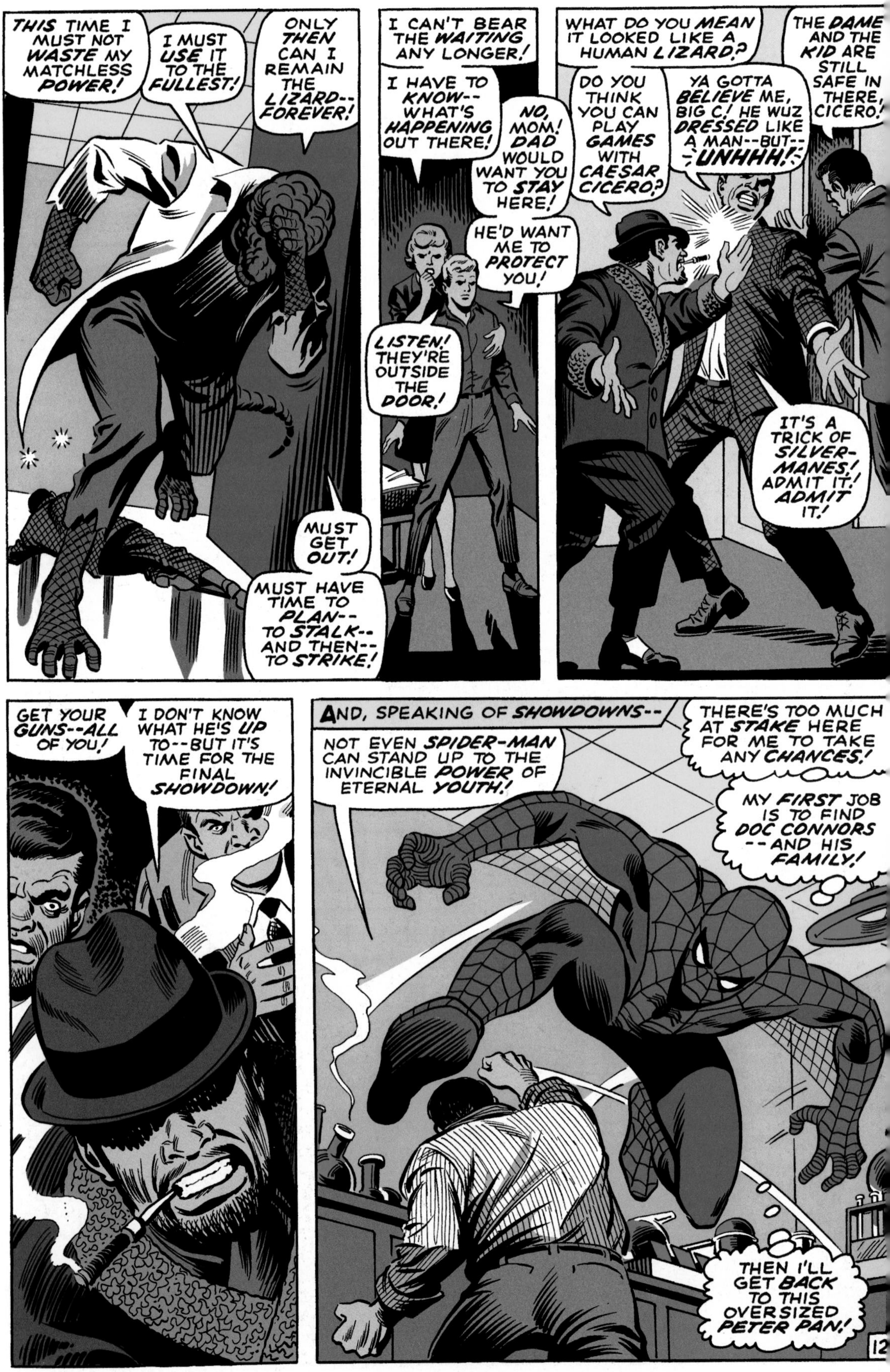
THIS TIME I MUST NOT WASTE MY MATCHLESS POWER!
I MUST USE IT TO THE FULLEST!
ONLY THEN CAN I REMAIN THE LIZARD--FOREVER!
MUST GET OUT!
MUST HAVE TIME TO PLAN--TO STALK--AND THEN--TO STRIKE!
I CAN'T BEAR THE WAITING ANY LONGER!
I HAVE TO KNOW--WHAT'S HAPPENING OUT THERE!
NO, MOM! DAD WOULD WANT YOU TO STAY HERE!
HE'D WANT ME TO PROTECT YOU!
LISTEN! THEY'RE OUTSIDE THE DOOR!
WHAT DO YOU MEAN IT LOOKED LIKE A HUMAN LIZARD?
DO YOU THINK YOU CAN PLAY GAMES WITH CAESAR CICERO?
YA GOTTA BELIEVE ME, BIG C! HE WUZ DRESSED LIKE A MAN--BUT--UNHHH!
THE DAME AND THE KID ARE STILL SAFE IN THERE, CICERO!
IT'S A TRICK OF SILVERMANES! ADMIT IT! ADMIT IT!
GET YOUR GUNS--ALL OF YOU!
I DON'T KNOW WHAT HE'S UP TO--BUT IT'S TIME FOR THE FINAL SHOWDOWN!
AND, SPEAKING OF SHOWDOWNS--
NOT EVEN SPIDER-MAN CAN STAND UP TO THE INVINCIBLE POWER OF ETERNAL YOUTH!
THERE'S TOO MUCH AT STAKE HERE FOR ME TO TAKE ANY CHANCES!
MY FIRST JOB IS TO FIND DOC CONNORS--AND HIS FAMILY!
THEN I'LL GET BACK TO THIS OVERSIZED PETER PAN!
12

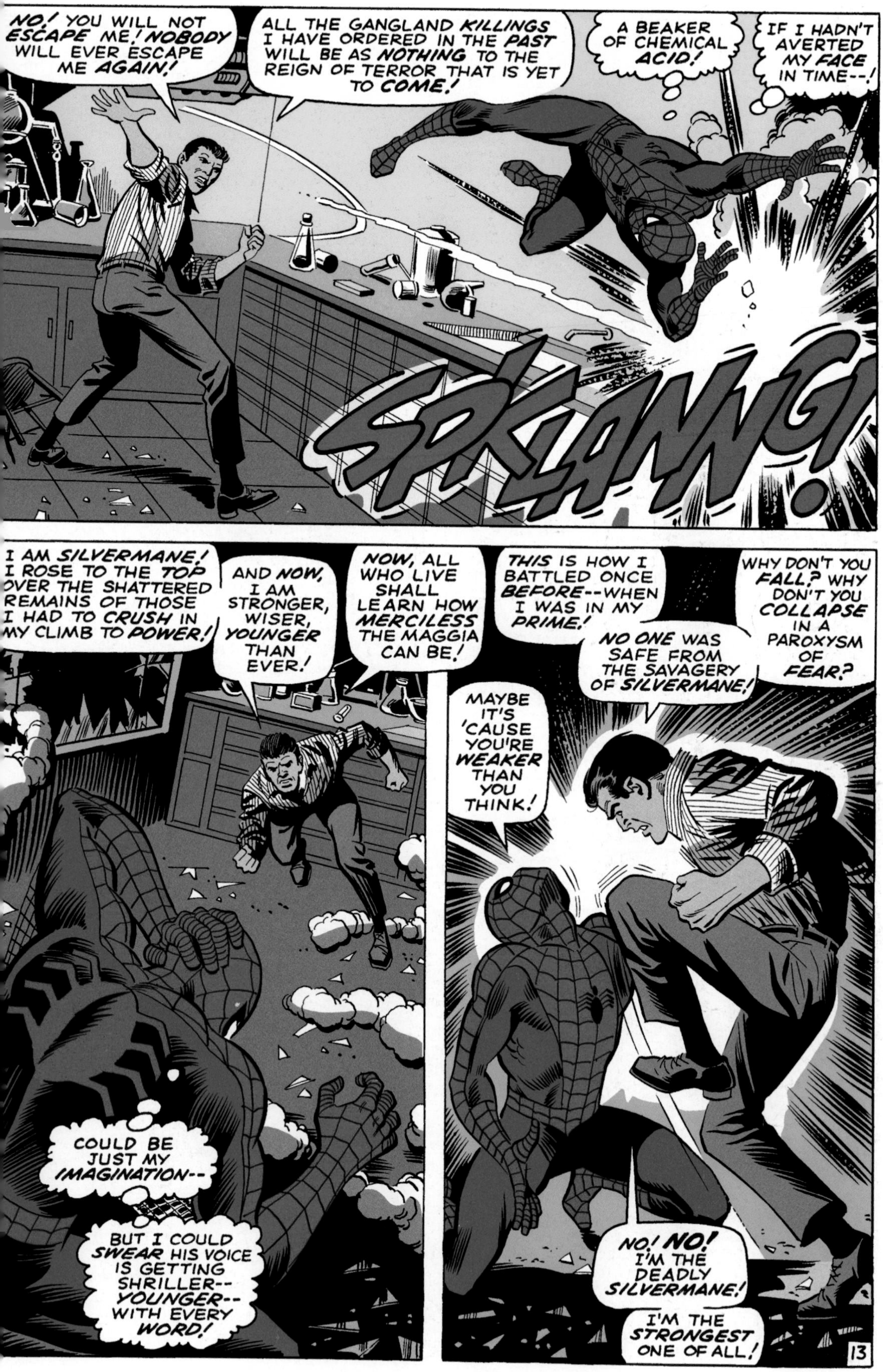

NO! YOU WILL NOT ESCAPE ME! NOBODY WILL EVER ESCAPE ME AGAIN!
ALL THE GANGLAND KILLINGS I HAVE ORDERED IN THE PAST WILL BE AS NOTHING TO THE REIGN OF TERROR THAT IS YET TO COME!
A BEAKER OF CHEMICAL ACID!
IF I HADN'T AVERTED MY FACE IN TIME--!
SPKLANNG!
I AM SILVERMANE! I ROSE TO THE TOP OVER THE SHATTERED REMAINS OF THOSE I HAD TO CRUSH IN MY CLIMB TO POWER!
AND NOW, I AM STRONGER, WISER, YOUNGER THAN EVER!
NOW, ALL WHO LIVE SHALL LEARN HOW MERCILESS THE MAGGIA CAN BE!
COULD BE JUST MY IMAGINATION--
BUT I COULD SWEAR HIS VOICE IS GETTING SHRILLER--YOUNGER--WITH EVERY WORD!
THIS IS HOW I BATTLED ONCE BEFORE--WHEN I WAS IN MY PRIME!
NO ONE WAS SAFE FROM THE SAVAGERY OF SILVERMANE!
WHY DON'T YOU FALL? WHY DON'T YOU COLLAPSE IN A PAROXYSM OF FEAR?
MAYBE IT'S 'CAUSE YOU'RE WEAKER THAN YOU THINK!
NO! NO! I'M THE DEADLY SILVERMANE!
I'M THE STRONGEST ONE OF ALL!

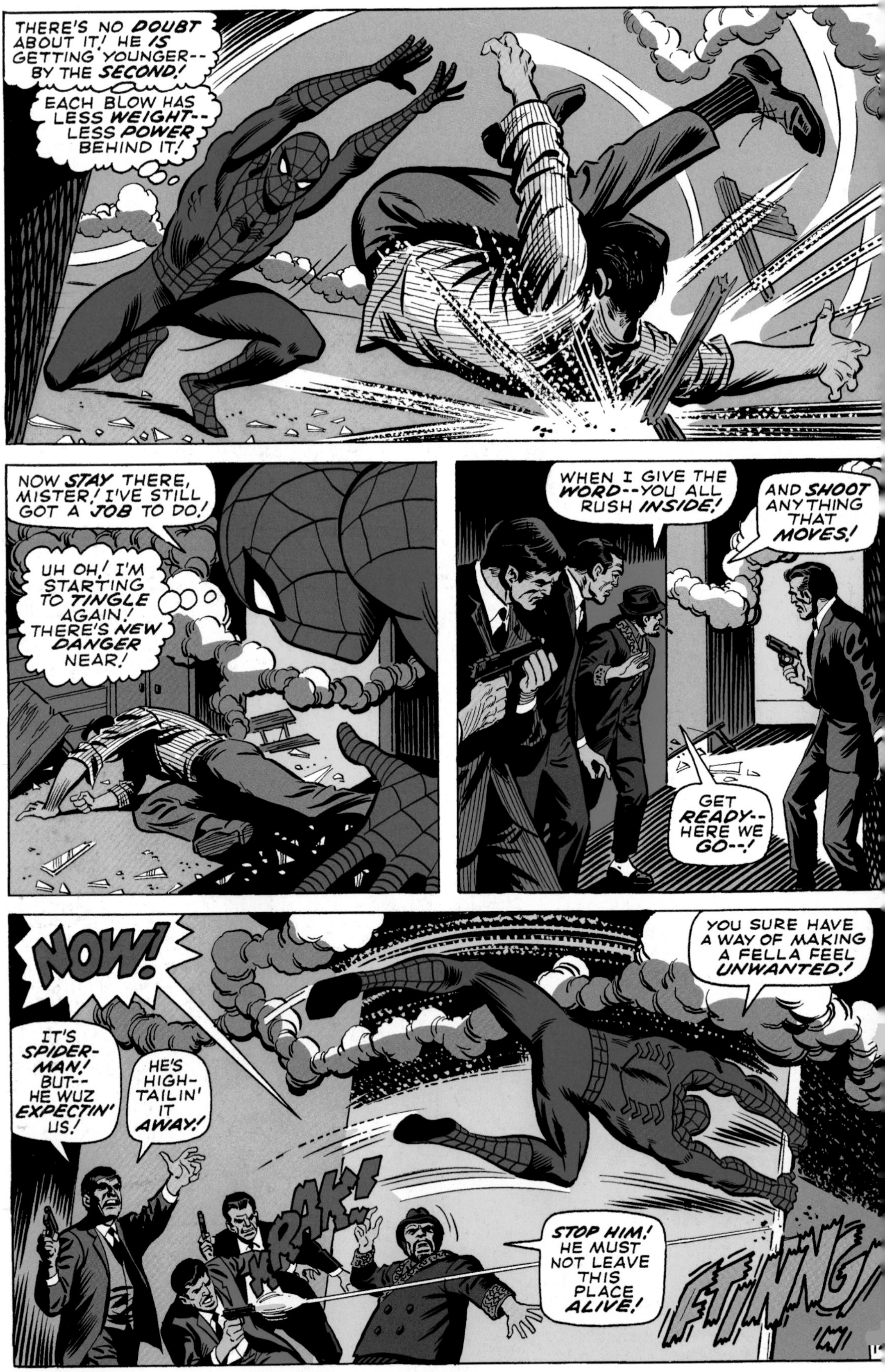

THERE'S NO DOUBT ABOUT IT! HE IS GETTING YOUNGER-- BY THE SECOND!
EACH BLOW HAS LESS WEIGHT-- LESS POWER BEHIND IT!
NOW STAY THERE, MISTER! I'VE STILL GOT A JOB TO DO!
UH OH! I'M STARTING TO TINGLE AGAIN! THERE'S NEW DANGER NEAR!
WHEN I GIVE THE WORD--YOU ALL RUSH INSIDE!
AND SHOOT ANYTHING THAT MOVES!
GET READY-- HERE WE GO--!
NOW!
YOU SURE HAVE A WAY OF MAKING A FELLA FEEL UNWANTED!
IT'S SPIDER-MAN! BUT-- HE WUZ EXPECTIN' US!
HE'S HIGH-TAILIN' IT AWAY!
THRAK!
STOP HIM! HE MUST NOT LEAVE THIS PLACE ALIVE!
FTNNG!

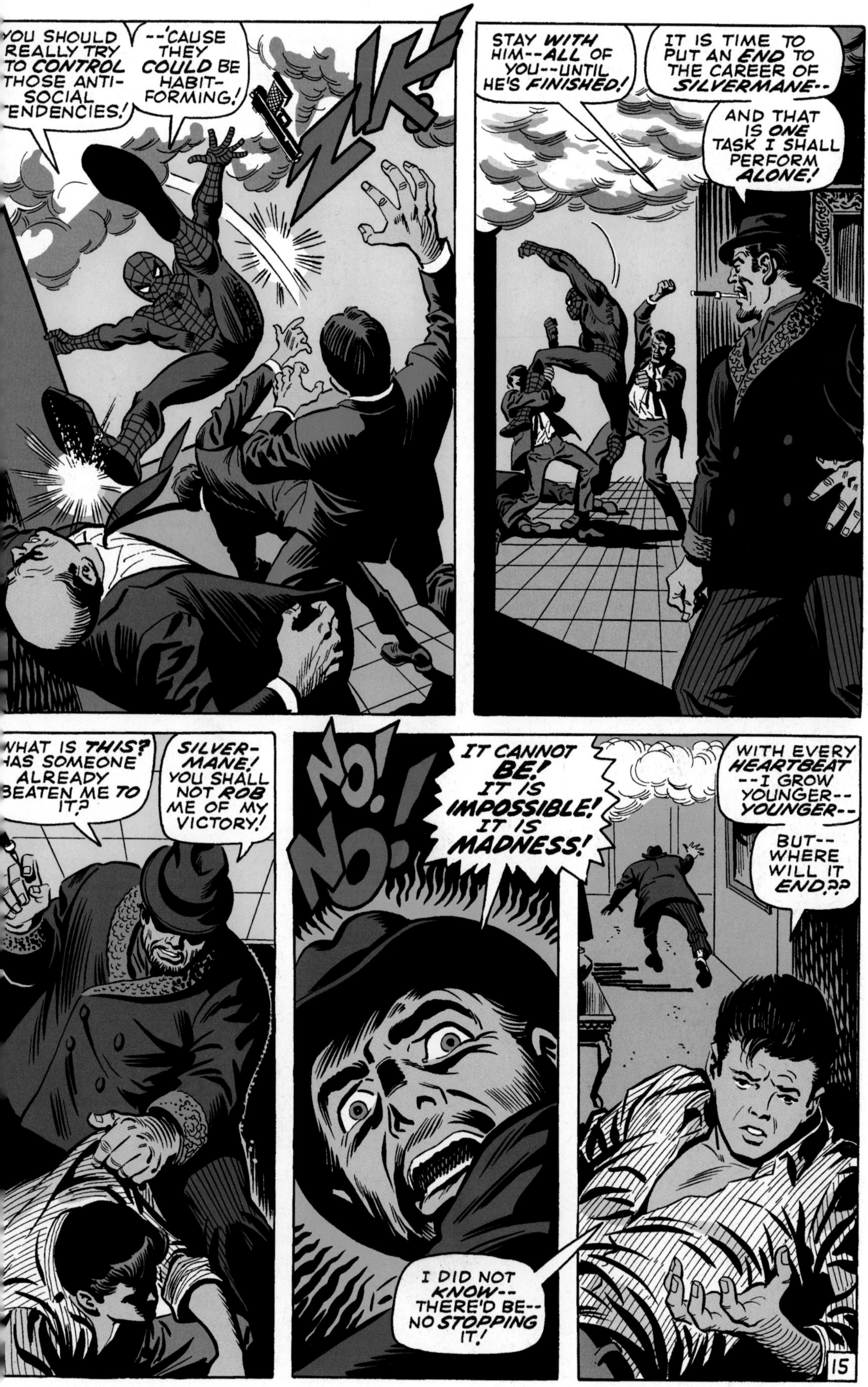

YOU SHOULD REALLY TRY TO CONTROL THOSE ANTI-SOCIAL TENDENCIES!
--'CAUSE THEY COULD BE HABIT-FORMING!
ZAK!
STAY WITH HIM--ALL OF YOU--UNTIL HE'S FINISHED!
IT IS TIME TO PUT AN END TO THE CAREER OF SILVERMANE--
AND THAT IS ONE TASK I SHALL PERFORM ALONE!
WHAT IS THIS? HAS SOMEONE ALREADY BEATEN ME TO IT?
SILVERMANE! YOU SHALL NOT ROB ME OF MY VICTORY!
NO! NO!
IT CANNOT BE! IT IS IMPOSSIBLE! IT IS MADNESS!
I DID NOT KNOW-- THERE'D BE-- NO STOPPING IT!
WITH EVERY HEARTBEAT --I GROW YOUNGER-- YOUNGER--
BUT-- WHERE WILL IT END??

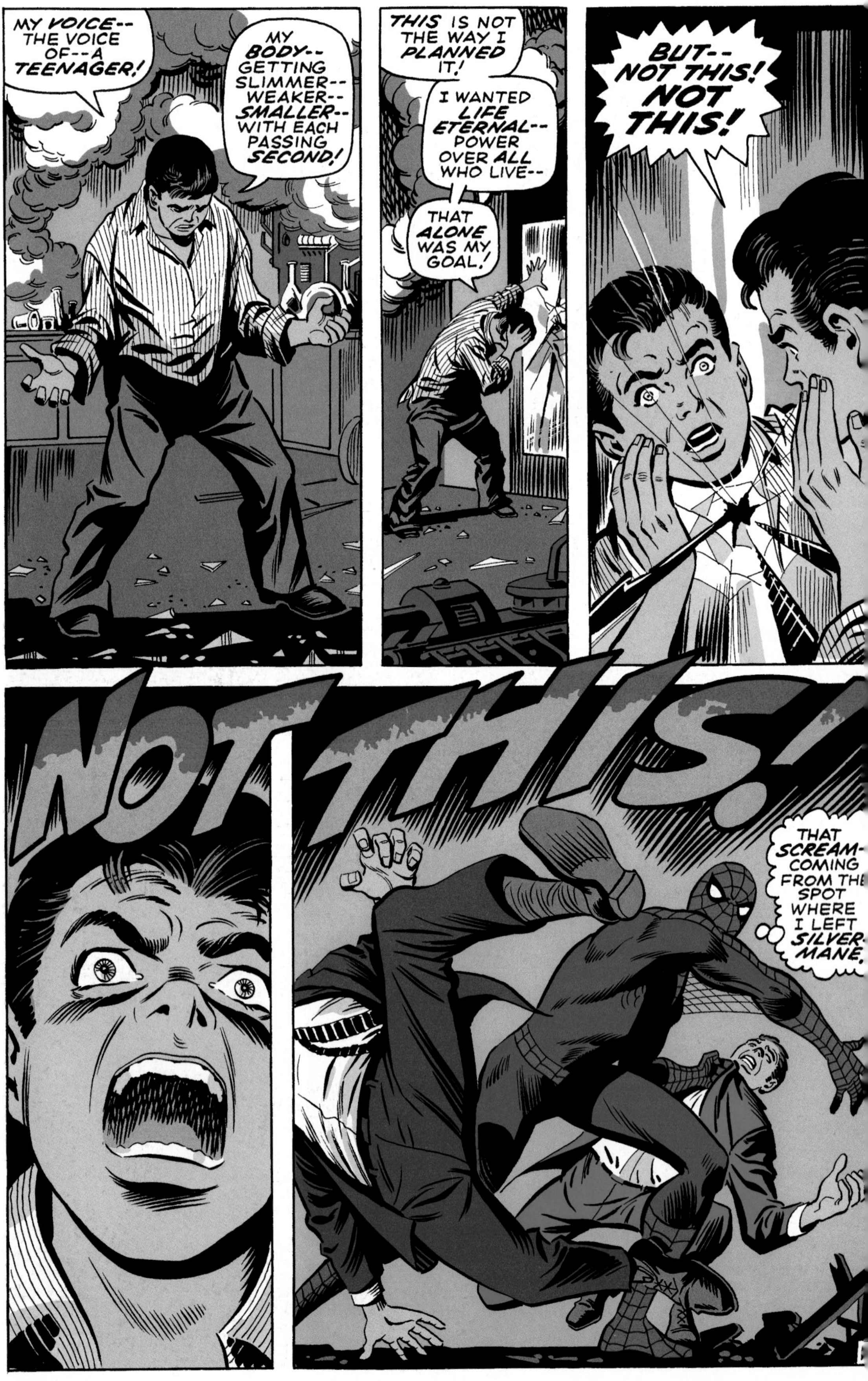
MY VOICE-- THE VOICE OF--A TEENAGER!
MY BODY-- GETTING SLIMMER-- WEAKER-- SMALLER-- WITH EACH PASSING SECOND!
THIS IS NOT THE WAY I PLANNED IT!
I WANTED LIFE ETERNAL-- POWER OVER ALL WHO LIVE--
THAT ALONE WAS MY GOAL!
BUT-- NOT THIS! NOT THIS!
NOT THIS!
THAT SCREAM-- COMING FROM THE SPOT WHERE I LEFT SILVERMANE!

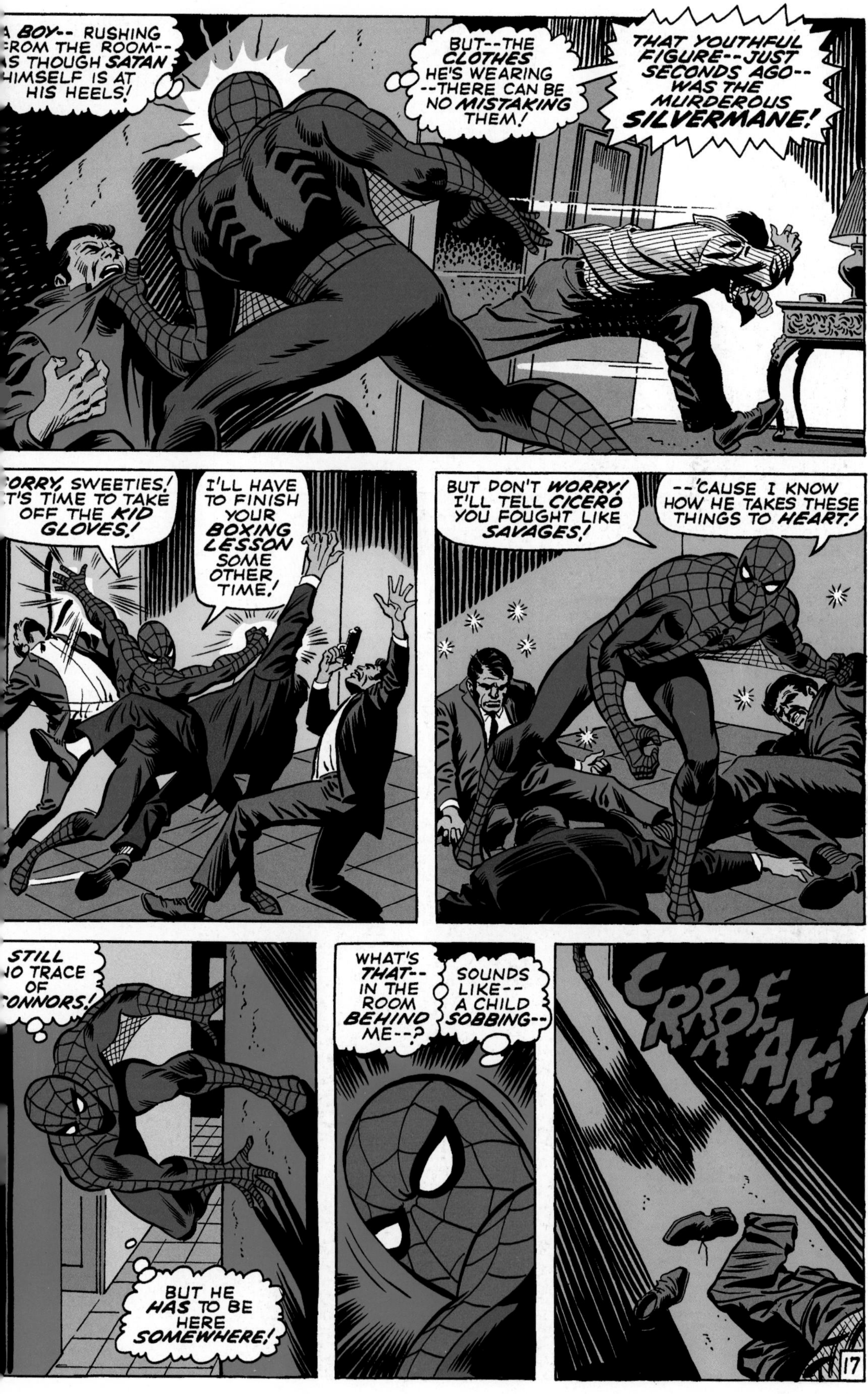
A BOY-- RUSHING FROM THE ROOM-- AS THOUGH SATAN HIMSELF IS AT HIS HEELS!
BUT--THE CLOTHES HE'S WEARING --THERE CAN BE NO MISTAKING THEM!
THAT YOUTHFUL FIGURE--JUST SECONDS AGO-- WAS THE MURDEROUS SILVERMANE!
SORRY, SWEETIES! IT'S TIME TO TAKE OFF THE KID GLOVES!
I'LL HAVE TO FINISH YOUR BOXING LESSON SOME OTHER TIME!
BUT DON'T WORRY! I'LL TELL CICERO YOU FOUGHT LIKE SAVAGES!
--'CAUSE I KNOW HOW HE TAKES THESE THINGS TO HEART!
STILL NO TRACE OF CONNORS!
BUT HE HAS TO BE HERE SOMEWHERE!
WHAT'S THAT-- IN THE ROOM BEHIND ME--?
SOUNDS LIKE-- A CHILD SOBBING--
CRREEAK!
17

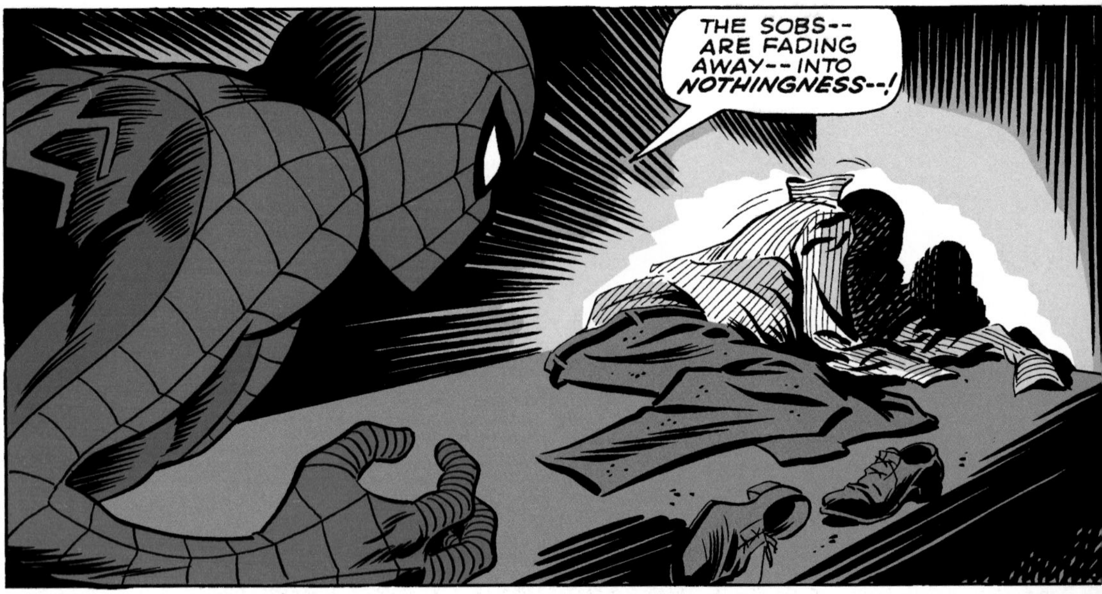
THE SOBS--
ARE FADING
AWAY-- INTO
NOTHINGNESS--!

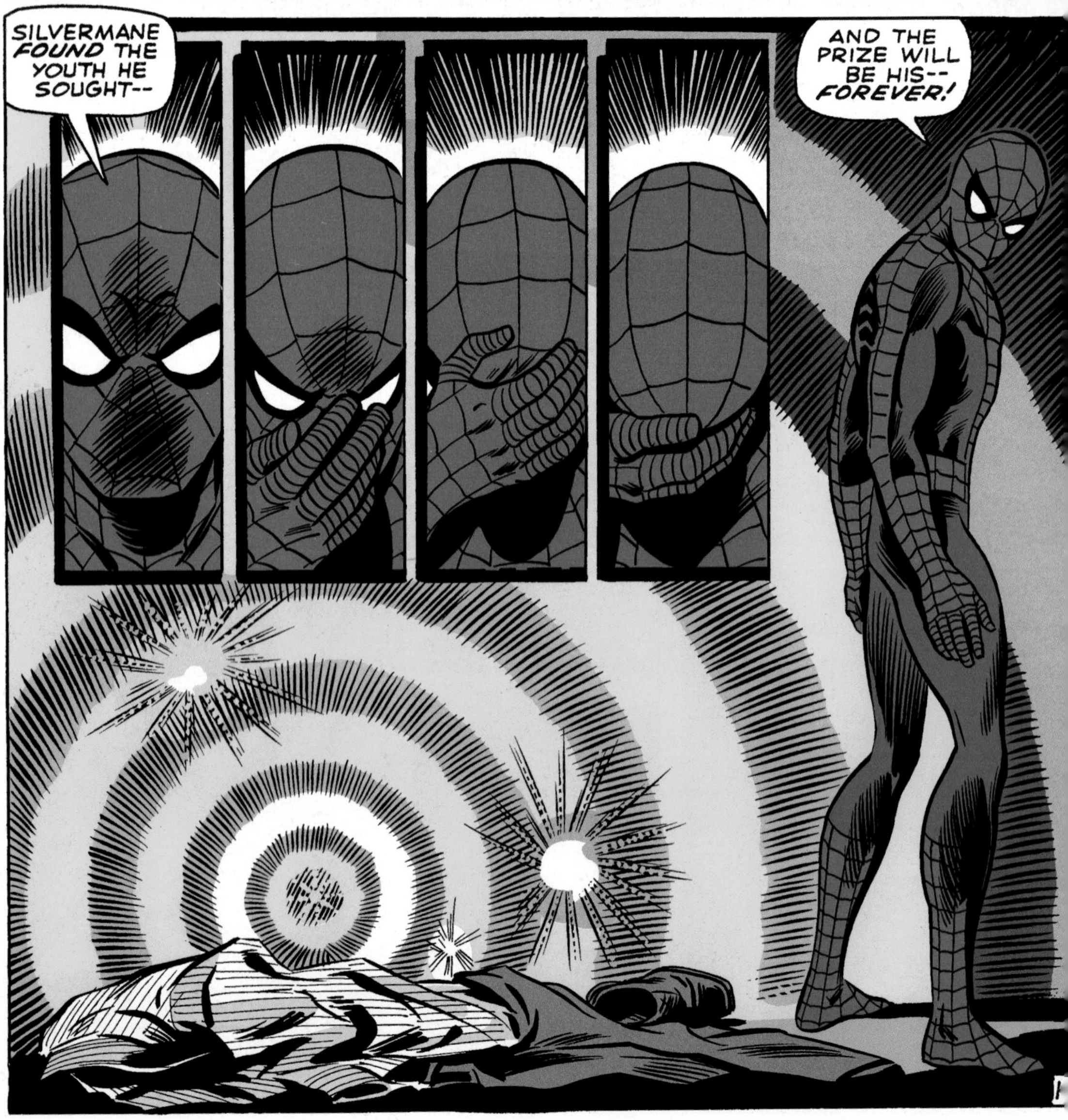
SILVERMANE FOUND THE YOUTH HE SOUGHT--
AND THE PRIZE WILL BE HIS-- FOREVER!

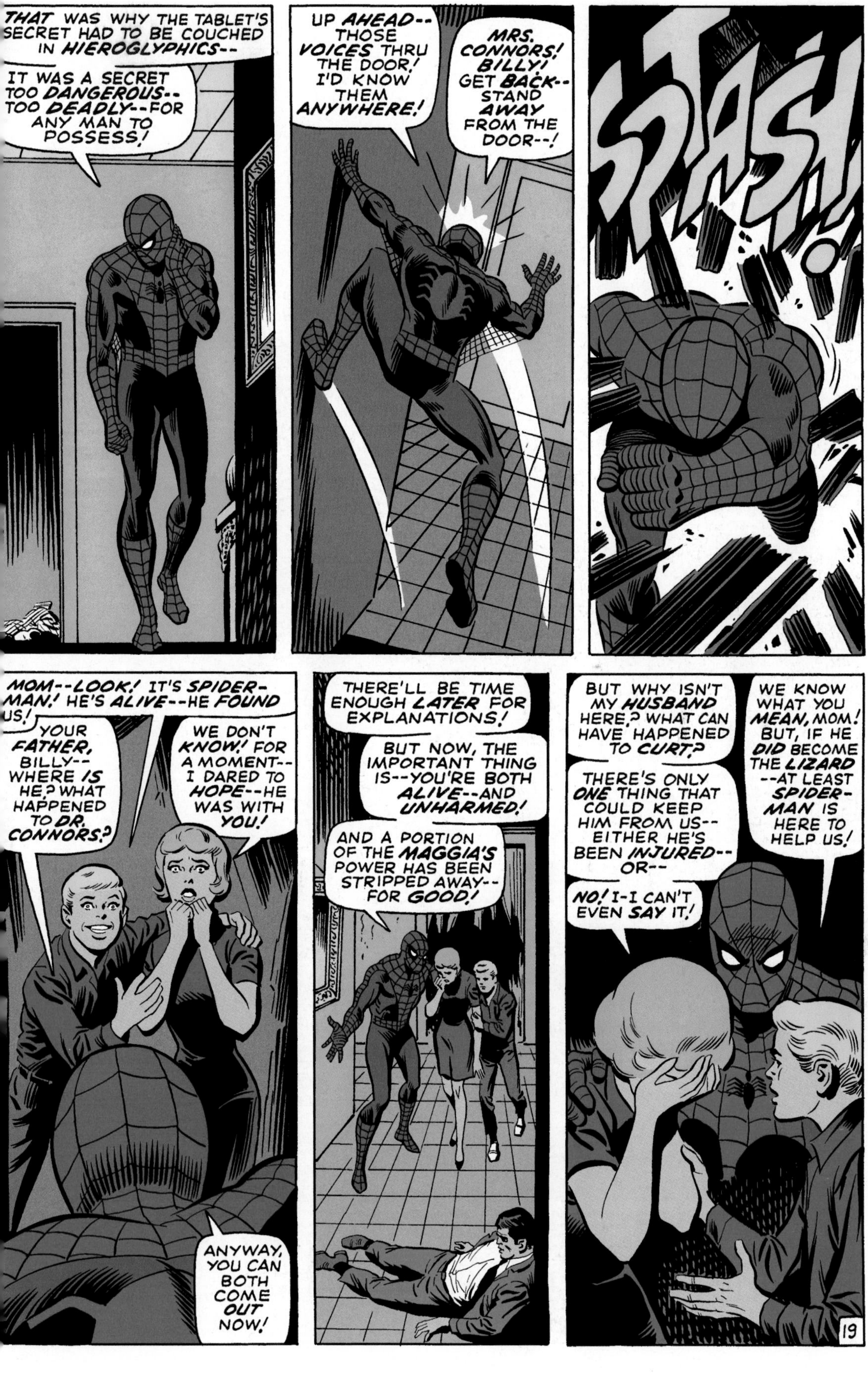
THAT WAS WHY THE TABLET'S SECRET HAD TO BE COUCHED IN HIEROGLYPHICS--
IT WAS A SECRET TOO DANGEROUS--TOO DEADLY--FOR ANY MAN TO POSSESS!
UP AHEAD--THOSE VOICES THRU THE DOOR! I'D KNOW THEM ANYWHERE!
MRS. CONNORS! BILLY! GET BACK--STAND AWAY FROM THE DOOR--!
SPASH!
MOM--LOOK! IT'S SPIDER-MAN! HE'S ALIVE--HE FOUND US!
YOUR FATHER, BILLY--WHERE IS HE? WHAT HAPPENED TO DR. CONNORS?
WE DON'T KNOW! FOR A MOMENT--I DARED TO HOPE--HE WAS WITH YOU!
ANYWAY, YOU CAN BOTH COME OUT NOW!
THERE'LL BE TIME ENOUGH LATER FOR EXPLANATIONS!
BUT NOW, THE IMPORTANT THING IS--YOU'RE BOTH ALIVE--AND UNHARMED!
AND A PORTION OF THE MAGGIA'S POWER HAS BEEN STRIPPED AWAY--FOR GOOD!
BUT WHY ISN'T MY HUSBAND HERE? WHAT CAN HAVE HAPPENED TO CURT?
THERE'S ONLY ONE THING THAT COULD KEEP HIM FROM US--EITHER HE'S BEEN INJURED--OR--
NO! I-I CAN'T EVEN SAY IT!
WE KNOW WHAT YOU MEAN, MOM! BUT, IF HE DID BECOME THE LIZARD--AT LEAST SPIDER-MAN IS HERE TO HELP US!
19

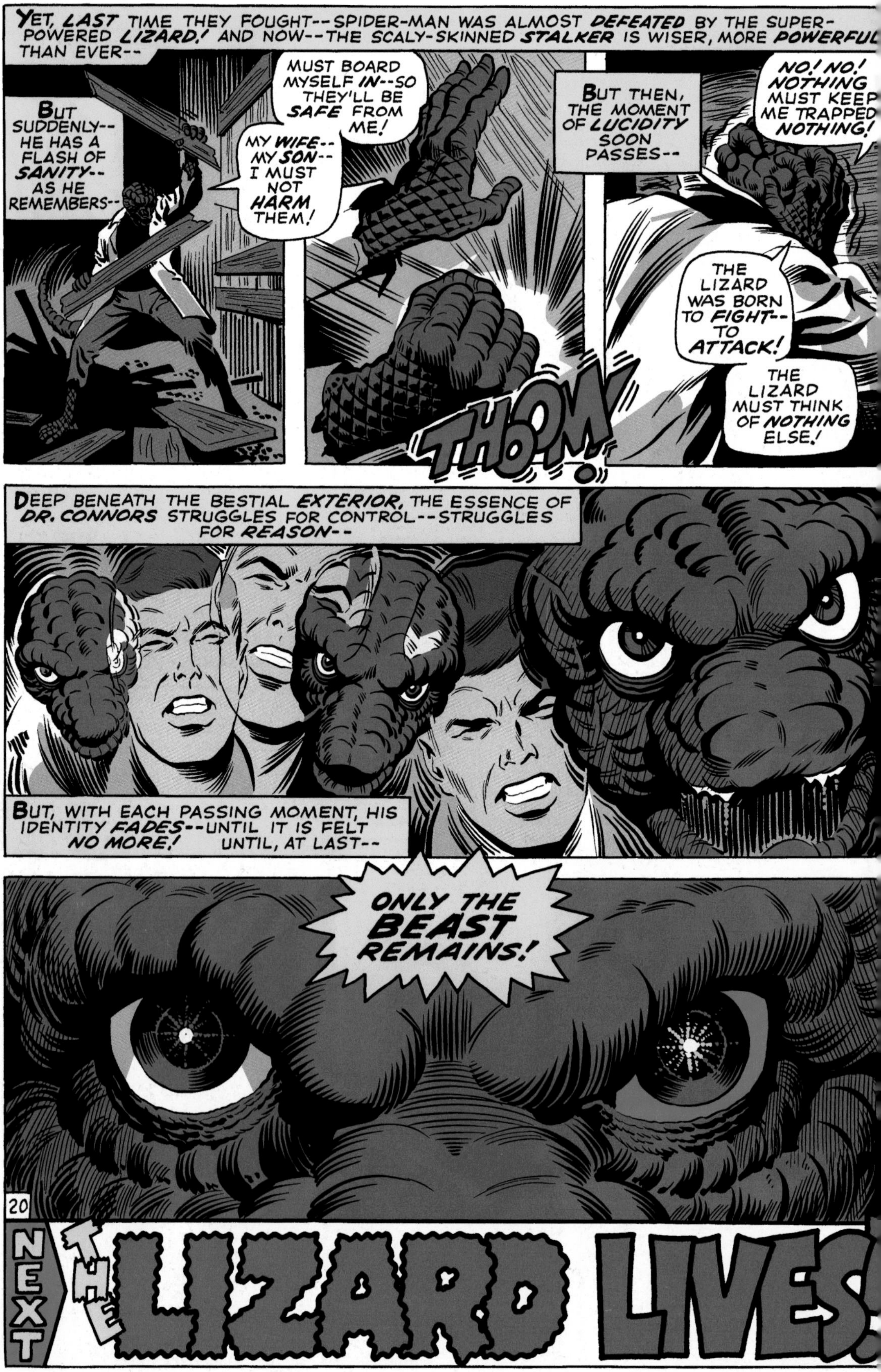

YET, LAST TIME THEY FOUGHT--SPIDER-MAN WAS ALMOST DEFEATED BY THE SUPER-POWERED LIZARD! AND NOW--THE SCALY-SKINNED STALKER IS WISER, MORE POWERFUL THAN EVER--
BUT SUDDENLY--HE HAS A FLASH OF SANITY--AS HE REMEMBERS--
MUST BOARD MYSELF IN--SO THEY'LL BE SAFE FROM ME!
MY WIFE--MY SON--I MUST NOT HARM THEM!
THOOM!
BUT THEN, THE MOMENT OF LUCIDITY SOON PASSES--
NO! NO! NOTHING MUST KEEP ME TRAPPED! NOTHING!
THE LIZARD WAS BORN TO FIGHT--TO ATTACK!
THE LIZARD MUST THINK OF NOTHING ELSE!
DEEP BENEATH THE BESTIAL EXTERIOR, THE ESSENCE OF DR. CONNORS STRUGGLES FOR CONTROL--STRUGGLES FOR REASON--
BUT, WITH EACH PASSING MOMENT, HIS IDENTITY FADES--UNTIL IT IS FELT NO MORE! UNTIL, AT LAST--
ONLY THE BEAST REMAINS!
20
NEXT THE LIZARD LIVES!

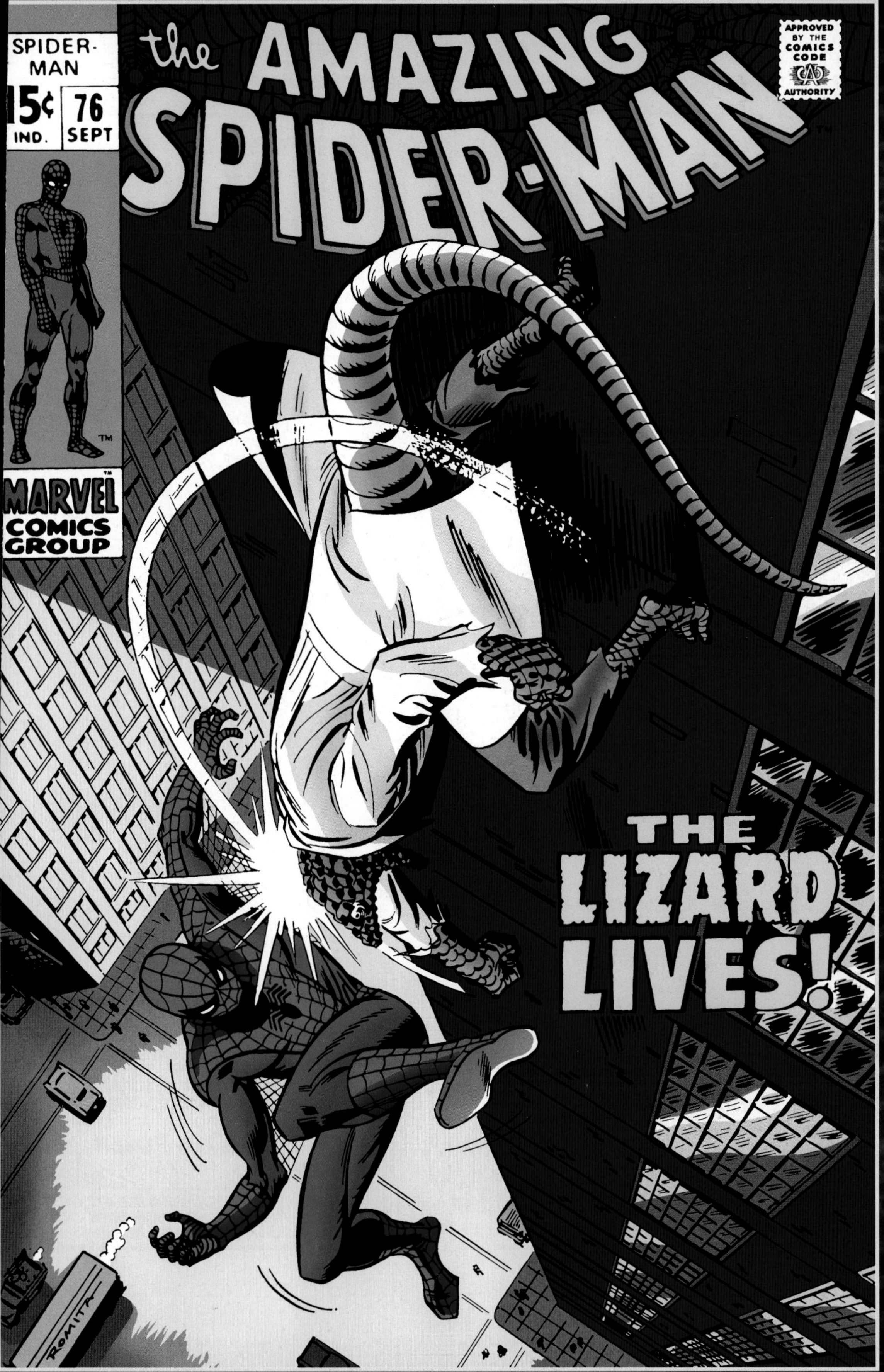
SPIDER-MAN
15¢ IND.
76 SEPT
the AMAZING SPIDER-MAN
APPROVED BY THE COMICS CODE AUTHORITY
MARVEL COMICS GROUP
THE LIZARD LIVES!
ROMITA

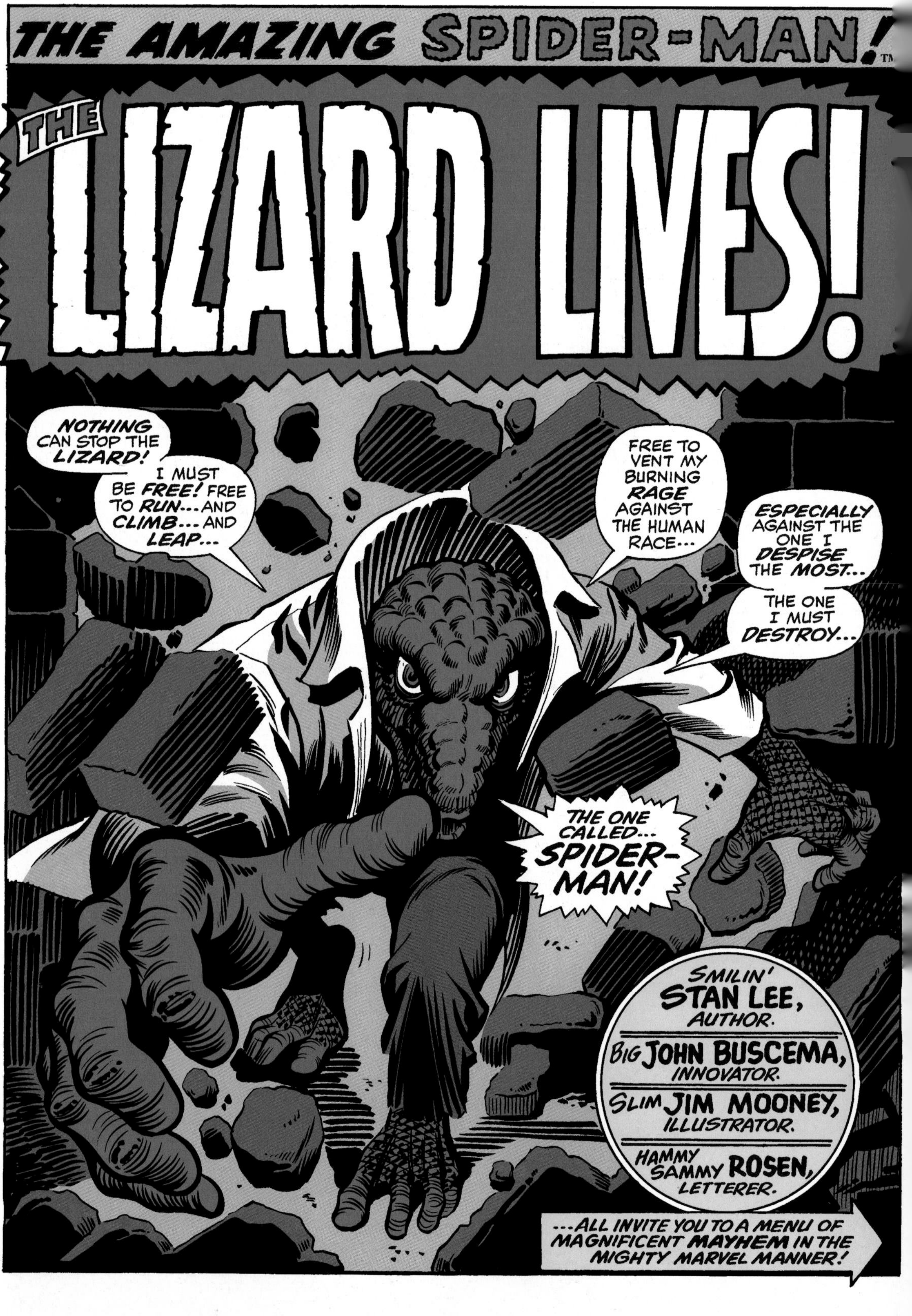
THE AMAZING SPIDER-MAN!™
THE LIZARD LIVES!
NOTHING CAN STOP THE LIZARD!
I MUST BE FREE! FREE TO RUN... AND CLIMB... AND LEAP...
FREE TO VENT MY BURNING RAGE AGAINST THE HUMAN RACE...
ESPECIALLY AGAINST THE ONE I DESPISE THE MOST...
THE ONE I MUST DESTROY...
THE ONE CALLED... SPIDER-MAN!
SMILIN' STAN LEE, AUTHOR.
BIG JOHN BUSCEMA, INNOVATOR.
SLIM JIM MOONEY, ILLUSTRATOR.
HAMMY SAMMY ROSEN, LETTERER.
...ALL INVITE YOU TO A MENU OF MAGNIFICENT MAYHEM IN THE MIGHTY MARVEL MANNER!

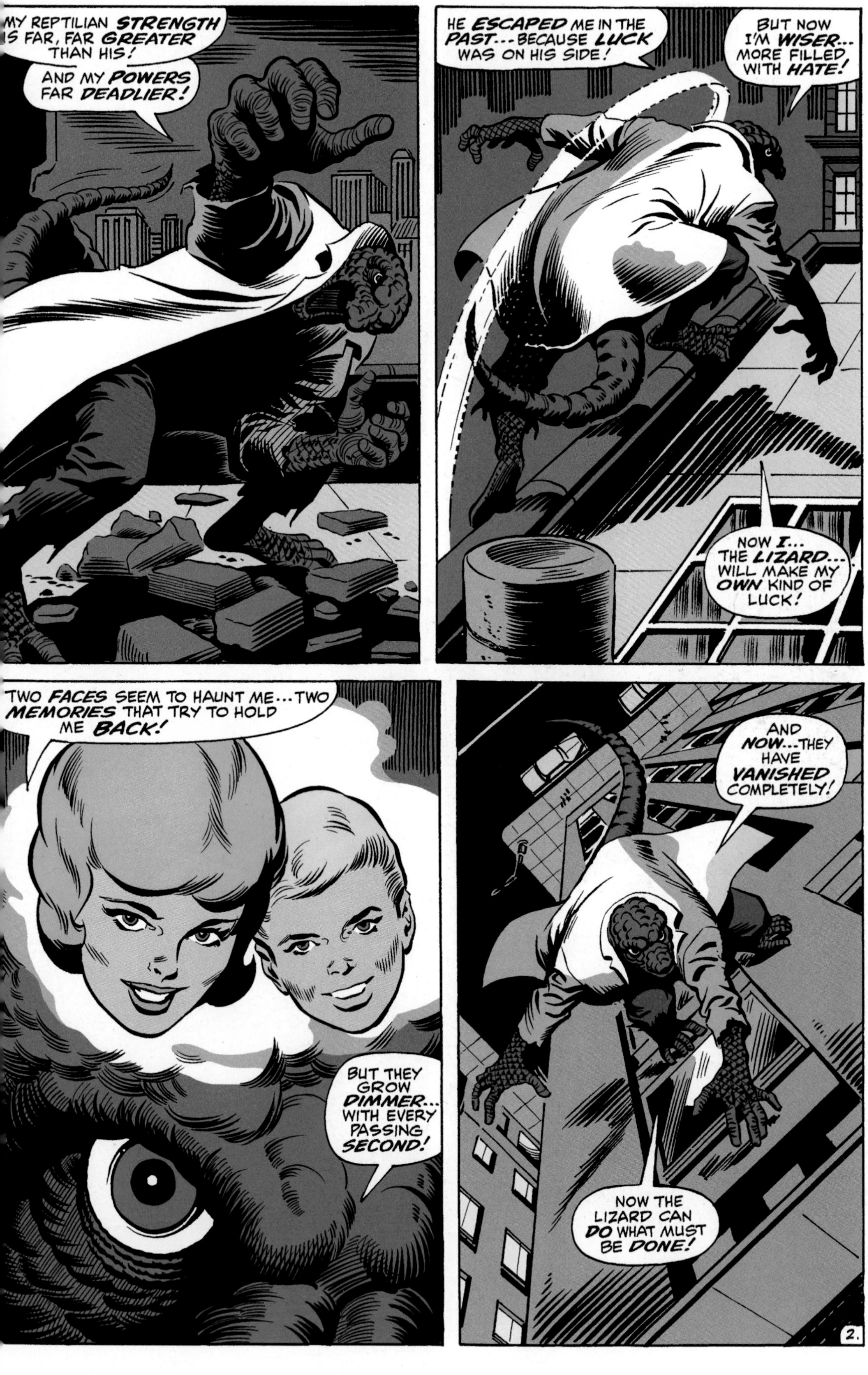

MY REPTILIAN STRENGTH IS FAR, FAR GREATER THAN HIS!
AND MY POWERS FAR DEADLIER!
HE ESCAPED ME IN THE PAST...BECAUSE LUCK WAS ON HIS SIDE!
BUT NOW I'M WISER... MORE FILLED WITH HATE!
NOW I... THE LIZARD... WILL MAKE MY OWN KIND OF LUCK!
TWO FACES SEEM TO HAUNT ME...TWO MEMORIES THAT TRY TO HOLD ME BACK!
BUT THEY GROW DIMMER... WITH EVERY PASSING SECOND!
AND NOW...THEY HAVE VANISHED COMPLETELY!
NOW THE LIZARD CAN DO WHAT MUST BE DONE!
2.

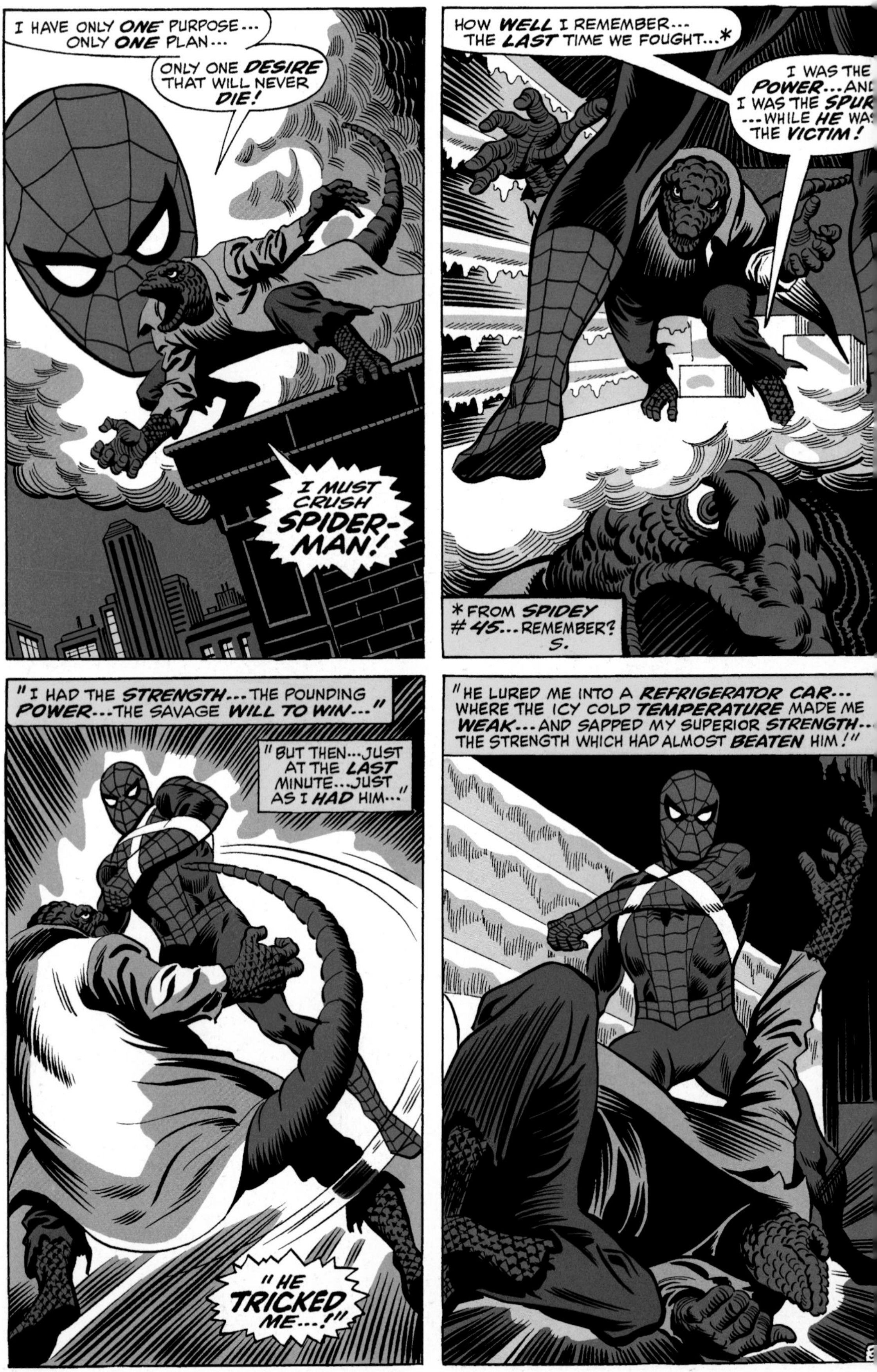
I HAVE ONLY ONE PURPOSE... ONLY ONE PLAN...
ONLY ONE DESIRE THAT WILL NEVER DIE!
I MUST CRUSH SPIDER-MAN!
HOW WELL I REMEMBER... THE LAST TIME WE FOUGHT...*
I WAS THE POWER...AN I WAS THE SPU ...WHILE HE WA THE VICTIM!
*FROM SPIDEY #45...REMEMBER? S.
"I HAD THE STRENGTH...THE POUNDING POWER...THE SAVAGE WILL TO WIN..."
"BUT THEN...JUST AT THE LAST MINUTE...JUST AS I HAD HIM..."
"HE TRICKED ME...!"
"HE LURED ME INTO A REFRIGERATOR CAR... WHERE THE ICY COLD TEMPERATURE MADE ME WEAK...AND SAPPED MY SUPERIOR STRENGTH... THE STRENGTH WHICH HAD ALMOST BEATEN HIM!"

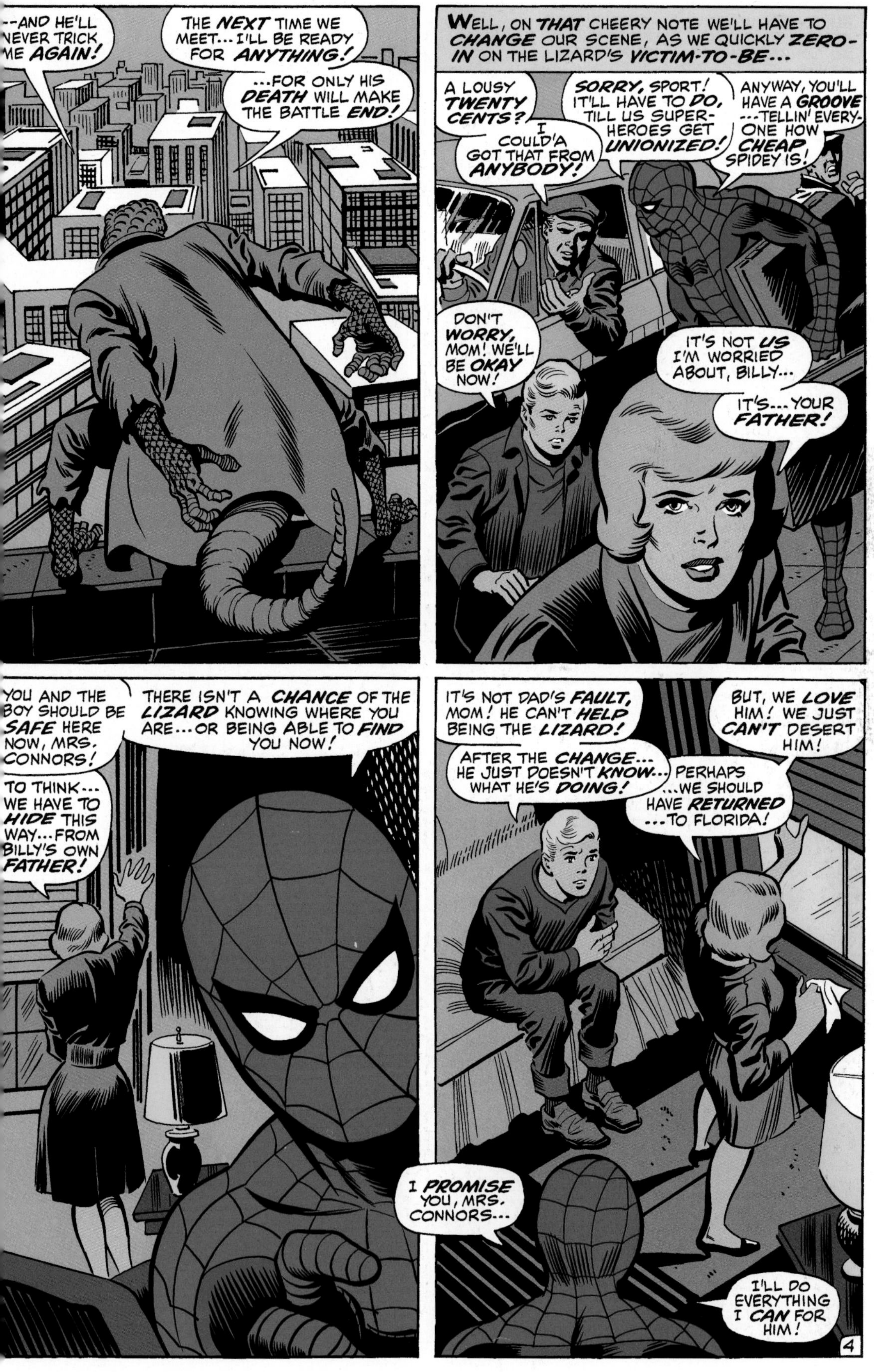
--AND HE'LL NEVER TRICK ME AGAIN!
THE NEXT TIME WE MEET... I'LL BE READY FOR ANYTHING!
...FOR ONLY HIS DEATH WILL MAKE THE BATTLE END!
WELL, ON THAT CHEERY NOTE WE'LL HAVE TO CHANGE OUR SCENE, AS WE QUICKLY ZERO-IN ON THE LIZARD'S VICTIM-TO-BE...
A LOUSY TWENTY CENTS?
I COULD'A GOT THAT FROM ANYBODY!
SORRY, SPORT! IT'LL HAVE TO DO, TILL US SUPER-HEROES GET UNIONIZED!
ANYWAY, YOU'LL HAVE A GROOVE --TELLIN' EVERY-ONE HOW CHEAP SPIDEY IS!
DON'T WORRY, MOM! WE'LL BE OKAY NOW!
IT'S NOT US I'M WORRIED ABOUT, BILLY...
IT'S... YOUR FATHER!
YOU AND THE BOY SHOULD BE SAFE HERE NOW, MRS. CONNORS!
THERE ISN'T A CHANCE OF THE LIZARD KNOWING WHERE YOU ARE... OR BEING ABLE TO FIND YOU NOW!
TO THINK... WE HAVE TO HIDE THIS WAY... FROM BILLY'S OWN FATHER!
IT'S NOT DAD'S FAULT, MOM! HE CAN'T HELP BEING THE LIZARD!
BUT, WE LOVE HIM! WE JUST CAN'T DESERT HIM!
AFTER THE CHANGE... HE JUST DOESN'T KNOW... WHAT HE'S DOING!
PERHAPS ...WE SHOULD HAVE RETURNED ...TO FLORIDA!
I PROMISE YOU, MRS. CONNORS...
I'LL DO EVERYTHING I CAN FOR HIM!
4

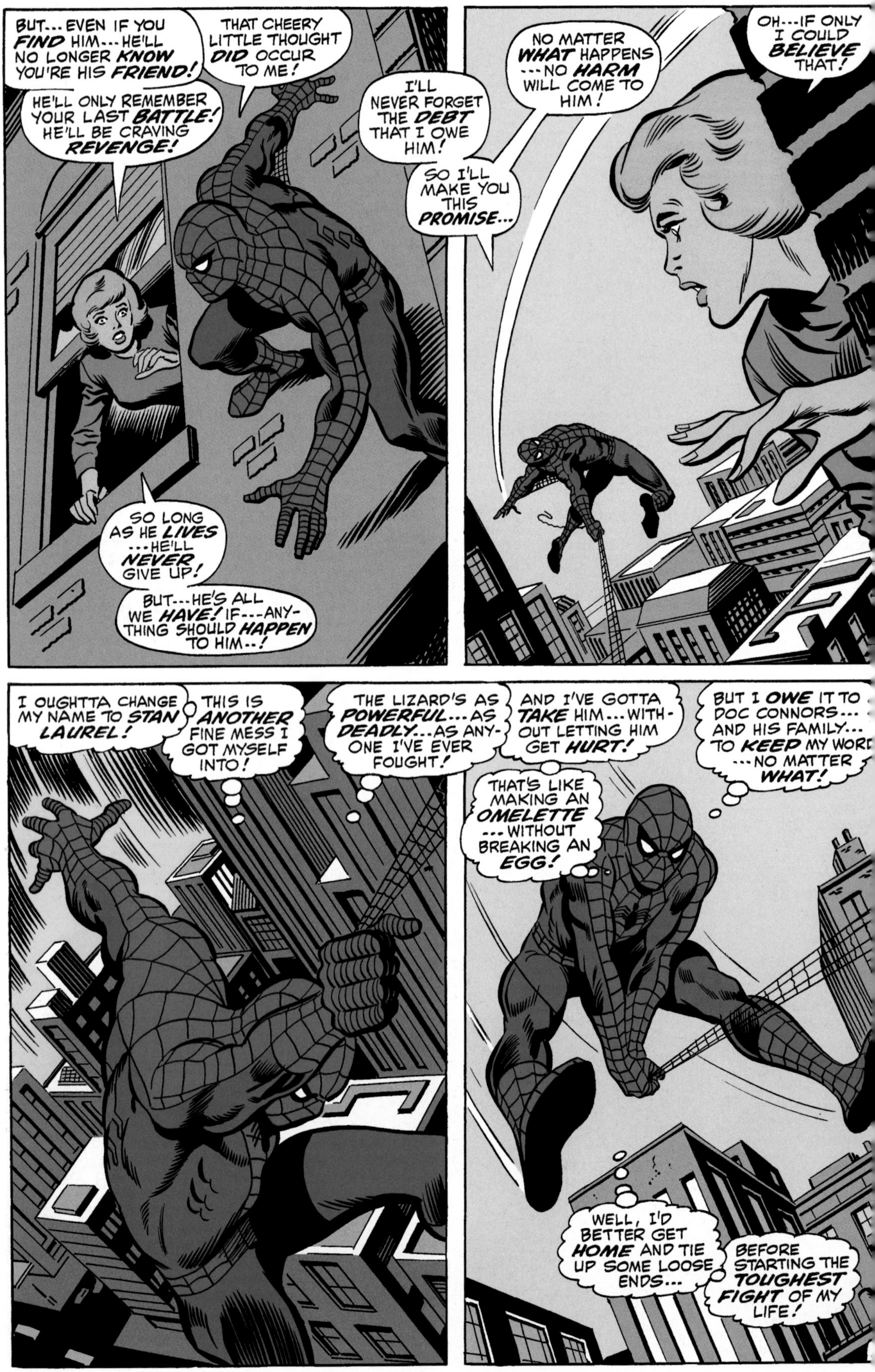

BUT... EVEN IF YOU FIND HIM... HE'LL NO LONGER KNOW YOU'RE HIS FRIEND!
HE'LL ONLY REMEMBER YOUR LAST BATTLE! HE'LL BE CRAVING REVENGE!
THAT CHEERY LITTLE THOUGHT DID OCCUR TO ME!
SO LONG AS HE LIVES ---HE'LL NEVER GIVE UP!
BUT---HE'S ALL WE HAVE! IF---ANY-THING SHOULD HAPPEN TO HIM--!
I'LL NEVER FORGET THE DEBT THAT I OWE HIM!
SO I'LL MAKE YOU THIS PROMISE...
NO MATTER WHAT HAPPENS ---NO HARM WILL COME TO HIM!
OH---IF ONLY I COULD BELIEVE THAT!
I OUGHTTA CHANGE MY NAME TO STAN LAUREL!
THIS IS ANOTHER FINE MESS I GOT MYSELF INTO!
THE LIZARD'S AS POWERFUL... AS DEADLY... AS ANY-ONE I'VE EVER FOUGHT!
AND I'VE GOTTA TAKE HIM... WITH-OUT LETTING HIM GET HURT!
THAT'S LIKE MAKING AN OMELETTE ... WITHOUT BREAKING AN EGG!
BUT I OWE IT TO DOC CONNORS... AND HIS FAMILY... TO KEEP MY WORD ---NO MATTER WHAT!
WELL, I'D BETTER GET HOME AND TIE UP SOME LOOSE ENDS...
BEFORE STARTING THE TOUGHEST FIGHT OF MY LIFE!

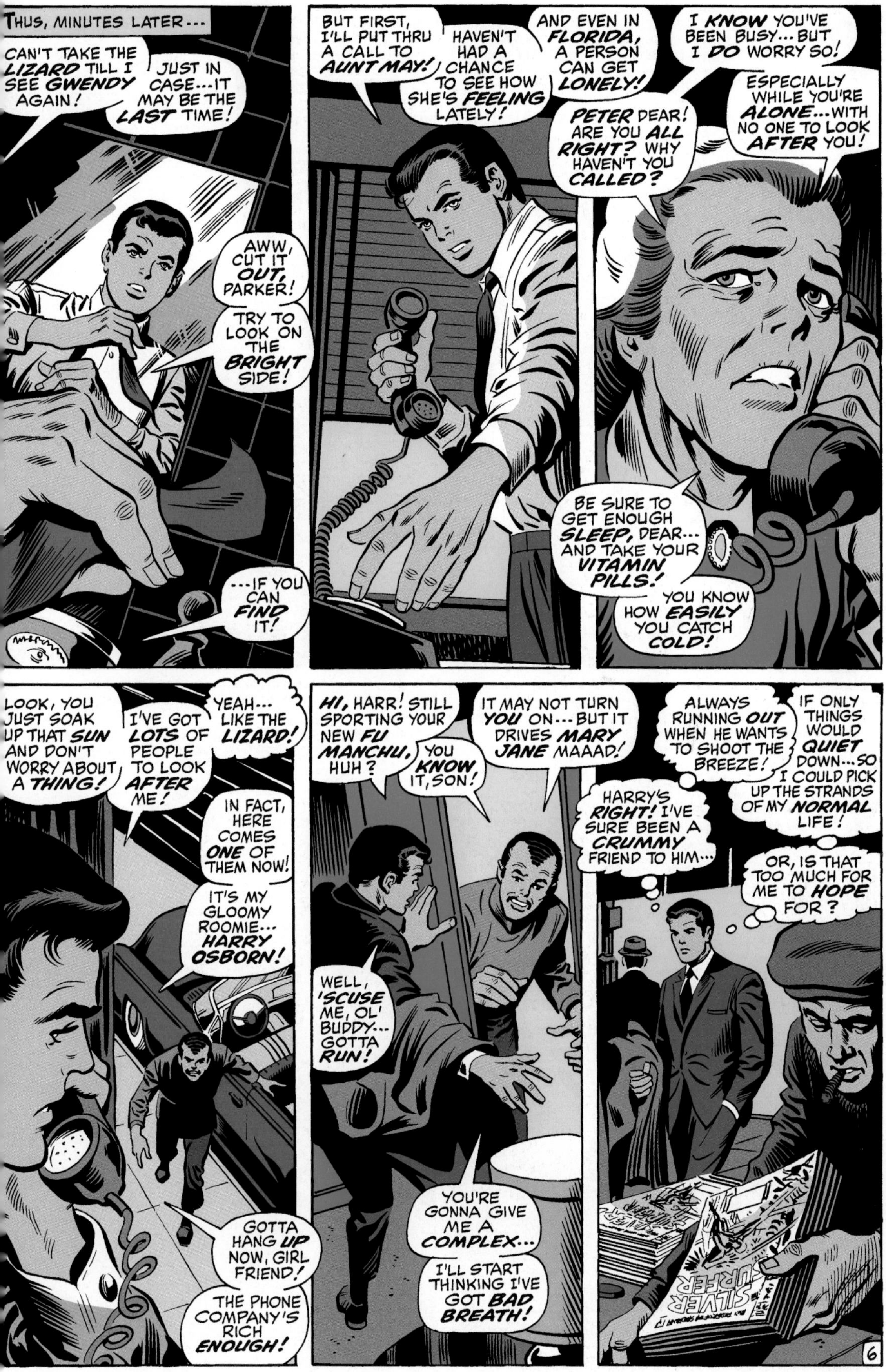

THUS, MINUTES LATER...
CAN'T TAKE THE LIZARD TILL I SEE GWENDY AGAIN!
JUST IN CASE...IT MAY BE THE LAST TIME!
AWW, CUT IT OUT, PARKER!
TRY TO LOOK ON THE BRIGHT SIDE!
...IF YOU CAN FIND IT!
BUT FIRST, I'LL PUT THRU A CALL TO AUNT MAY!
HAVEN'T HAD A CHANCE TO SEE HOW SHE'S FEELING LATELY!
AND EVEN IN FLORIDA, A PERSON CAN GET LONELY!
PETER DEAR! ARE YOU ALL RIGHT? WHY HAVEN'T YOU CALLED?
I KNOW YOU'VE BEEN BUSY... BUT I DO WORRY SO!
ESPECIALLY WHILE YOU'RE ALONE...WITH NO ONE TO LOOK AFTER YOU!
BE SURE TO GET ENOUGH SLEEP, DEAR... AND TAKE YOUR VITAMIN PILLS!
YOU KNOW HOW EASILY YOU CATCH COLD!
LOOK, YOU JUST SOAK UP THAT SUN AND DON'T WORRY ABOUT A THING!
I'VE GOT LOTS OF PEOPLE TO LOOK AFTER ME!
YEAH... LIKE THE LIZARD!
IN FACT, HERE COMES ONE OF THEM NOW!
IT'S MY GLOOMY ROOMIE... HARRY OSBORN!
GOTTA HANG UP NOW, GIRL FRIEND!
THE PHONE COMPANY'S RICH ENOUGH!
HI, HARR! STILL SPORTING YOUR NEW FU MANCHU, HUH?
YOU KNOW IT, SON!
IT MAY NOT TURN YOU ON---BUT IT DRIVES MARY JANE MAAAD!
WELL, 'SCUSE ME, OL' BUDDY... GOTTA RUN!
YOU'RE GONNA GIVE ME A COMPLEX...
I'LL START THINKING I'VE GOT BAD BREATH!
ALWAYS RUNNING OUT WHEN HE WANTS TO SHOOT THE BREEZE!
HARRY'S RIGHT! I'VE SURE BEEN A CRUMMY FRIEND TO HIM...
IF ONLY THINGS WOULD QUIET DOWN...SO I COULD PICK UP THE STRANDS OF MY NORMAL LIFE!
OR, IS THAT TOO MUCH FOR ME TO HOPE FOR?
SILVER SURFER

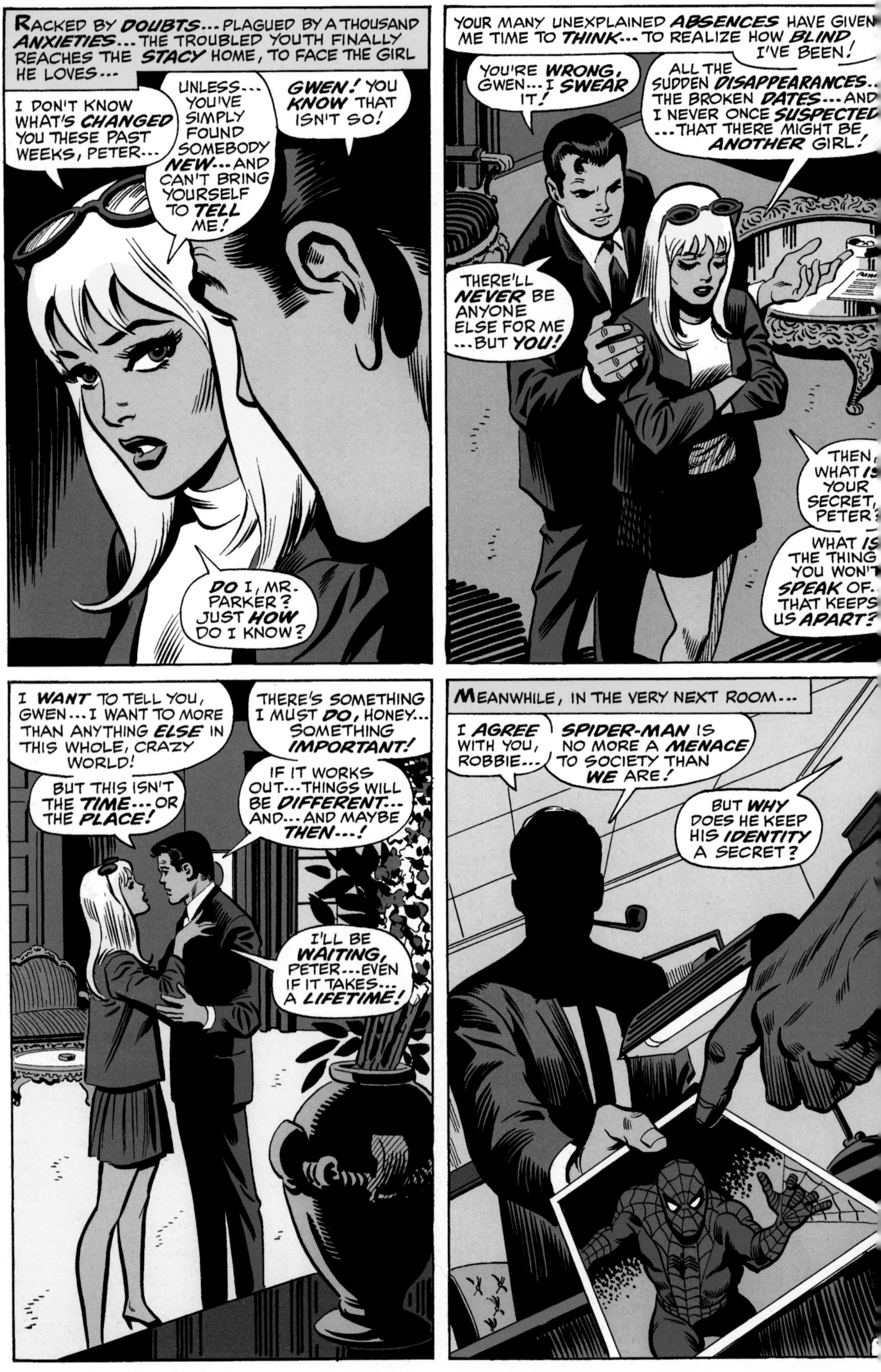

RACKED BY DOUBTS... PLAGUED BY A THOUSAND ANXIETIES... THE TROUBLED YOUTH FINALLY REACHES THE STACY HOME, TO FACE THE GIRL HE LOVES...
I DON'T KNOW WHAT'S CHANGED YOU THESE PAST WEEKS, PETER...
UNLESS... YOU'VE SIMPLY FOUND SOMEBODY NEW... AND CAN'T BRING YOURSELF TO TELL ME!
GWEN! YOU KNOW THAT ISN'T SO!
DO I, MR. PARKER? JUST HOW DO I KNOW?
YOUR MANY UNEXPLAINED ABSENCES HAVE GIVEN ME TIME TO THINK... TO REALIZE HOW BLIND I'VE BEEN!
YOU'RE WRONG, GWEN... I SWEAR IT!
ALL THE SUDDEN DISAPPEARANCES... THE BROKEN DATES... AND I NEVER ONCE SUSPECTED ...THAT THERE MIGHT BE ANOTHER GIRL!
THERE'LL NEVER BE ANYONE ELSE FOR ME ...BUT YOU!
THEN, WHAT IS YOUR SECRET, PETER?
WHAT IS THE THING YOU WON'T SPEAK OF... THAT KEEPS US APART?
I WANT TO TELL YOU, GWEN... I WANT TO MORE THAN ANYTHING ELSE IN THIS WHOLE, CRAZY WORLD!
BUT THIS ISN'T THE TIME... OR THE PLACE!
THERE'S SOMETHING I MUST DO, HONEY... SOMETHING IMPORTANT!
IF IT WORKS OUT... THINGS WILL BE DIFFERENT... AND... AND MAYBE THEN...!
I'LL BE WAITING, PETER... EVEN IF IT TAKES... A LIFETIME!
MEANWHILE, IN THE VERY NEXT ROOM...
I AGREE WITH YOU, ROBBIE...
SPIDER-MAN IS NO MORE A MENACE TO SOCIETY THAN WE ARE!
BUT WHY DOES HE KEEP HIS IDENTITY A SECRET?

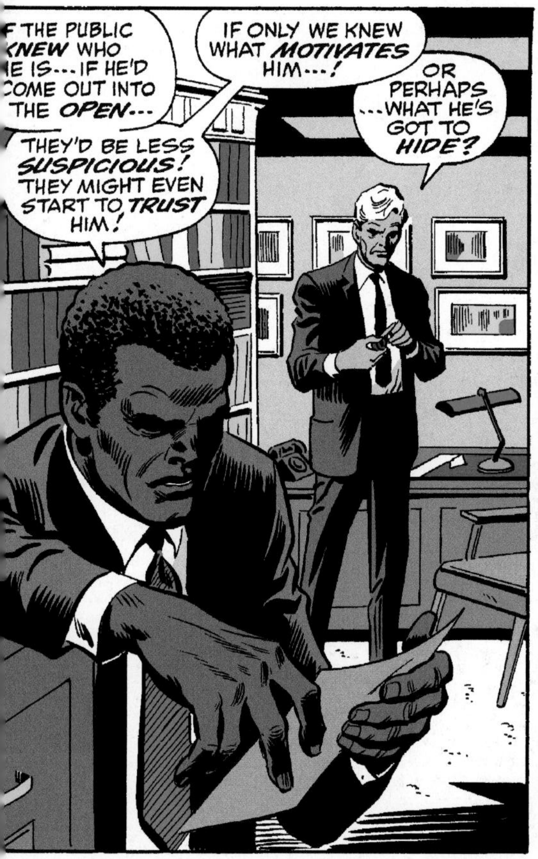
F THE PUBLIC KNEW WHO IE IS--- IF HE'D COME OUT INTO THE OPEN---
THEY'D BE LESS SUSPICIOUS! THEY MIGHT EVEN START TO TRUST HIM!
IF ONLY WE KNEW WHAT MOTIVATES HIM---!
OR PERHAPS ---WHAT HE'S GOT TO HIDE?

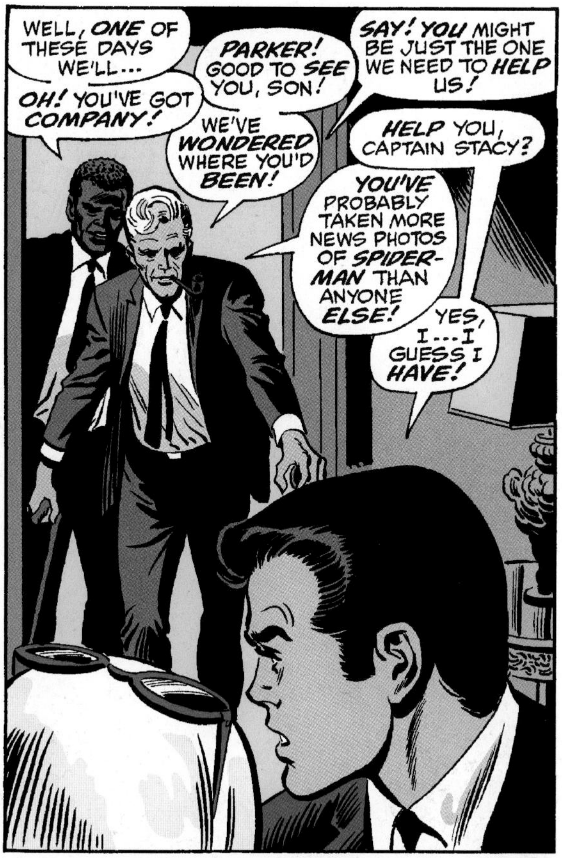
WELL, ONE OF THESE DAYS WE'LL---
OH! YOU'VE GOT COMPANY!
PARKER! GOOD TO SEE YOU, SON!
WE'VE WONDERED WHERE YOU'D BEEN!
SAY! YOU MIGHT BE JUST THE ONE WE NEED TO HELP US!
HELP YOU, CAPTAIN STACY?
YOU'VE PROBABLY TAKEN MORE NEWS PHOTOS OF SPIDER-MAN THAN ANYONE ELSE!
YES, I---I GUESS I HAVE!

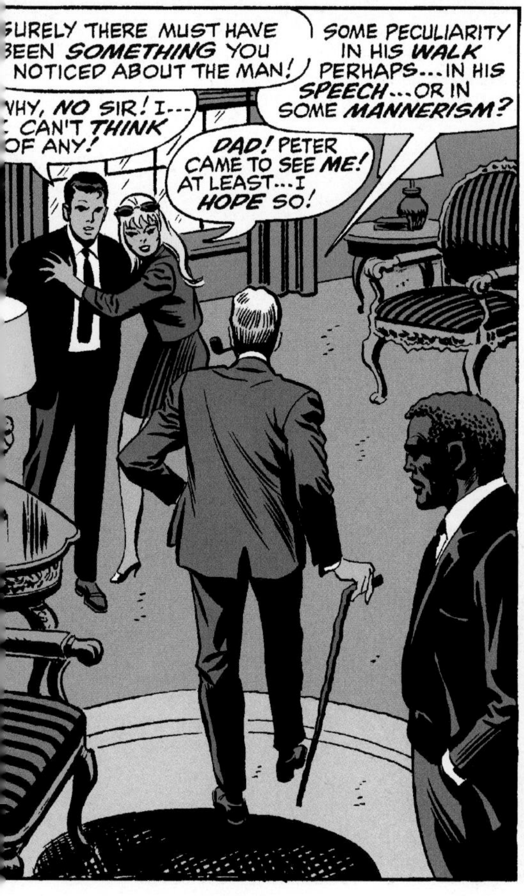
SURELY THERE MUST HAVE BEEN SOMETHING YOU NOTICED ABOUT THE MAN!
SOME PECULIARITY IN HIS WALK PERHAPS---IN HIS SPEECH---OR IN SOME MANNERISM?
WHY, NO SIR! I--- I CAN'T THINK OF ANY!
DAD! PETER CAME TO SEE ME! AT LEAST---I HOPE SO!

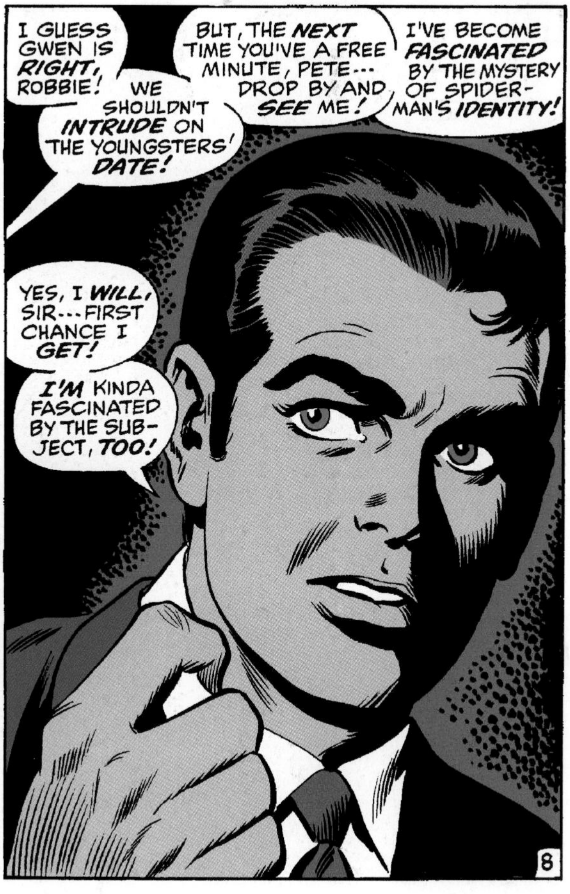
I GUESS GWEN IS RIGHT, ROBBIE!
WE SHOULDN'T INTRUDE ON THE YOUNGSTERS' DATE!
BUT, THE NEXT TIME YOU'VE A FREE MINUTE, PETE--- DROP BY AND SEE ME!
I'VE BECOME FASCINATED BY THE MYSTERY OF SPIDER-MAN'S IDENTITY!
YES, I WILL, SIR---FIRST CHANCE I GET!
I'M KINDA FASCINATED BY THE SUB-JECT, TOO!
8

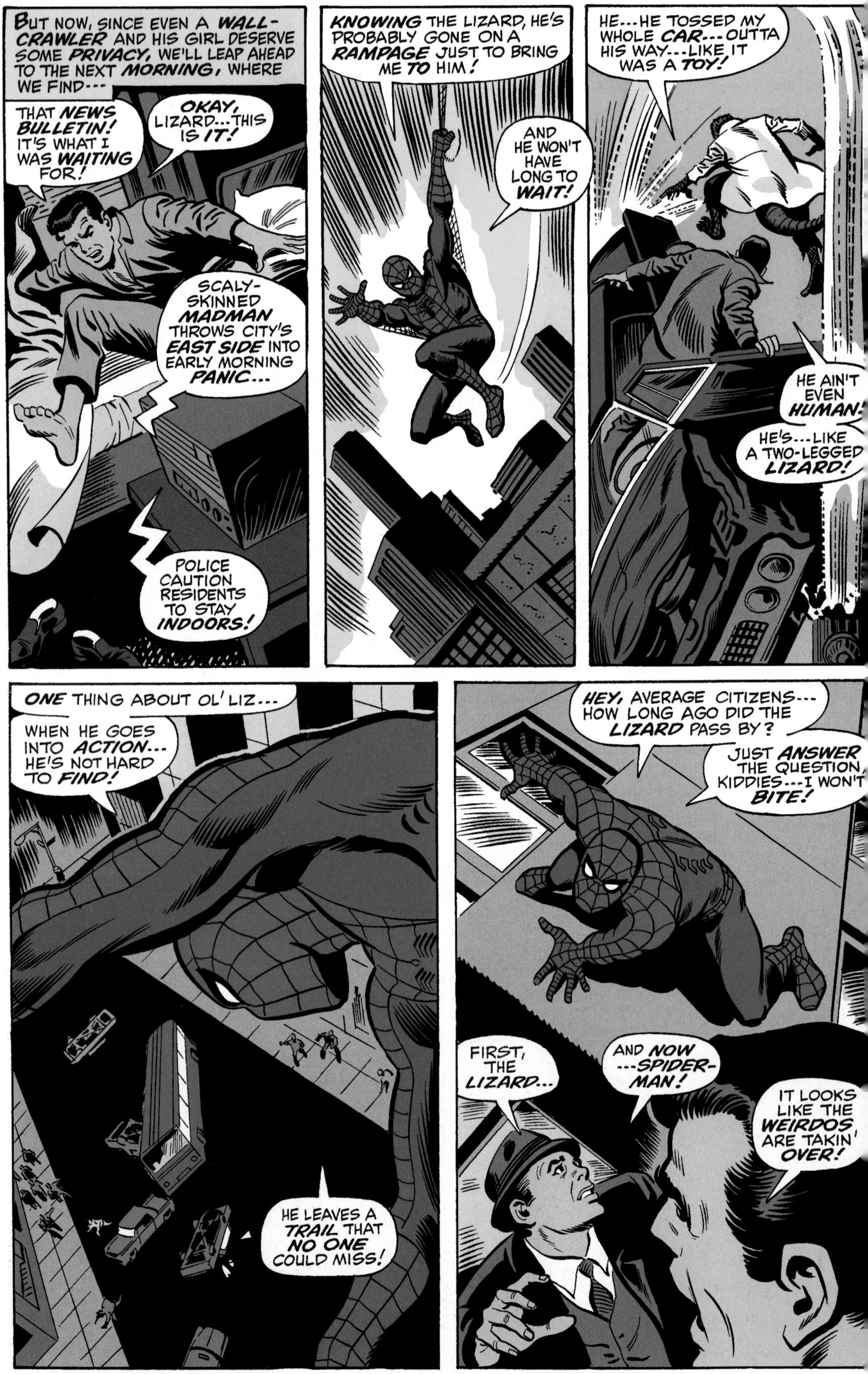
BUT NOW, SINCE EVEN A WALL-CRAWLER AND HIS GIRL DESERVE SOME PRIVACY, WE'LL LEAP AHEAD TO THE NEXT MORNING, WHERE WE FIND---
THAT NEWS BULLETIN! IT'S WHAT I WAS WAITING FOR!
OKAY, LIZARD...THIS IS IT!
SCALY-SKINNED MADMAN THROWS CITY'S EAST SIDE INTO EARLY MORNING PANIC...
POLICE CAUTION RESIDENTS TO STAY INDOORS!
KNOWING THE LIZARD, HE'S PROBABLY GONE ON A RAMPAGE JUST TO BRING ME TO HIM!
AND HE WON'T HAVE LONG TO WAIT!
HE---HE TOSSED MY WHOLE CAR---OUTTA HIS WAY---LIKE IT WAS A TOY!
HE AIN'T EVEN HUMAN!
HE'S---LIKE A TWO-LEGGED LIZARD!
ONE THING ABOUT OL' LIZ---
WHEN HE GOES INTO ACTION--- HE'S NOT HARD TO FIND!
HE LEAVES A TRAIL THAT NO ONE COULD MISS!
HEY, AVERAGE CITIZENS--- HOW LONG AGO DID THE LIZARD PASS BY?
JUST ANSWER THE QUESTION, KIDDIES---I WON'T BITE!
FIRST, THE LIZARD...
AND NOW ---SPIDER-MAN!
IT LOOKS LIKE THE WEIRDOS ARE TAKIN' OVER!

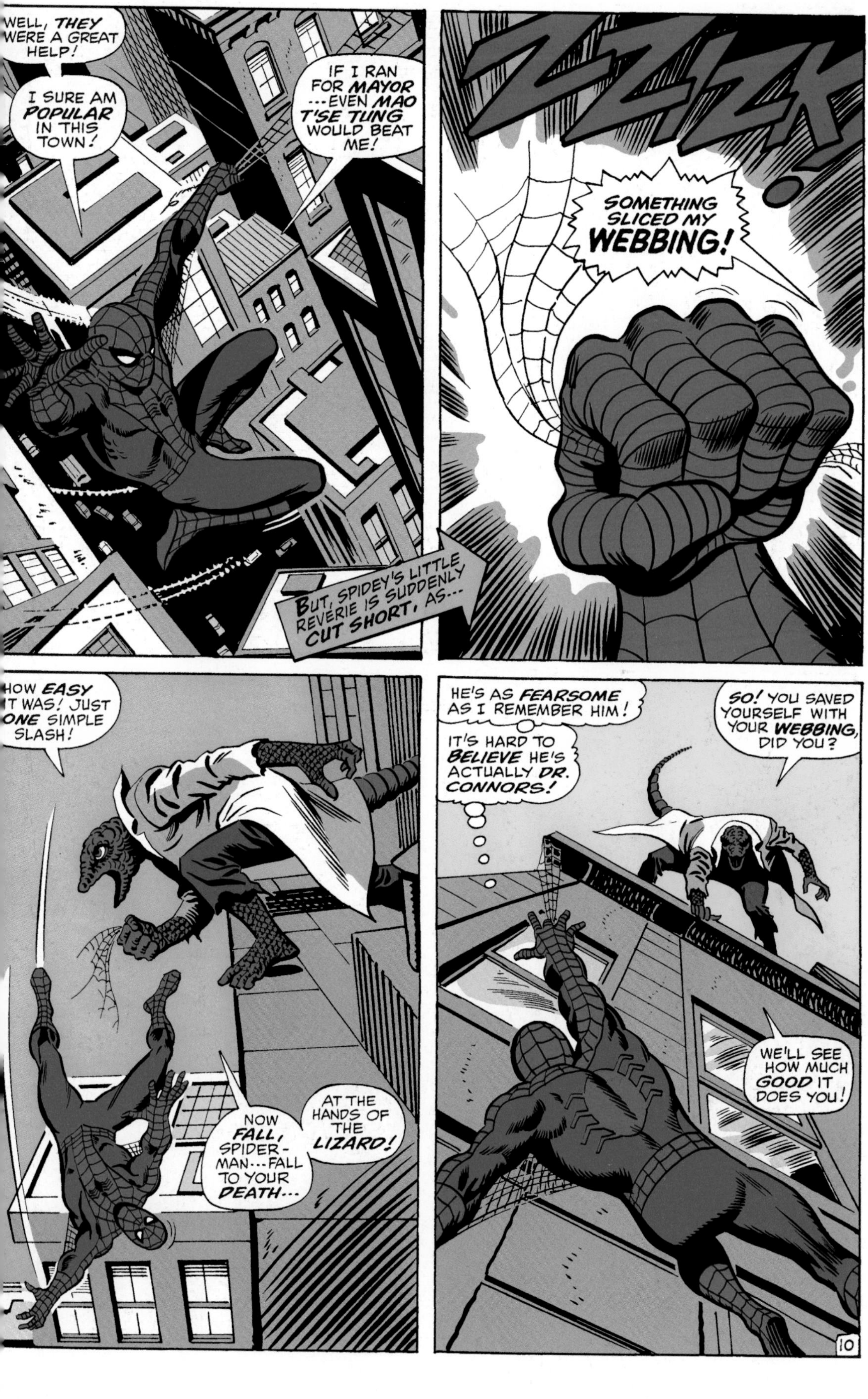
WELL, THEY WERE A GREAT HELP!
I SURE AM POPULAR IN THIS TOWN!
IF I RAN FOR MAYOR ---EVEN MAO T'SE TUNG WOULD BEAT ME!
BUT, SPIDEY'S LITTLE REVERIE IS SUDDENLY CUT SHORT, AS...
ZZZK!
SOMETHING SLICED MY WEBBING!
HOW EASY IT WAS! JUST ONE SIMPLE SLASH!
NOW FALL, SPIDER-MAN---FALL TO YOUR DEATH---
AT THE HANDS OF THE LIZARD!
HE'S AS FEARSOME AS I REMEMBER HIM!
IT'S HARD TO BELIEVE HE'S ACTUALLY DR. CONNORS!
SO! YOU SAVED YOURSELF WITH YOUR WEBBING, DID YOU?
WE'LL SEE HOW MUCH GOOD IT DOES YOU!

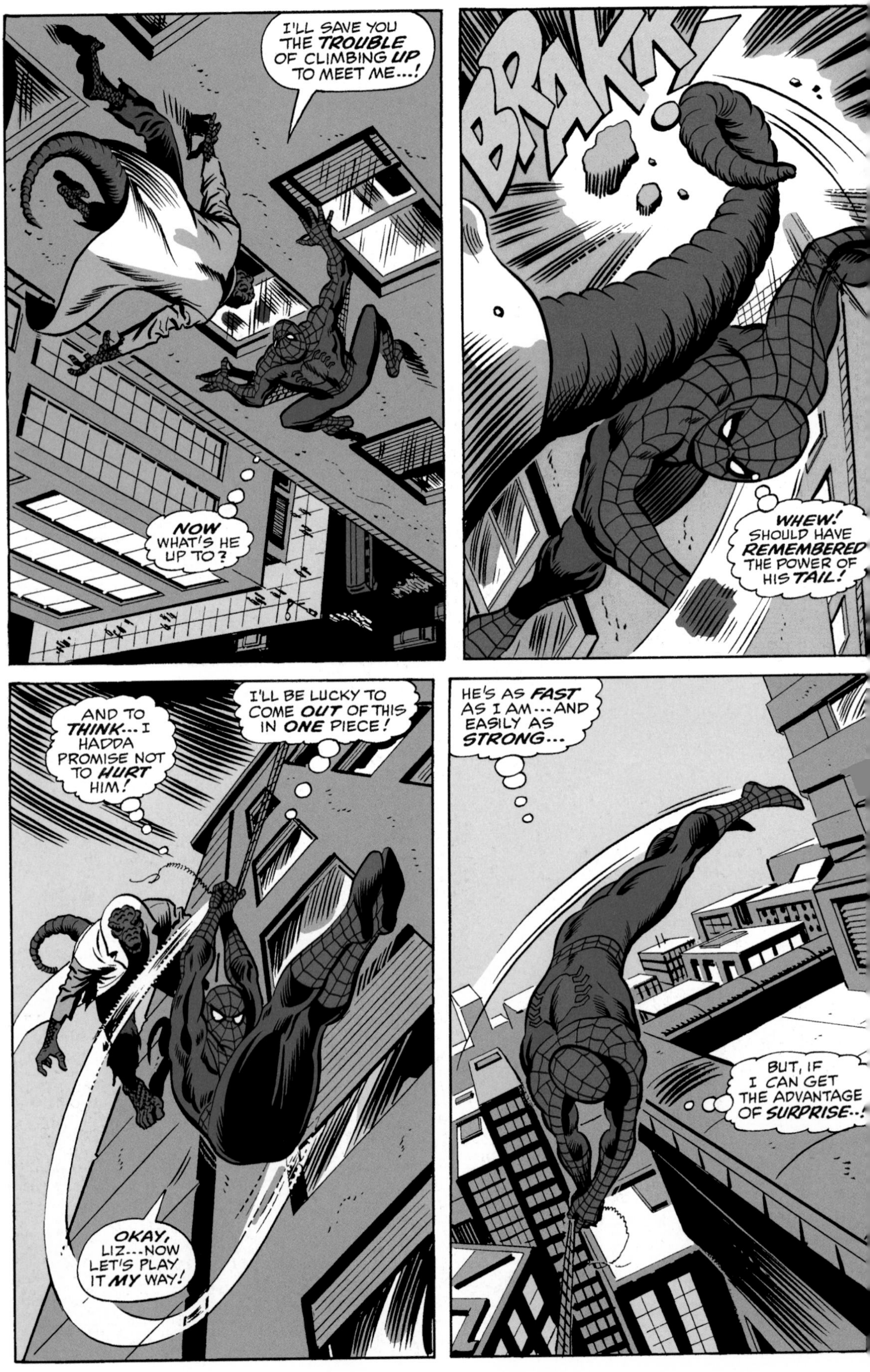
I'LL SAVE YOU THE TROUBLE OF CLIMBING UP TO MEET ME...!
NOW WHAT'S HE UP TO?
BRAKK!
WHEW! SHOULD HAVE REMEMBERED THE POWER OF HIS TAIL!
AND TO THINK...I HADDA PROMISE NOT TO HURT HIM!
I'LL BE LUCKY TO COME OUT OF THIS IN ONE PIECE!
OKAY, LIZ...NOW LET'S PLAY IT MY WAY!
HE'S AS FAST AS I AM...AND EASILY AS STRONG...
BUT, IF I CAN GET THE ADVANTAGE OF SURPRISE...!

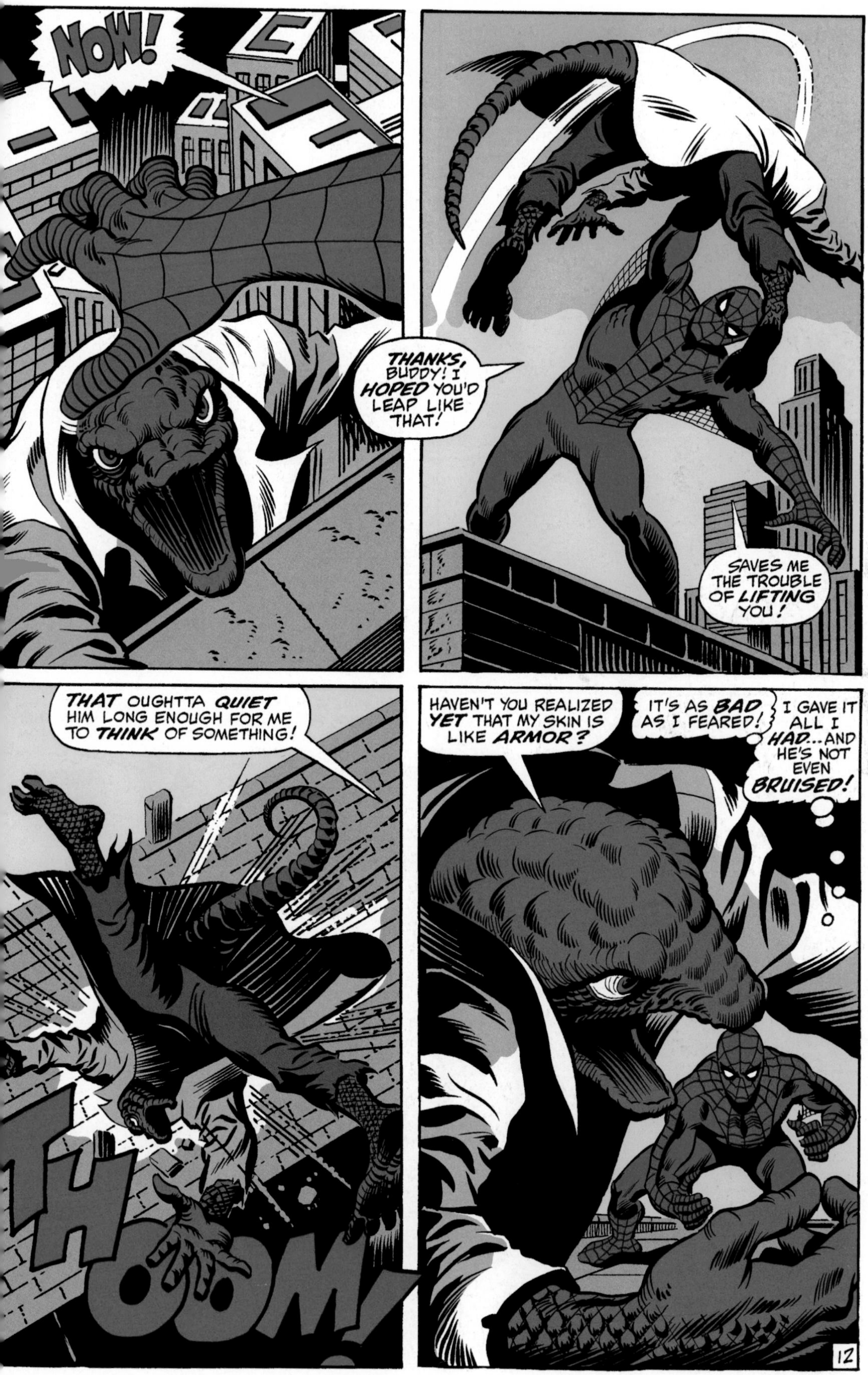

NOW!
THANKS, BUDDY! I HOPED YOU'D LEAP LIKE THAT!
SAVES ME THE TROUBLE OF LIFTING YOU!
THAT OUGHTTA QUIET HIM LONG ENOUGH FOR ME TO THINK OF SOMETHING!
THOOM!
HAVEN'T YOU REALIZED YET THAT MY SKIN IS LIKE ARMOR?
IT'S AS BAD AS I FEARED!
I GAVE IT ALL I HAD... AND HE'S NOT EVEN BRUISED!
12

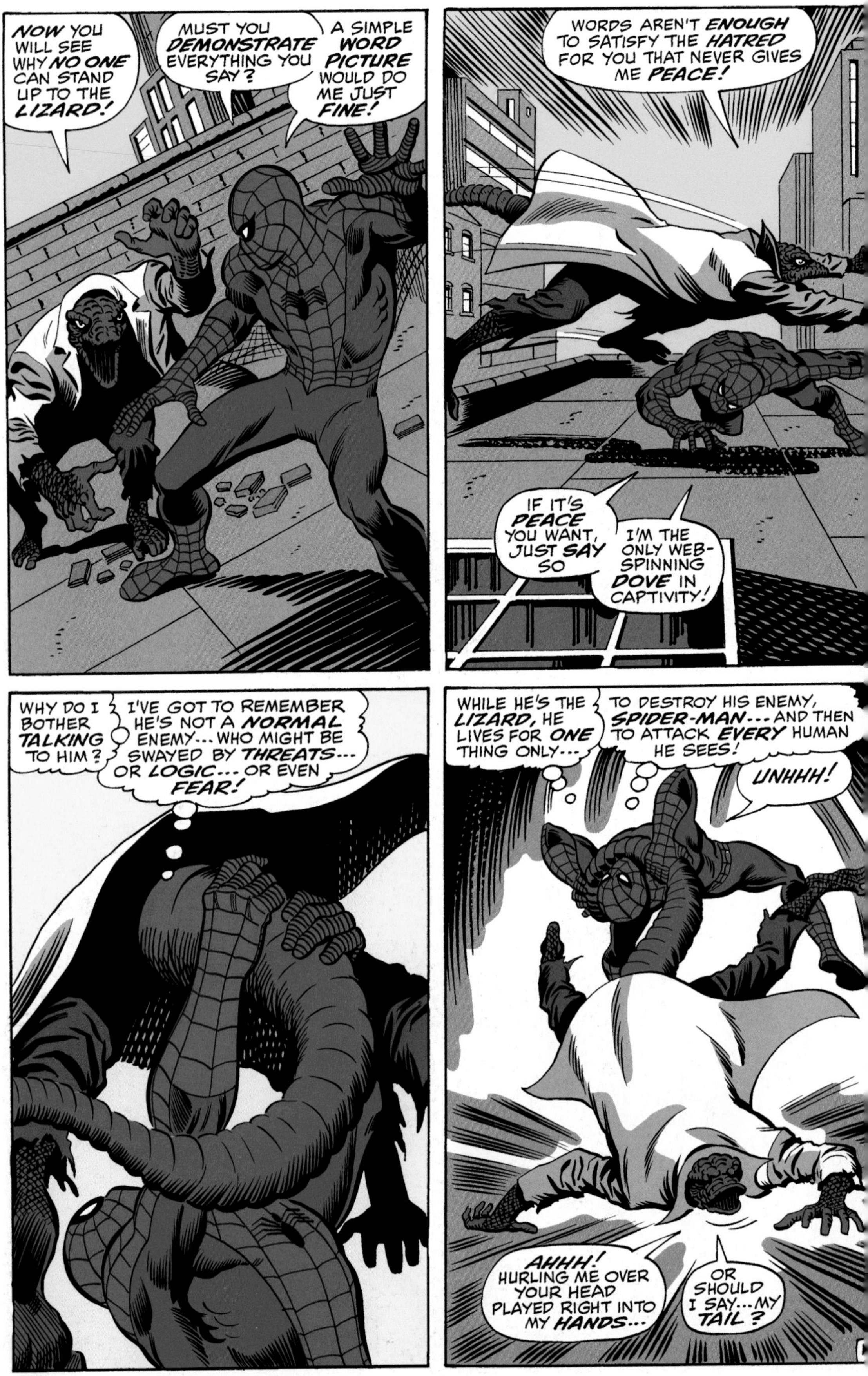
NOW YOU WILL SEE WHY NO ONE CAN STAND UP TO THE LIZARD!
MUST YOU DEMONSTRATE EVERYTHING YOU SAY?
A SIMPLE WORD PICTURE WOULD DO ME JUST FINE!
WORDS AREN'T ENOUGH TO SATISFY THE HATRED FOR YOU THAT NEVER GIVES ME PEACE!
IF IT'S PEACE YOU WANT, JUST SAY SO
I'M THE ONLY WEB-SPINNING DOVE IN CAPTIVITY!
WHY DO I BOTHER TALKING TO HIM?
I'VE GOT TO REMEMBER HE'S NOT A NORMAL ENEMY... WHO MIGHT BE SWAYED BY THREATS... OR LOGIC... OR EVEN FEAR!
WHILE HE'S THE LIZARD, HE LIVES FOR ONE THING ONLY...
TO DESTROY HIS ENEMY, SPIDER-MAN... AND THEN TO ATTACK EVERY HUMAN HE SEES!
UNHHH!
AHHH! HURLING ME OVER YOUR HEAD PLAYED RIGHT INTO MY HANDS...
OR SHOULD I SAY... MY TAIL?

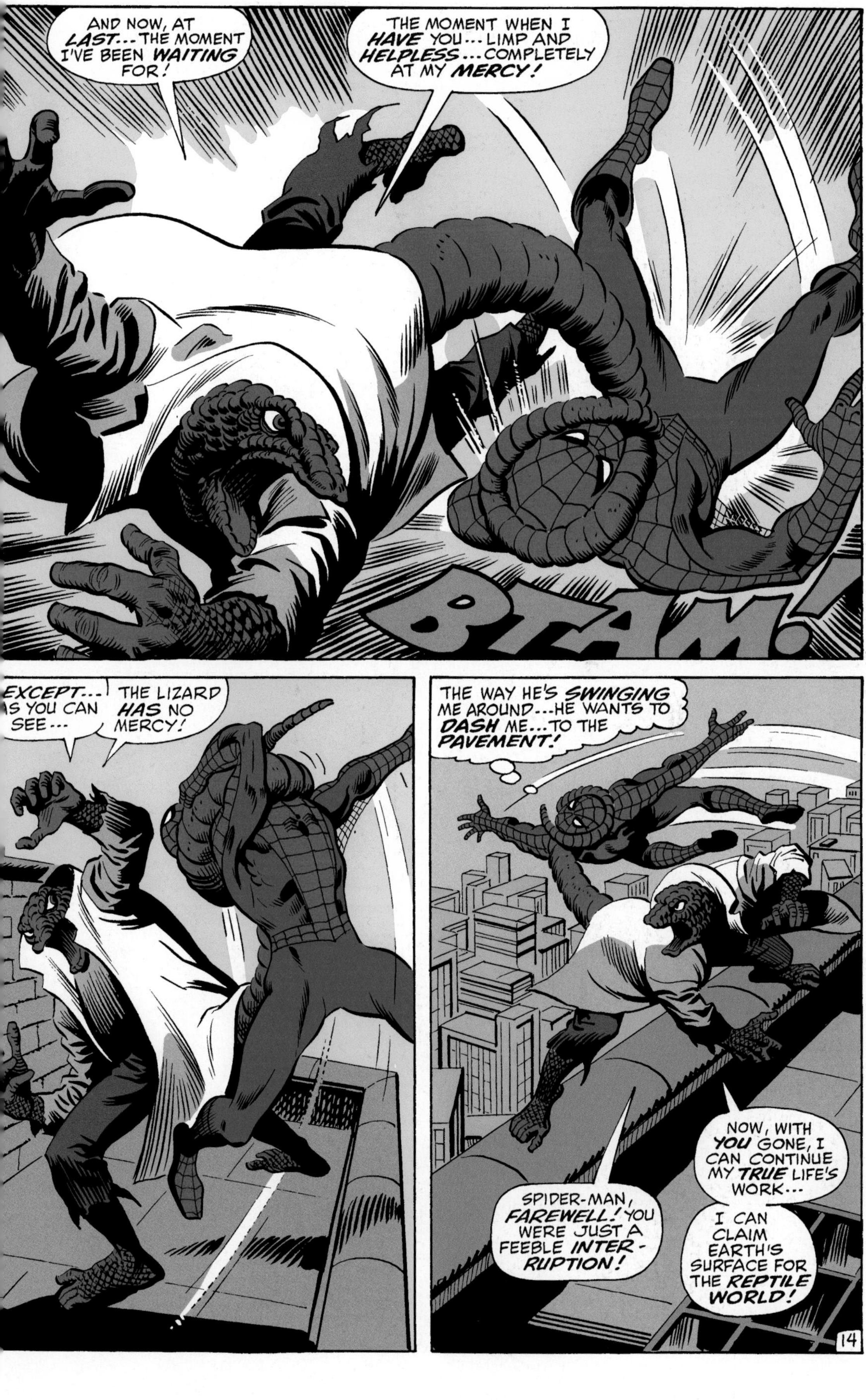
AND NOW, AT LAST... THE MOMENT I'VE BEEN WAITING FOR!
THE MOMENT WHEN I HAVE YOU... LIMP AND HELPLESS... COMPLETELY AT MY MERCY!
BLAM!
EXCEPT... AS YOU CAN SEE...
THE LIZARD HAS NO MERCY!
THE WAY HE'S SWINGING ME AROUND... HE WANTS TO DASH ME... TO THE PAVEMENT!
SPIDER-MAN, FAREWELL! YOU WERE JUST A FEEBLE INTER-RUPTION!
NOW, WITH YOU GONE, I CAN CONTINUE MY TRUE LIFE'S WORK...
I CAN CLAIM EARTH'S SURFACE FOR THE REPTILE WORLD!
14

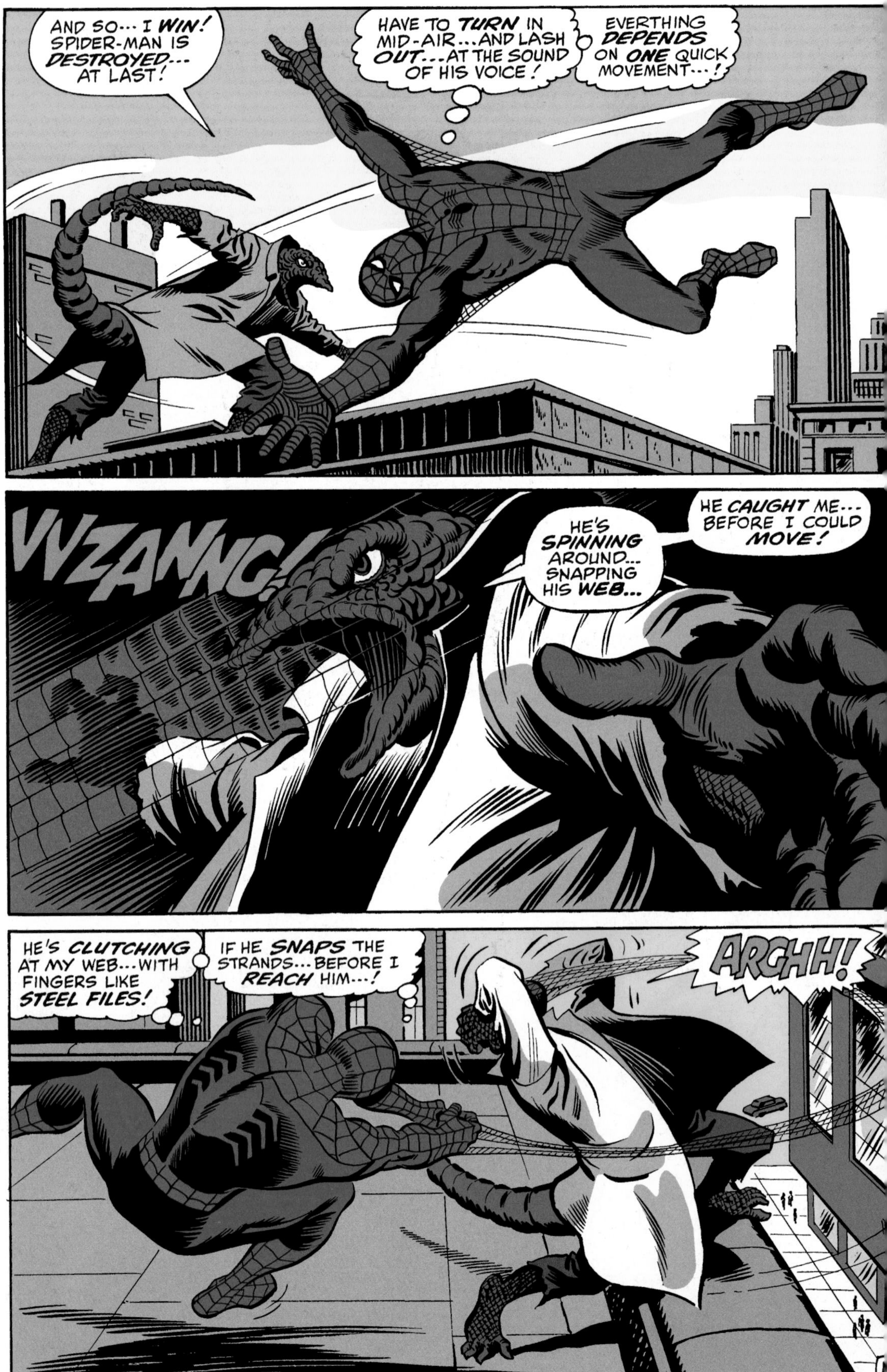
AND SO... I WIN! SPIDER-MAN IS DESTROYED... AT LAST!
HAVE TO TURN IN MID-AIR... AND LASH OUT... AT THE SOUND OF HIS VOICE!
EVERTHING DEPENDS ON ONE QUICK MOVEMENT...!
VVZANNG!
HE'S SPINNING AROUND... SNAPPING HIS WEB...
HE CAUGHT ME... BEFORE I COULD MOVE!
HE'S CLUTCHING AT MY WEB... WITH FINGERS LIKE STEEL FILES!
IF HE SNAPS THE STRANDS... BEFORE I REACH HIM...!
ARGHH!

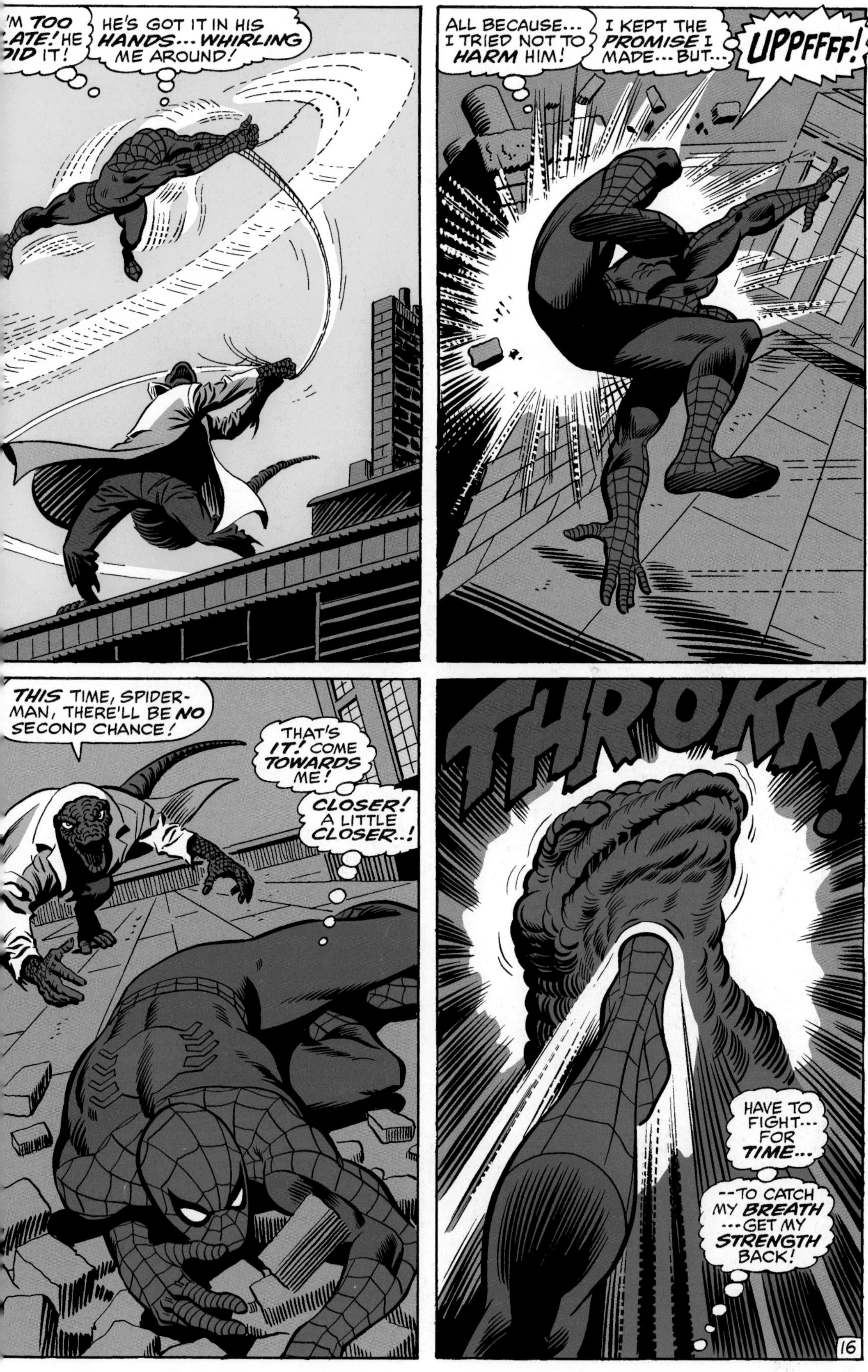
'M TOO
ATE! HE
DID IT!
HE'S GOT IT IN HIS HANDS... WHIRLING ME AROUND!
ALL BECAUSE... I TRIED NOT TO HARM HIM!
I KEPT THE PROMISE I MADE... BUT...
UPPFFFF!
THIS TIME, SPIDER-MAN, THERE'LL BE NO SECOND CHANCE!
THAT'S IT! COME TOWARDS ME!
CLOSER! A LITTLE CLOSER..!
THROKK!
HAVE TO FIGHT... FOR TIME...
--TO CATCH MY BREATH ...GET MY STRENGTH BACK!
16

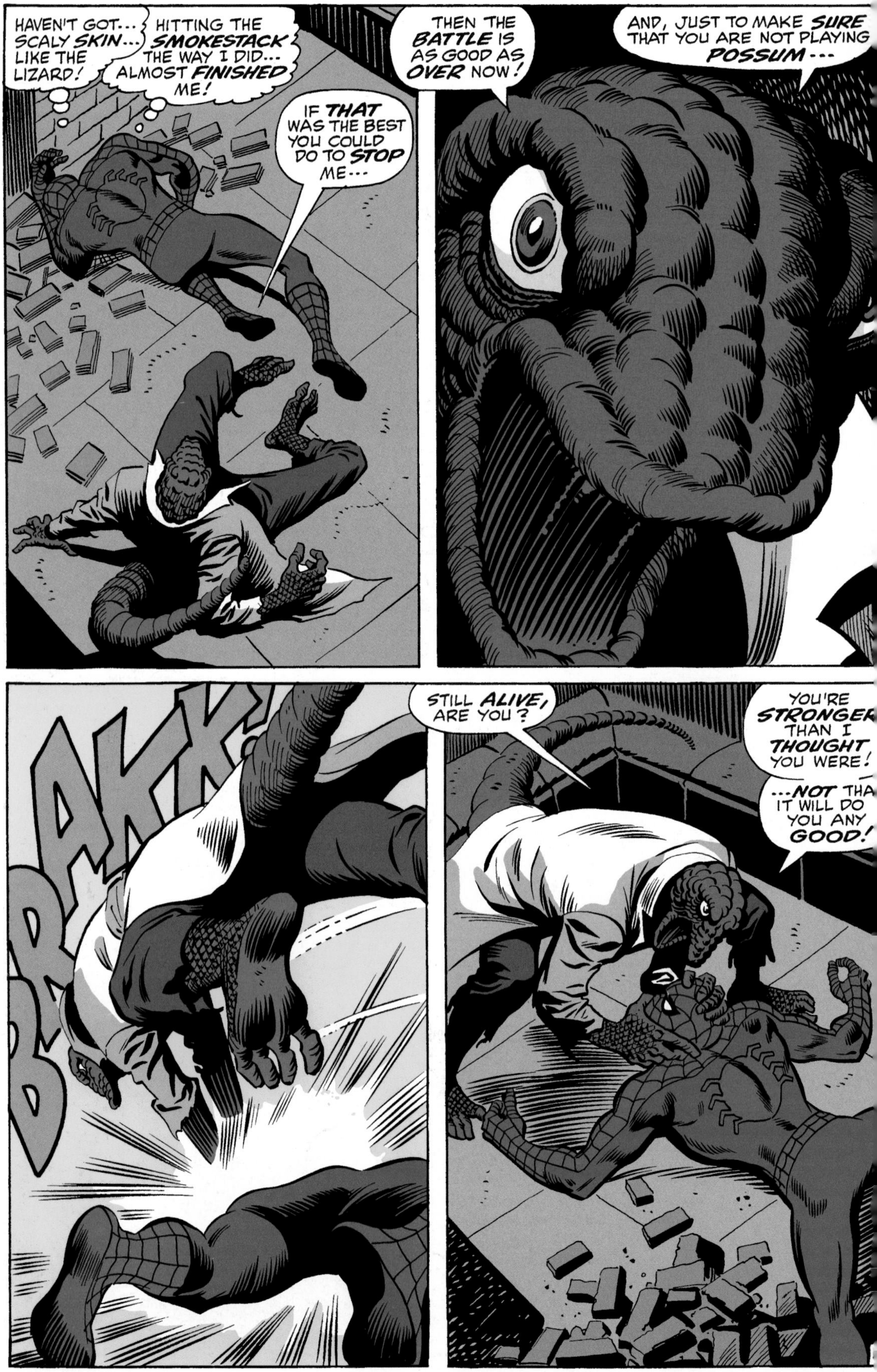

HAVEN'T GOT... SCALY SKIN... LIKE THE LIZARD!
HITTING THE SMOKESTACK THE WAY I DID... ALMOST FINISHED ME!
IF THAT WAS THE BEST YOU COULD DO TO STOP ME---
THEN THE BATTLE IS AS GOOD AS OVER NOW!
AND, JUST TO MAKE SURE THAT YOU ARE NOT PLAYING POSSUM---
BRAKK!
STILL ALIVE, ARE YOU?
YOU'RE STRONGER THAN I THOUGHT YOU WERE!
...NOT THA IT WILL DO YOU ANY GOOD!

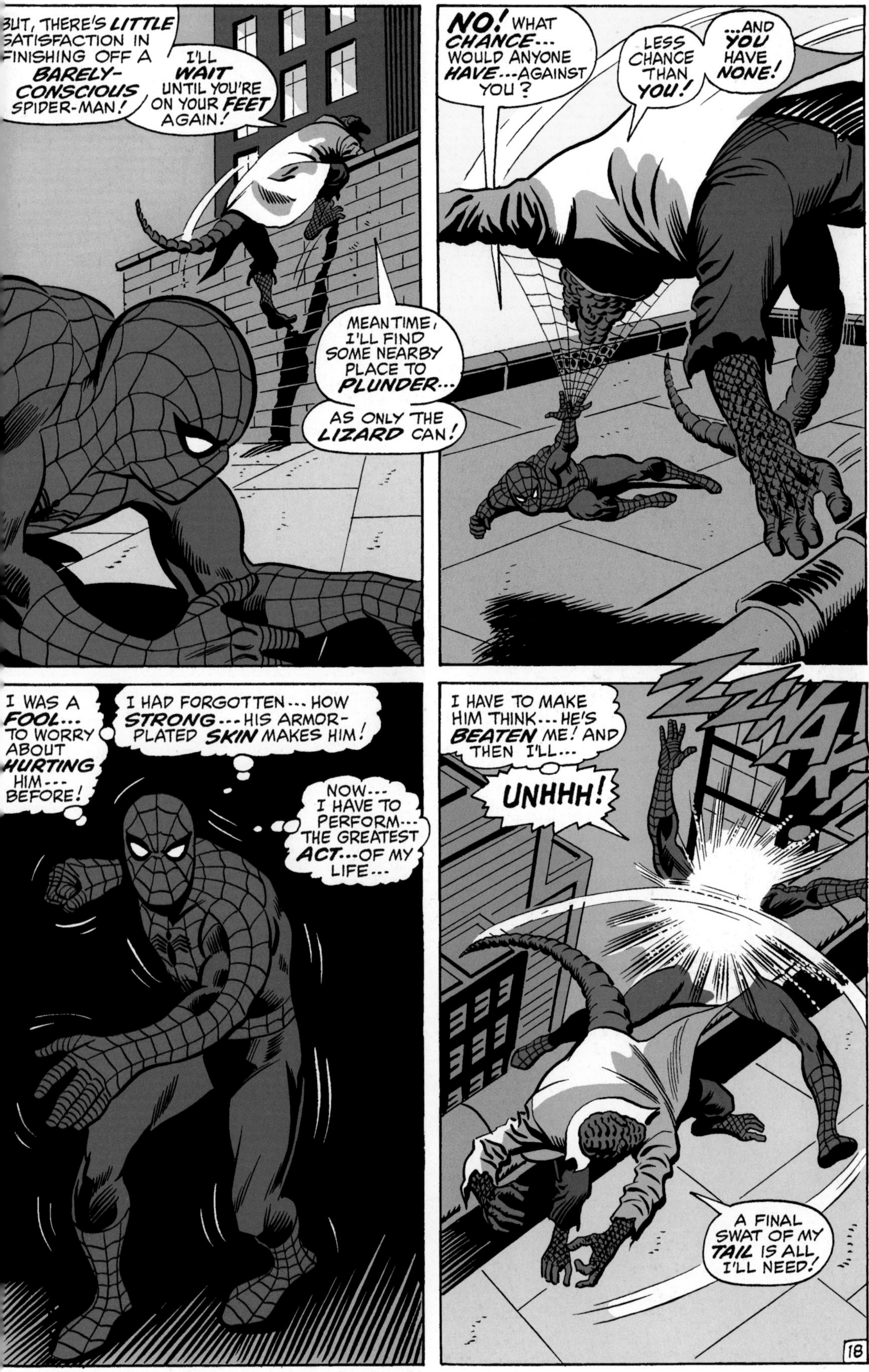
BUT, THERE'S LITTLE SATISFACTION IN FINISHING OFF A BARELY-CONSCIOUS SPIDER-MAN!
I'LL WAIT UNTIL YOU'RE ON YOUR FEET AGAIN!
MEANTIME, I'LL FIND SOME NEARBY PLACE TO PLUNDER...
AS ONLY THE LIZARD CAN!
NO! WHAT CHANCE... WOULD ANYONE HAVE...AGAINST YOU?
LESS CHANCE THAN YOU!
...AND YOU HAVE NONE!
I WAS A FOOL... TO WORRY ABOUT HURTING HIM... BEFORE!
I HAD FORGOTTEN... HOW STRONG... HIS ARMOR-PLATED SKIN MAKES HIM!
NOW... I HAVE TO PERFORM... THE GREATEST ACT...OF MY LIFE...
I HAVE TO MAKE HIM THINK... HE'S BEATEN ME! AND THEN I'LL...
UNHHH!
A FINAL SWAT OF MY TAIL IS ALL I'LL NEED!
18

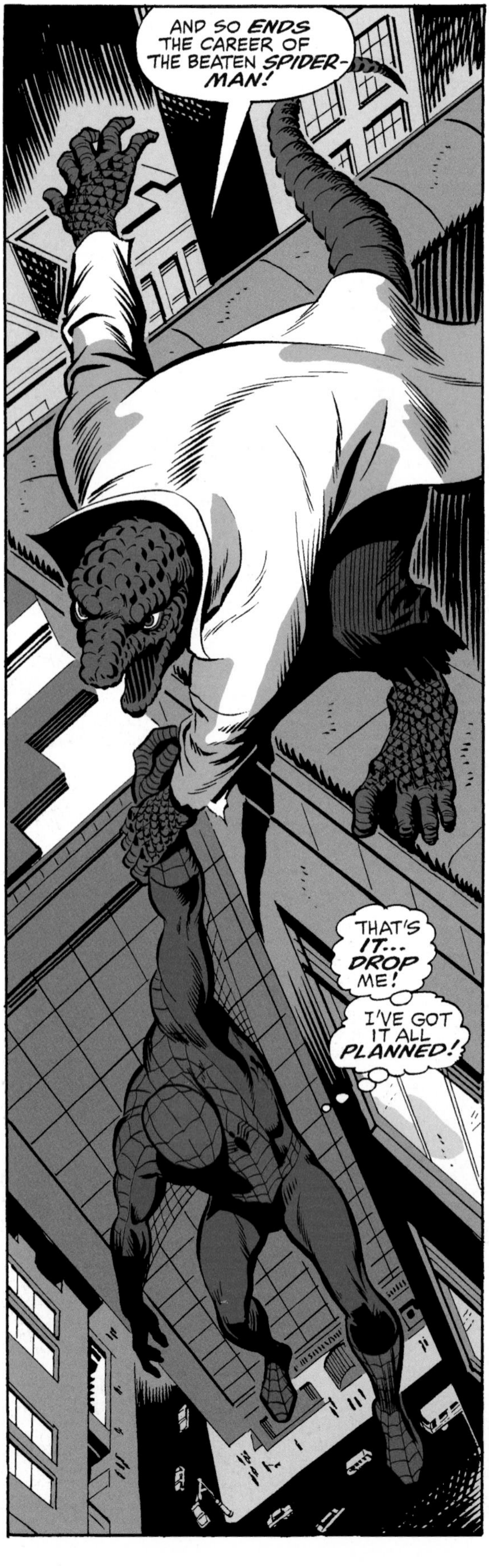
AND SO ENDS THE CAREER OF THE BEATEN SPIDER-MAN!
THAT'S IT... DROP ME!
I'VE GOT IT ALL PLANNED!

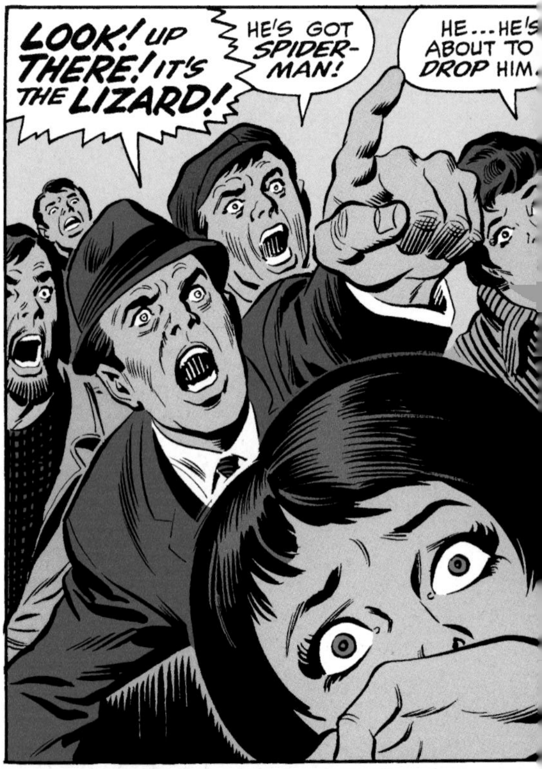
LOOK! UP THERE! IT'S THE LIZARD!
HE'S GOT SPIDER-MAN!
HE...HE'S ABOUT TO DROP HIM.

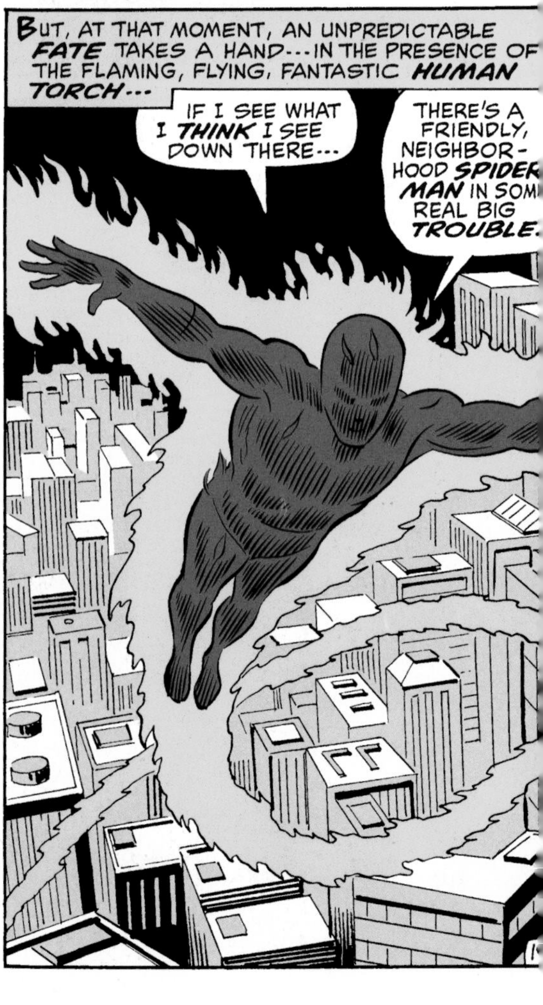
BUT, AT THAT MOMENT, AN UNPREDICTABLE FATE TAKES A HAND---IN THE PRESENCE OF THE FLAMING, FLYING, FANTASTIC HUMAN TORCH---
IF I SEE WHAT I THINK I SEE DOWN THERE---
THERE'S A FRIENDLY, NEIGHBOR-HOOD SPIDER-MAN IN SOME REAL BIG TROUBLE.

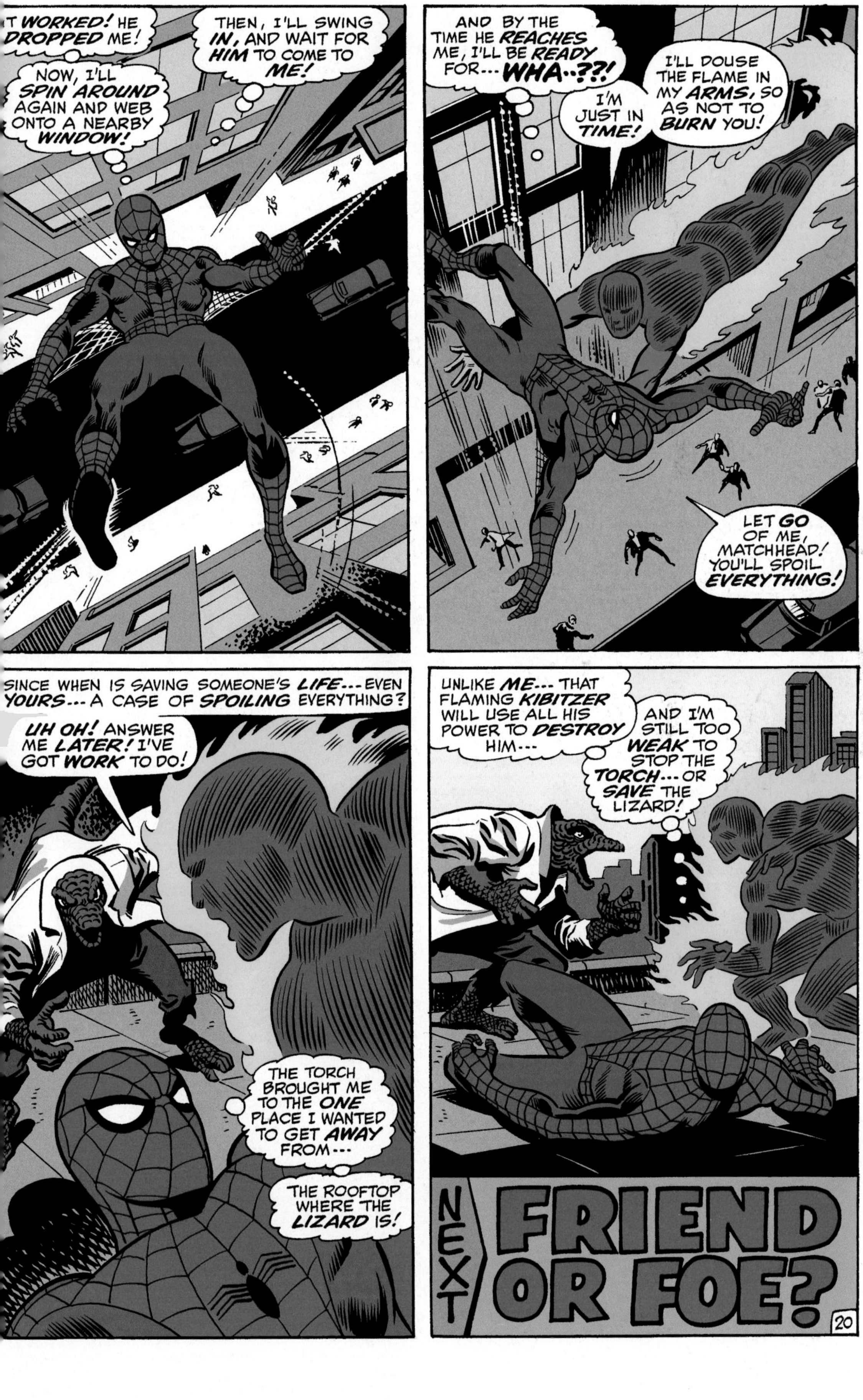
T WORKED! HE DROPPED ME!
NOW, I'LL SPIN AROUND AGAIN AND WEB ONTO A NEARBY WINDOW!
THEN, I'LL SWING IN, AND WAIT FOR HIM TO COME TO ME!
AND BY THE TIME HE REACHES ME, I'LL BE READY FOR--- WHA--??!
I'M JUST IN TIME!
I'LL DOUSE THE FLAME IN MY ARMS, SO AS NOT TO BURN YOU!
LET GO OF ME, MATCHHEAD! YOU'LL SPOIL EVERYTHING!
SINCE WHEN IS SAVING SOMEONE'S LIFE--- EVEN YOURS--- A CASE OF SPOILING EVERYTHING?
UH OH! ANSWER ME LATER! I'VE GOT WORK TO DO!
THE TORCH BROUGHT ME TO THE ONE PLACE I WANTED TO GET AWAY FROM---
THE ROOFTOP WHERE THE LIZARD IS!
UNLIKE ME--- THAT FLAMING KIBITZER WILL USE ALL HIS POWER TO DESTROY HIM---
AND I'M STILL TOO WEAK TO STOP THE TORCH--- OR SAVE THE LIZARD!
NEXT
FRIEND OR FOE?
20

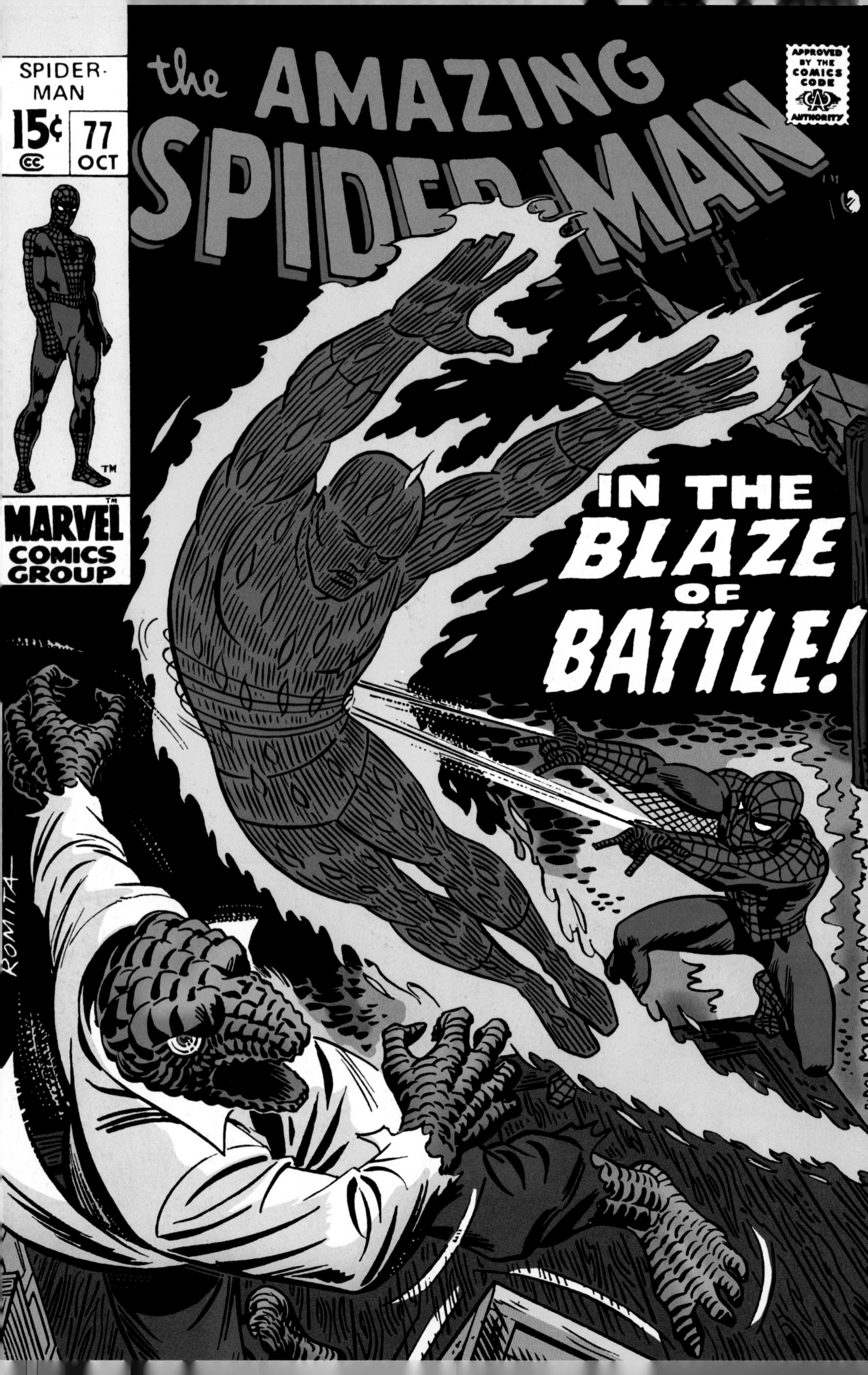

SPIDER-MAN
15¢
77
OCT
the AMAZING
SPIDER-MAN
APPROVED BY THE COMICS CODE AUTHORITY
MARVEL COMICS GROUP
IN THE BLAZE OF BATTLE!
ROMITA

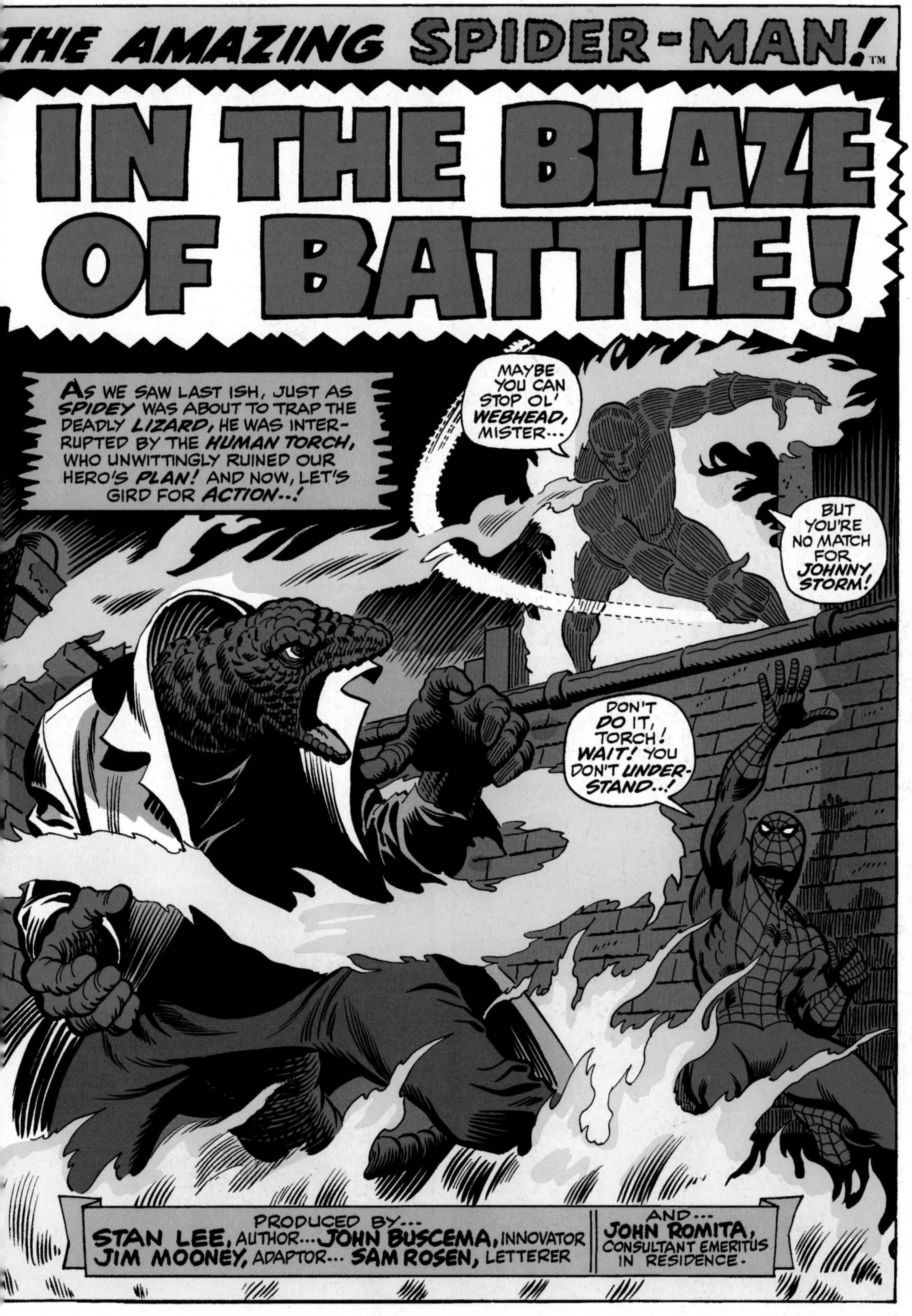

THE AMAZING SPIDER-MAN!™
IN THE BLAZE OF BATTLE!
AS WE SAW LAST ISH, JUST AS SPIDEY WAS ABOUT TO TRAP THE DEADLY LIZARD, HE WAS INTERRUPTED BY THE HUMAN TORCH, WHO UNWITTINGLY RUINED OUR HERO'S PLAN! AND NOW, LET'S GIRD FOR ACTION..!
MAYBE YOU CAN STOP OL' WEBHEAD, MISTER...
BUT YOU'RE NO MATCH FOR JOHNNY STORM!
DON'T DO IT, TORCH! WAIT! YOU DON'T UNDERSTAND..!
PRODUCED BY...
STAN LEE, AUTHOR... JOHN BUSCEMA, INNOVATOR
JIM MOONEY, ADAPTOR... SAM ROSEN, LETTERER
AND... JOHN ROMITA, CONSULTANT EMERITUS IN RESIDENCE.

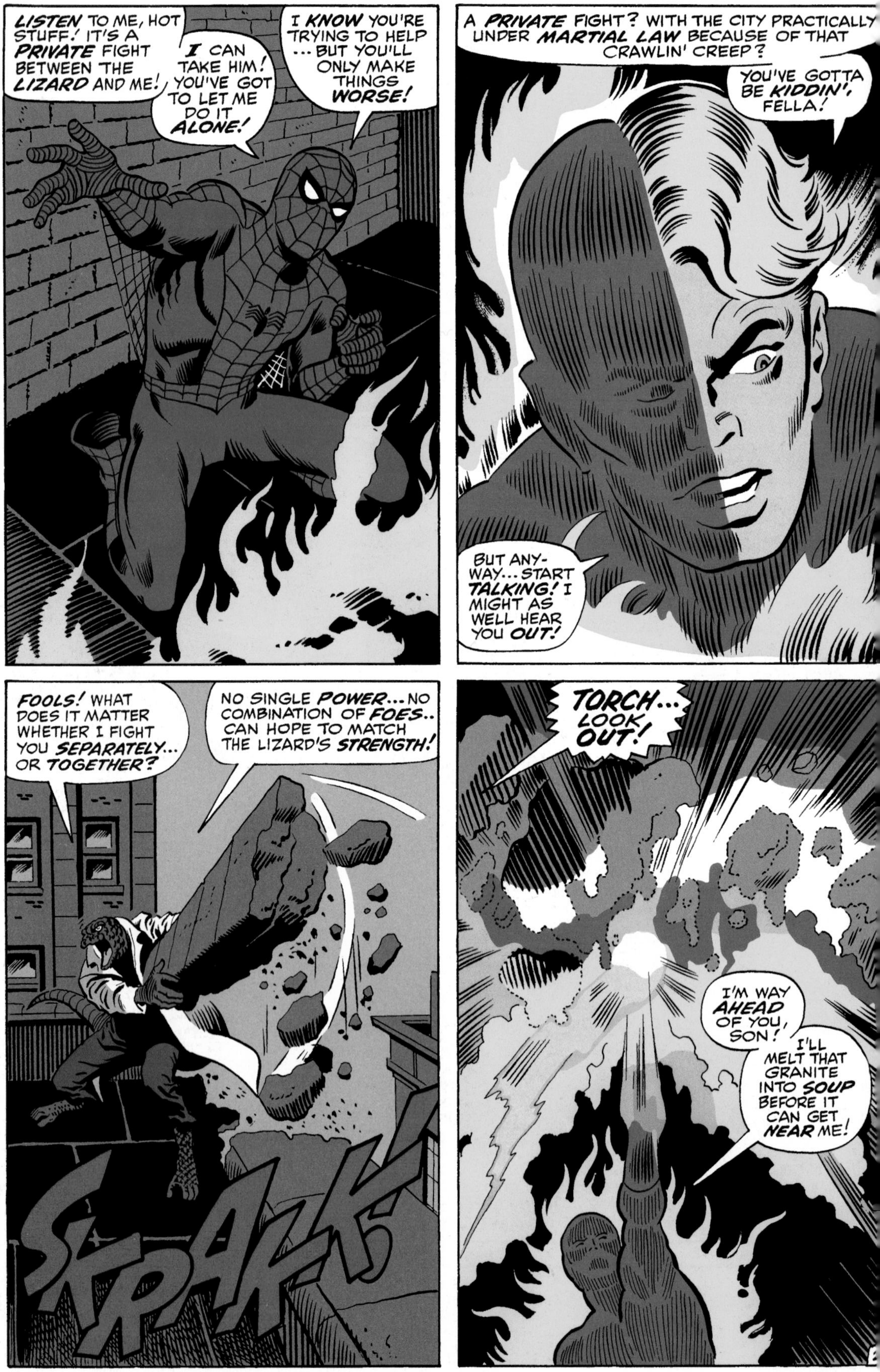

LISTEN TO ME, HOT STUFF! IT'S A PRIVATE FIGHT BETWEEN THE LIZARD AND ME!
I CAN TAKE HIM! YOU'VE GOT TO LET ME DO IT ALONE!
I KNOW YOU'RE TRYING TO HELP ...BUT YOU'LL ONLY MAKE THINGS WORSE!
A PRIVATE FIGHT? WITH THE CITY PRACTICALLY UNDER MARTIAL LAW BECAUSE OF THAT CRAWLIN' CREEP?
YOU'VE GOTTA BE KIDDIN', FELLA!
BUT ANY-WAY...START TALKING! I MIGHT AS WELL HEAR YOU OUT!
FOOLS! WHAT DOES IT MATTER WHETHER I FIGHT YOU SEPARATELY... OR TOGETHER?
NO SINGLE POWER...NO COMBINATION OF FOES.. CAN HOPE TO MATCH THE LIZARD'S STRENGTH!
SKRAK
TORCH... LOOK OUT!
I'M WAY AHEAD OF YOU, SON!
I'LL MELT THAT GRANITE INTO SOUP BEFORE IT CAN GET NEAR ME!

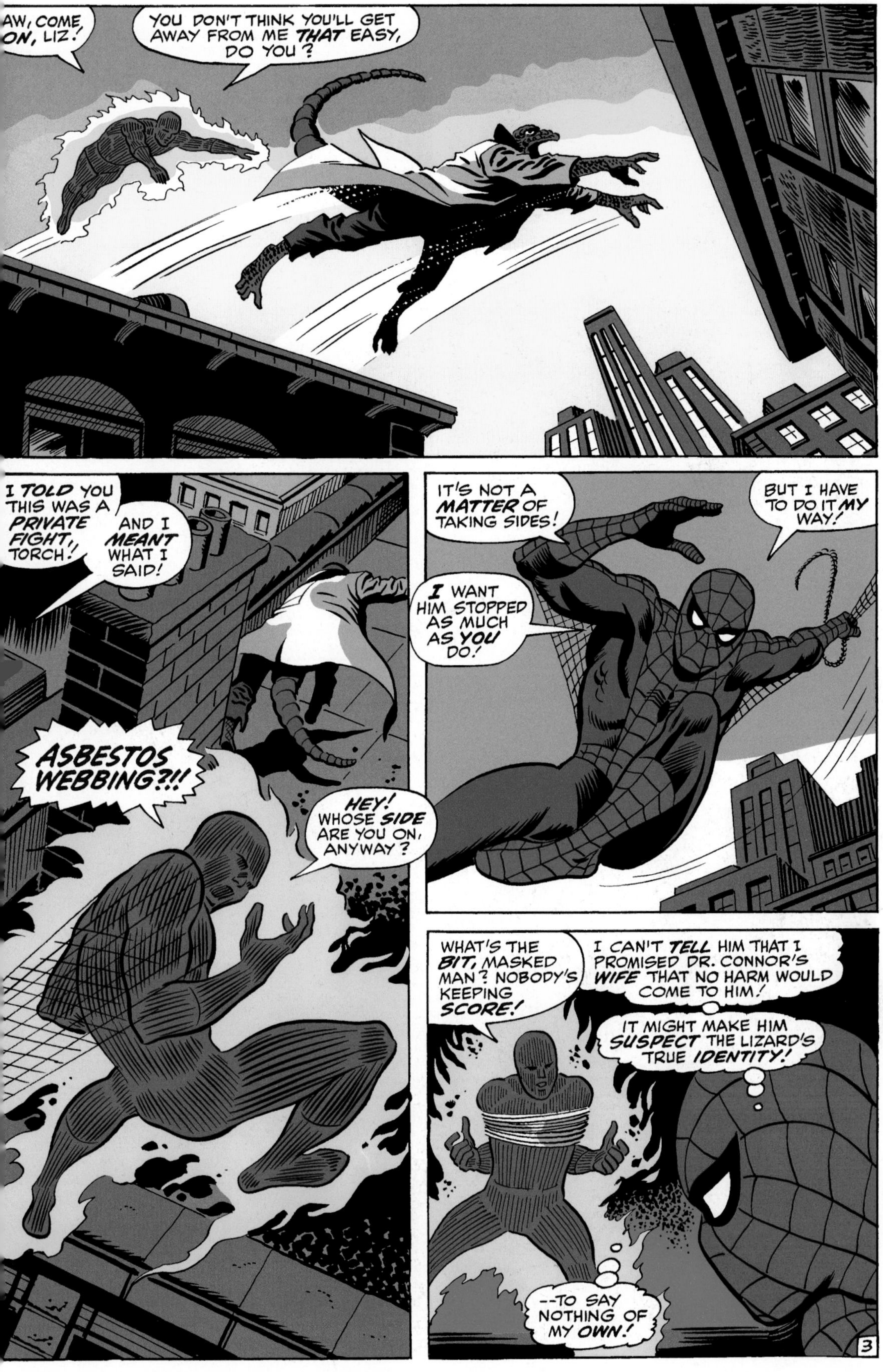
AW, COME ON, LIZ!
YOU DON'T THINK YOU'LL GET AWAY FROM ME THAT EASY, DO YOU?
I TOLD YOU THIS WAS A PRIVATE FIGHT, TORCH!
AND I MEANT WHAT I SAID!
ASBESTOS WEBBING?!!
HEY! WHOSE SIDE ARE YOU ON, ANYWAY?
IT'S NOT A MATTER OF TAKING SIDES!
BUT I HAVE TO DO IT MY WAY!
I WANT HIM STOPPED AS MUCH AS YOU DO!
WHAT'S THE BIT, MASKED MAN? NOBODY'S KEEPING SCORE!
I CAN'T TELL HIM THAT I PROMISED DR. CONNOR'S WIFE THAT NO HARM WOULD COME TO HIM!
IT MIGHT MAKE HIM SUSPECT THE LIZARD'S TRUE IDENTITY!
--TO SAY NOTHING OF MY OWN!
3

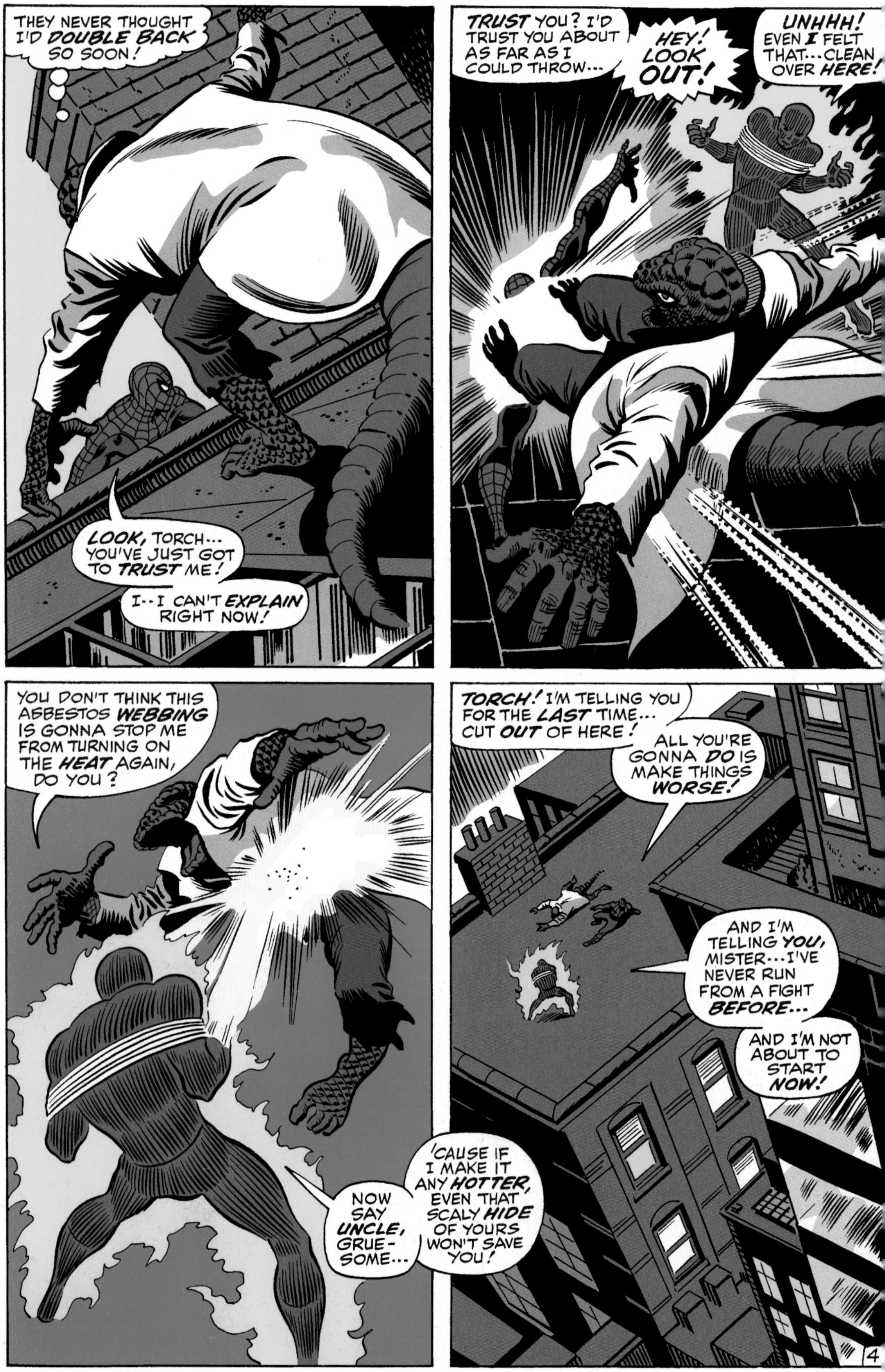

THEY NEVER THOUGHT I'D DOUBLE BACK SO SOON!
LOOK, TORCH... YOU'VE JUST GOT TO TRUST ME!
I--I CAN'T EXPLAIN RIGHT NOW!
TRUST YOU? I'D TRUST YOU ABOUT AS FAR AS I COULD THROW...
HEY! LOOK OUT!
UNHHH! EVEN I FELT THAT...CLEAN OVER HERE!
YOU DON'T THINK THIS ASBESTOS WEBBING IS GONNA STOP ME FROM TURNING ON THE HEAT AGAIN, DO YOU?
NOW SAY UNCLE, GRUE-SOME...
'CAUSE IF I MAKE IT ANY HOTTER, EVEN THAT SCALY HIDE OF YOURS WON'T SAVE YOU!
TORCH! I'M TELLING YOU FOR THE LAST TIME... CUT OUT OF HERE!
ALL YOU'RE GONNA DO IS MAKE THINGS WORSE!
AND I'M TELLING YOU, MISTER...I'VE NEVER RUN FROM A FIGHT BEFORE...
AND I'M NOT ABOUT TO START NOW!
4

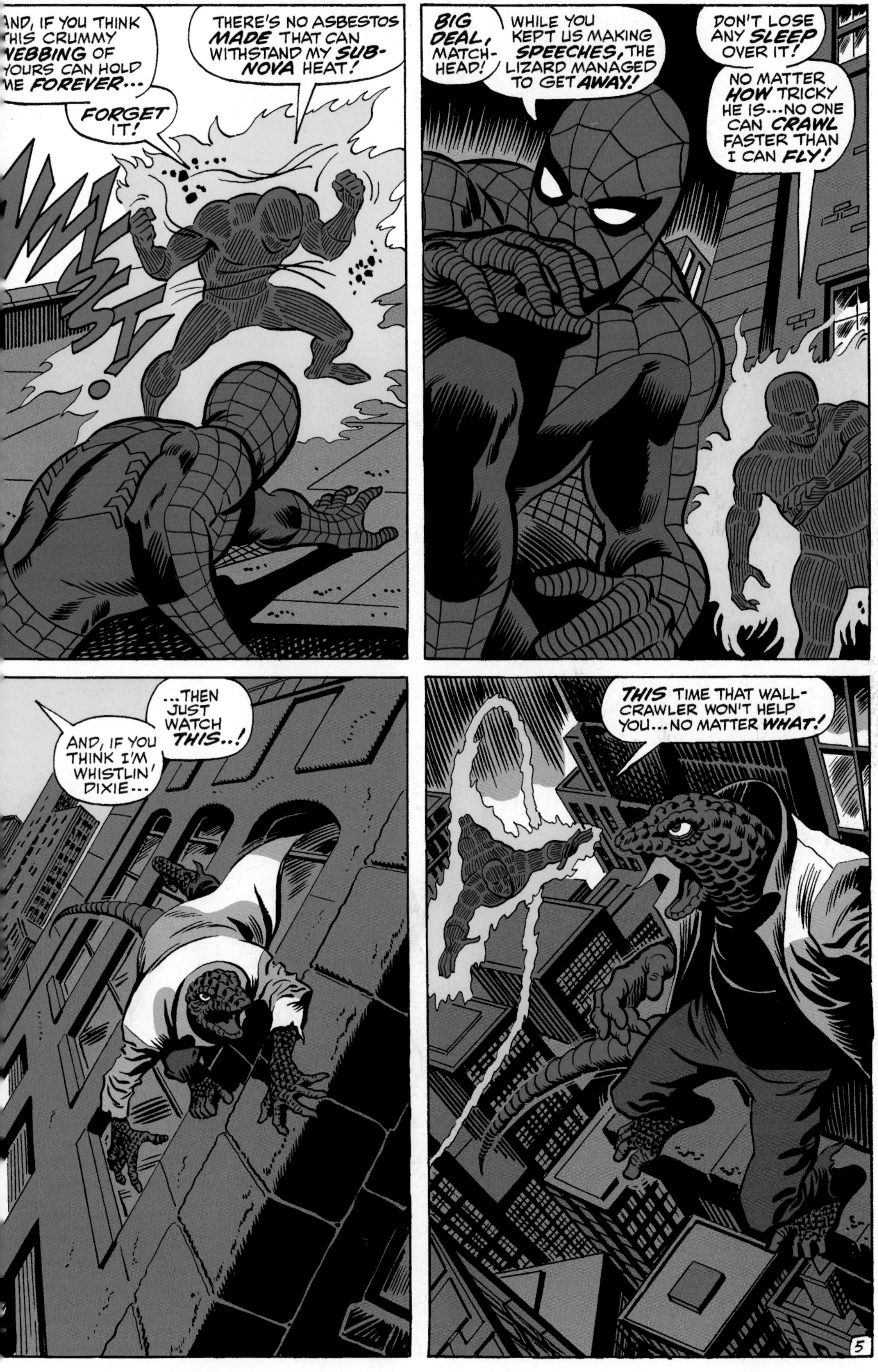
AND, IF YOU THINK THIS CRUMMY WEBBING OF YOURS CAN HOLD ME FOREVER...
FORGET IT!
THERE'S NO ASBESTOS MADE THAT CAN WITHSTAND MY SUB-NOVA HEAT!
BIG DEAL, MATCH-HEAD!
WHILE YOU KEPT US MAKING SPEECHES, THE LIZARD MANAGED TO GET AWAY!
DON'T LOSE ANY SLEEP OVER IT!
NO MATTER HOW TRICKY HE IS...NO ONE CAN CRAWL FASTER THAN I CAN FLY!
AND, IF YOU THINK I'M WHISTLIN' DIXIE...
...THEN JUST WATCH THIS..!
THIS TIME THAT WALL-CRAWLER WON'T HELP YOU...NO MATTER WHAT!
5

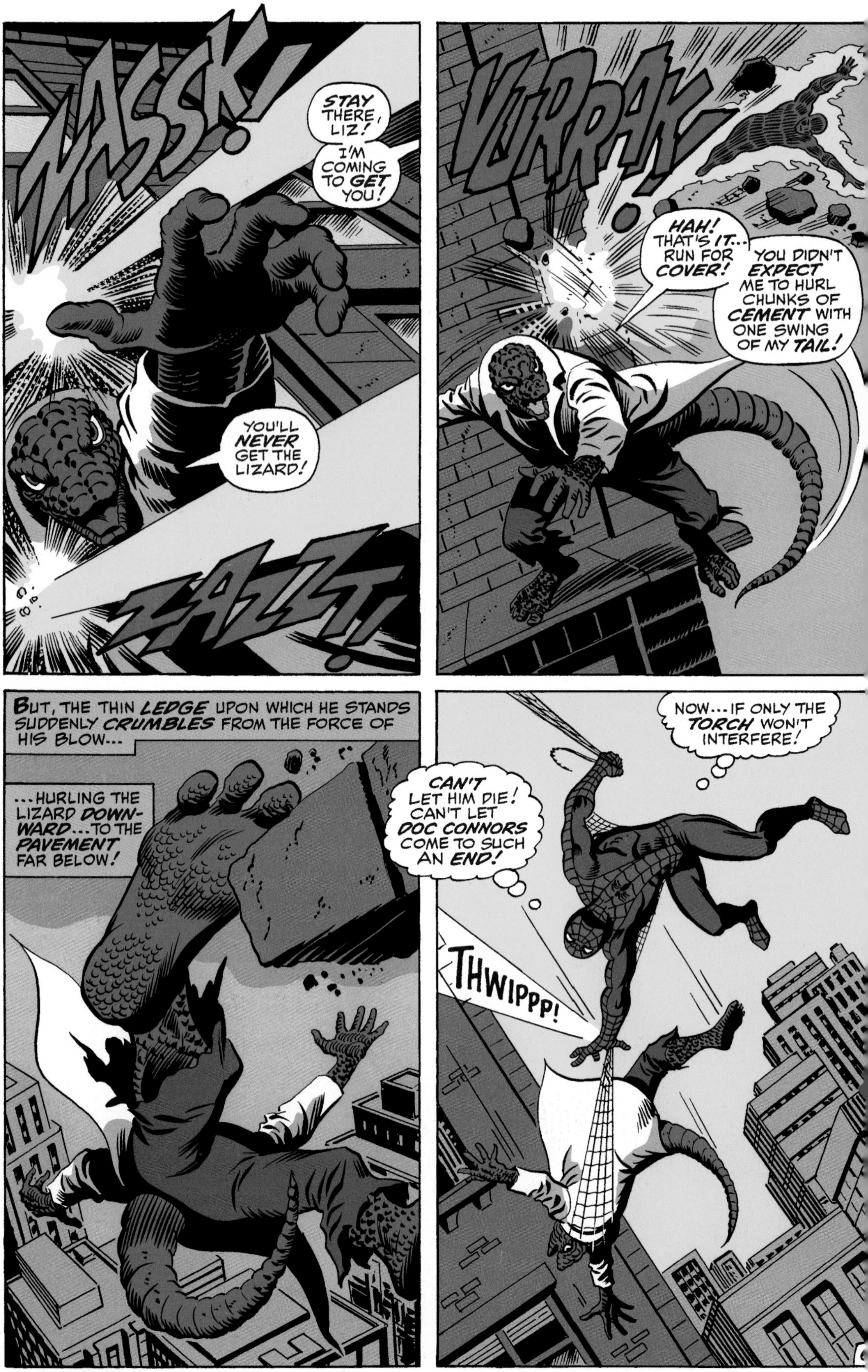

ZASSK!
STAY THERE, LIZ!
I'M COMING TO GET YOU!
YOU'LL NEVER GET THE LIZARD!
ZAZZT!
VURRAK!
HAH! THAT'S IT... RUN FOR COVER!
YOU DIDN'T EXPECT ME TO HURL CHUNKS OF CEMENT WITH ONE SWING OF MY TAIL!
BUT, THE THIN LEDGE UPON WHICH HE STANDS SUDDENLY CRUMBLES FROM THE FORCE OF HIS BLOW...
...HURLING THE LIZARD DOWNWARD...TO THE PAVEMENT FAR BELOW!
CAN'T LET HIM DIE! CAN'T LET DOC CONNORS COME TO SUCH AN END!
NOW...IF ONLY THE TORCH WON'T INTERFERE!
THWIPPP!

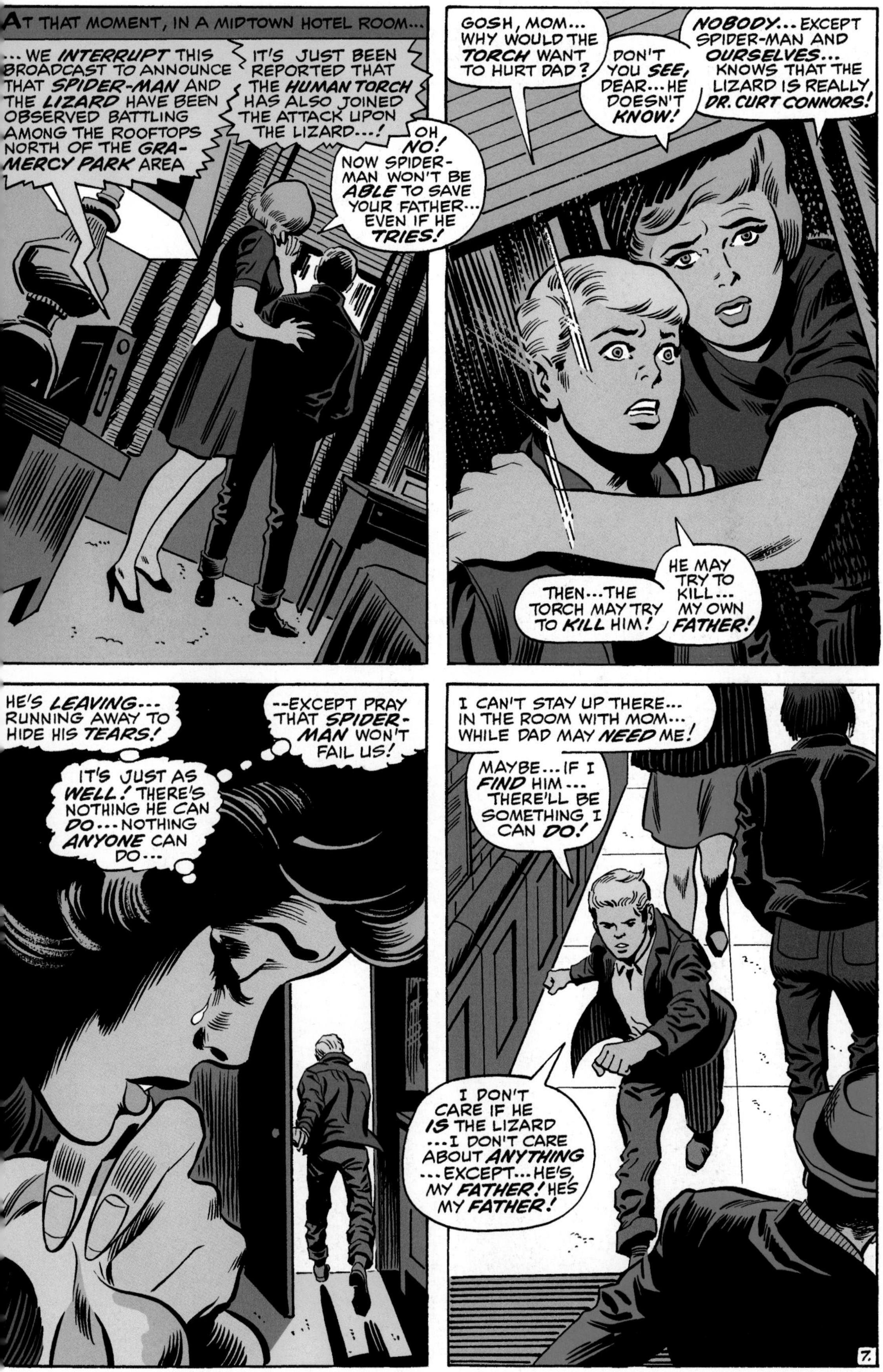
AT THAT MOMENT, IN A MIDTOWN HOTEL ROOM...
...WE INTERRUPT THIS BROADCAST TO ANNOUNCE THAT SPIDER-MAN AND THE LIZARD HAVE BEEN OBSERVED BATTLING AMONG THE ROOFTOPS NORTH OF THE GRAMERCY PARK AREA
IT'S JUST BEEN REPORTED THAT THE HUMAN TORCH HAS ALSO JOINED THE ATTACK UPON THE LIZARD...!
OH NO! NOW SPIDER-MAN WON'T BE ABLE TO SAVE YOUR FATHER... EVEN IF HE TRIES!
GOSH, MOM... WHY WOULD THE TORCH WANT TO HURT DAD?
DON'T YOU SEE, DEAR... HE DOESN'T KNOW!
NOBODY... EXCEPT SPIDER-MAN AND OURSELVES... KNOWS THAT THE LIZARD IS REALLY DR. CURT CONNORS!
THEN... THE TORCH MAY TRY TO KILL HIM!
HE MAY TRY TO KILL... MY OWN FATHER!
HE'S LEAVING... RUNNING AWAY TO HIDE HIS TEARS!
IT'S JUST AS WELL! THERE'S NOTHING HE CAN DO... NOTHING ANYONE CAN DO...
--EXCEPT PRAY THAT SPIDER-MAN WON'T FAIL US!
I CAN'T STAY UP THERE... IN THE ROOM WITH MOM... WHILE DAD MAY NEED ME!
MAYBE... IF I FIND HIM... THERE'LL BE SOMETHING I CAN DO!
I DON'T CARE IF HE IS THE LIZARD ...I DON'T CARE ABOUT ANYTHING ...EXCEPT... HE'S, MY FATHER! HE'S MY FATHER!
7.

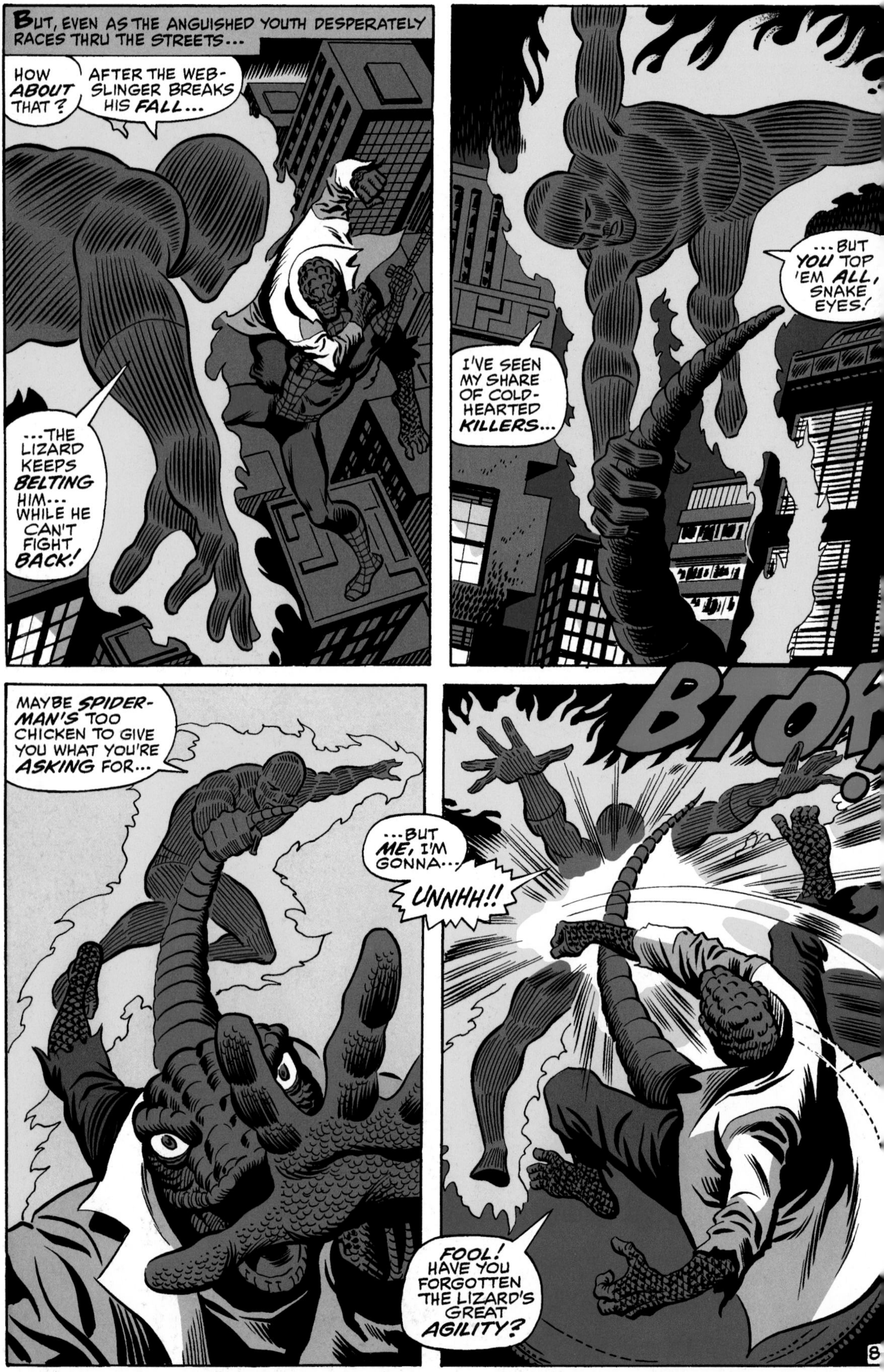

BUT, EVEN AS THE ANGUISHED YOUTH DESPERATELY RACES THRU THE STREETS...
HOW ABOUT THAT?
AFTER THE WEB-SLINGER BREAKS HIS FALL...
...THE LIZARD KEEPS BELTING HIM... WHILE HE CAN'T FIGHT BACK!
I'VE SEEN MY SHARE OF COLD-HEARTED KILLERS...
...BUT YOU TOP 'EM ALL, SNAKE EYES!
MAYBE SPIDER-MAN'S TOO CHICKEN TO GIVE YOU WHAT YOU'RE ASKING FOR...
...BUT ME, I'M GONNA...
UNNHH!!
BTOK
FOOL! HAVE YOU FORGOTTEN THE LIZARD'S GREAT AGILITY?

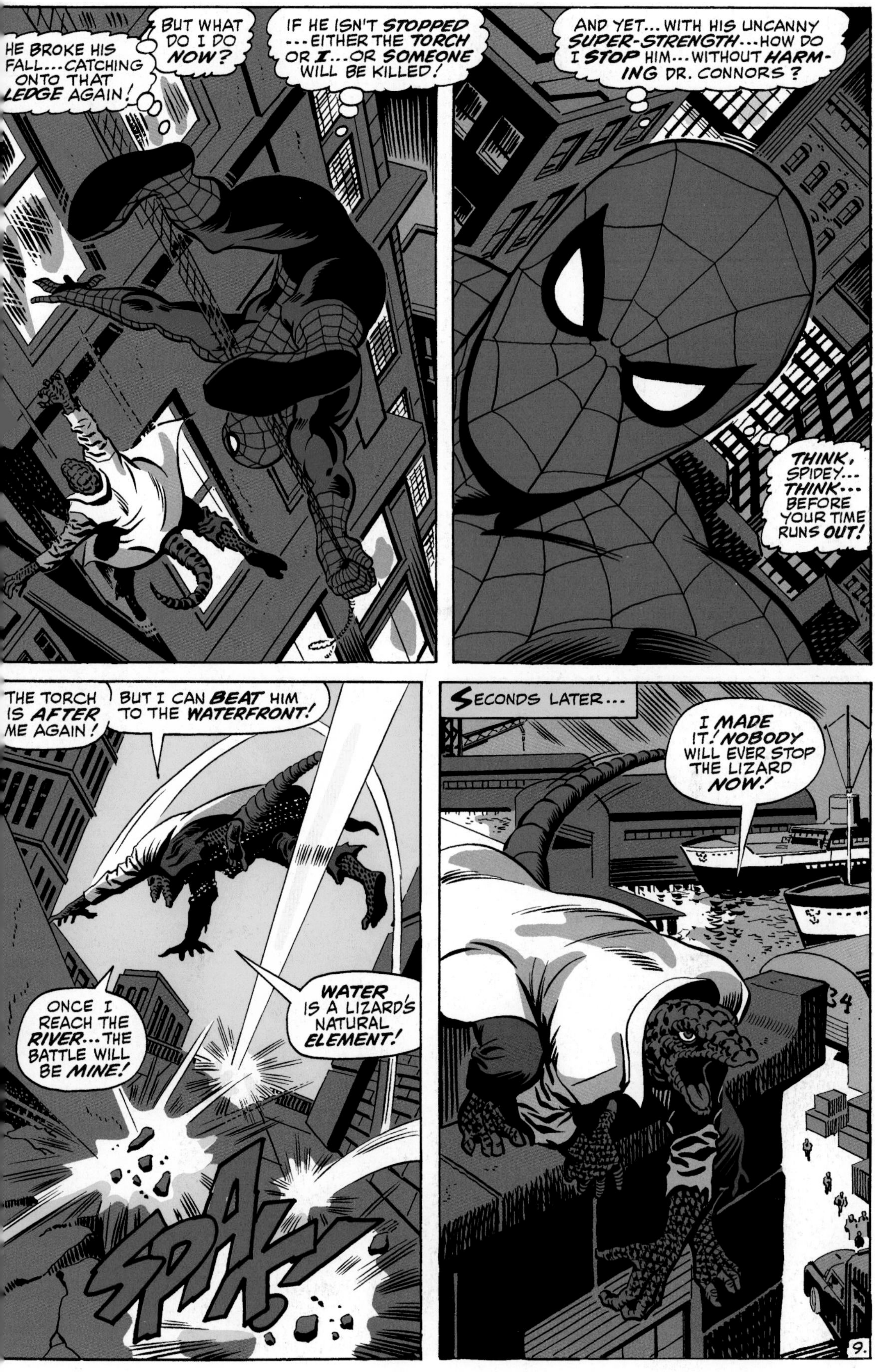

HE BROKE HIS FALL... CATCHING ONTO THAT LEDGE AGAIN!
BUT WHAT DO I DO NOW?
IF HE ISN'T STOPPED ...EITHER THE TORCH OR I...OR SOMEONE WILL BE KILLED!
AND YET... WITH HIS UNCANNY SUPER-STRENGTH...HOW DO I STOP HIM... WITHOUT HARMING DR. CONNORS?
THINK, SPIDEY... THINK... BEFORE YOUR TIME RUNS OUT!
THE TORCH IS AFTER ME AGAIN!
BUT I CAN BEAT HIM TO THE WATERFRONT!
ONCE I REACH THE RIVER...THE BATTLE WILL BE MINE!
WATER IS A LIZARD'S NATURAL ELEMENT!
SPAK
SECONDS LATER...
I MADE IT! NOBODY WILL EVER STOP THE LIZARD NOW!

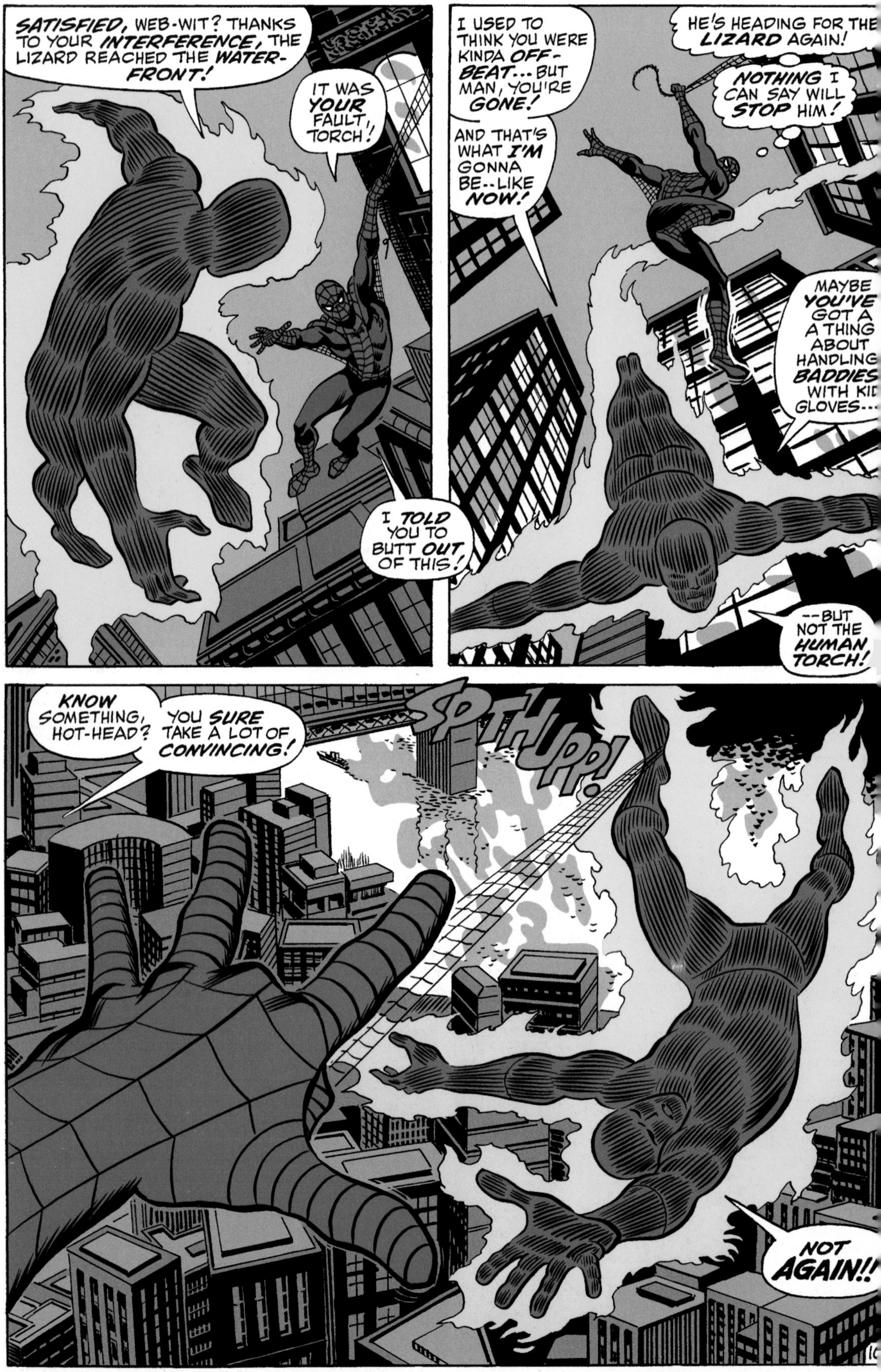
SATISFIED, WEB-WIT? THANKS TO YOUR INTERFERENCE, THE LIZARD REACHED THE WATER-FRONT!
IT WAS YOUR FAULT, TORCH!
I TOLD YOU TO BUTT OUT OF THIS!
I USED TO THINK YOU WERE KINDA OFF-BEAT... BUT MAN, YOU'RE GONE!
AND THAT'S WHAT I'M GONNA BE--LIKE NOW!
HE'S HEADING FOR THE LIZARD AGAIN!
NOTHING I CAN SAY WILL STOP HIM!
MAYBE YOU'VE GOT A A THING ABOUT HANDLING BADDIES WITH KID GLOVES...
--BUT NOT THE HUMAN TORCH!
KNOW SOMETHING, HOT-HEAD?
YOU SURE TAKE A LOT OF CONVINCING!
SPTHUPP!
NOT AGAIN!!

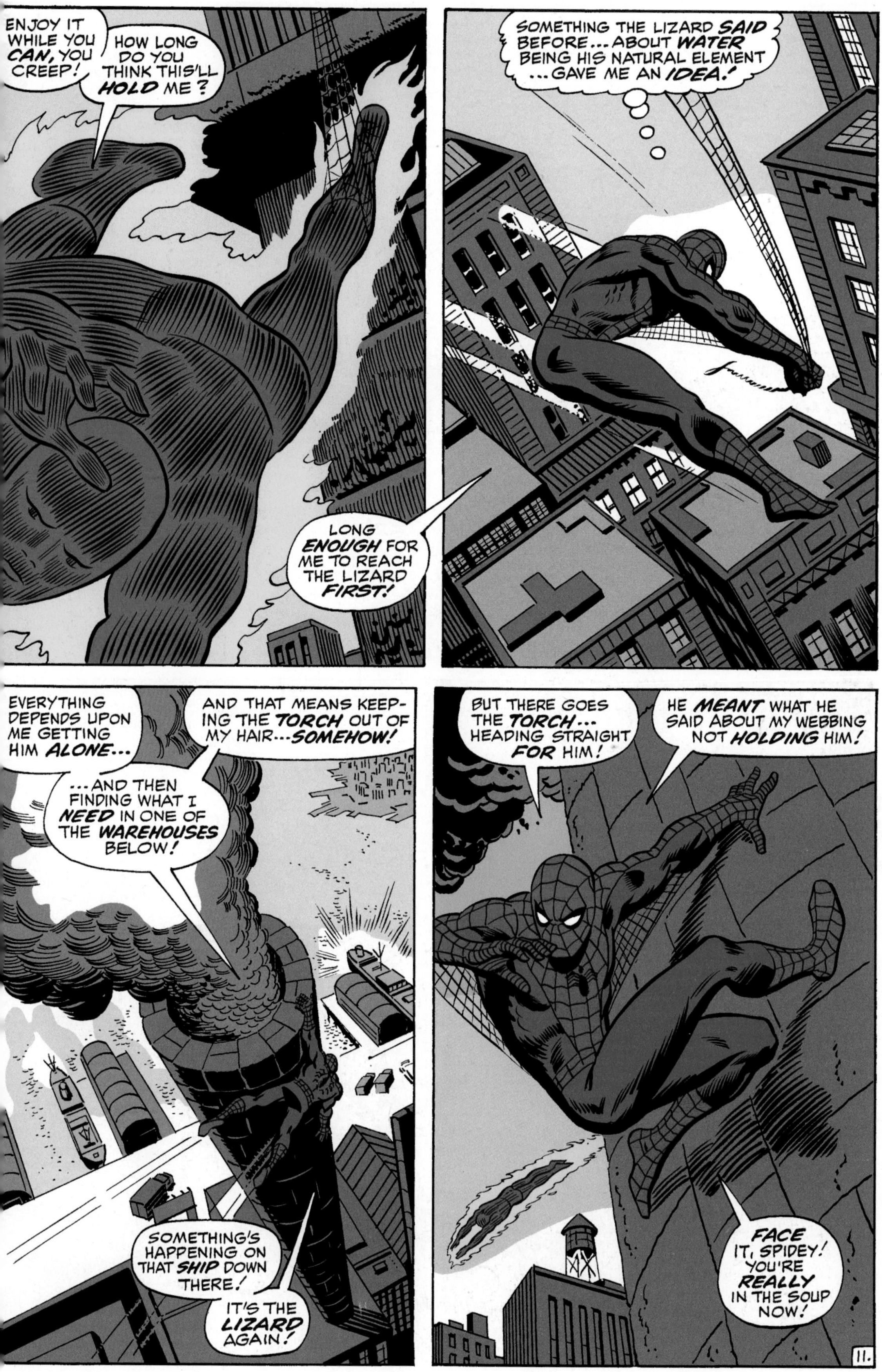

ENJOY IT WHILE YOU CAN, YOU CREEP!
HOW LONG DO YOU THINK THIS'LL HOLD ME?
LONG ENOUGH FOR ME TO REACH THE LIZARD FIRST!
SOMETHING THE LIZARD SAID BEFORE... ABOUT WATER BEING HIS NATURAL ELEMENT ...GAVE ME AN IDEA!
EVERYTHING DEPENDS UPON ME GETTING HIM ALONE...
AND THAT MEANS KEEPING THE TORCH OUT OF MY HAIR... SOMEHOW!
...AND THEN FINDING WHAT I NEED IN ONE OF THE WAREHOUSES BELOW!
SOMETHING'S HAPPENING ON THAT SHIP DOWN THERE!
IT'S THE LIZARD AGAIN!
BUT THERE GOES THE TORCH... HEADING STRAIGHT FOR HIM!
HE MEANT WHAT HE SAID ABOUT MY WEBBING NOT HOLDING HIM!
FACE IT, SPIDEY! YOU'RE REALLY IN THE SOUP NOW!
11.

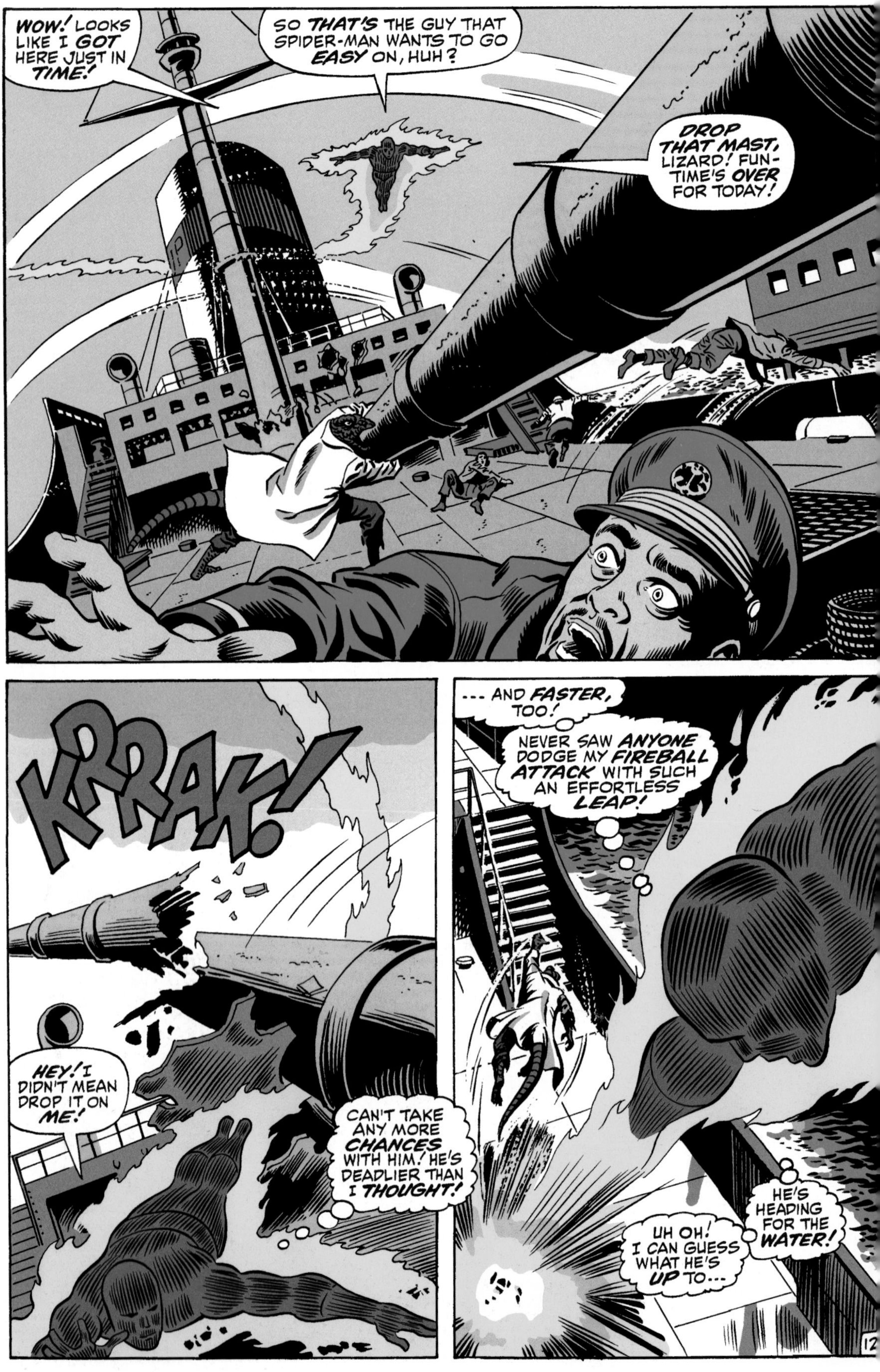
WOW! LOOKS LIKE I GOT HERE JUST IN TIME!
SO THAT'S THE GUY THAT SPIDER-MAN WANTS TO GO EASY ON, HUH?
DROP THAT MAST, LIZARD! FUN-TIME'S OVER FOR TODAY!
KRRAK!
HEY! I DIDN'T MEAN DROP IT ON ME!
CAN'T TAKE ANY MORE CHANCES WITH HIM! HE'S DEADLIER THAN I THOUGHT!
--- AND FASTER, TOO!
NEVER SAW ANYONE DODGE MY FIREBALL ATTACK WITH SUCH AN EFFORTLESS LEAP!
HE'S HEADING FOR THE WATER!
UH OH! I CAN GUESS WHAT HE'S UP TO...
12

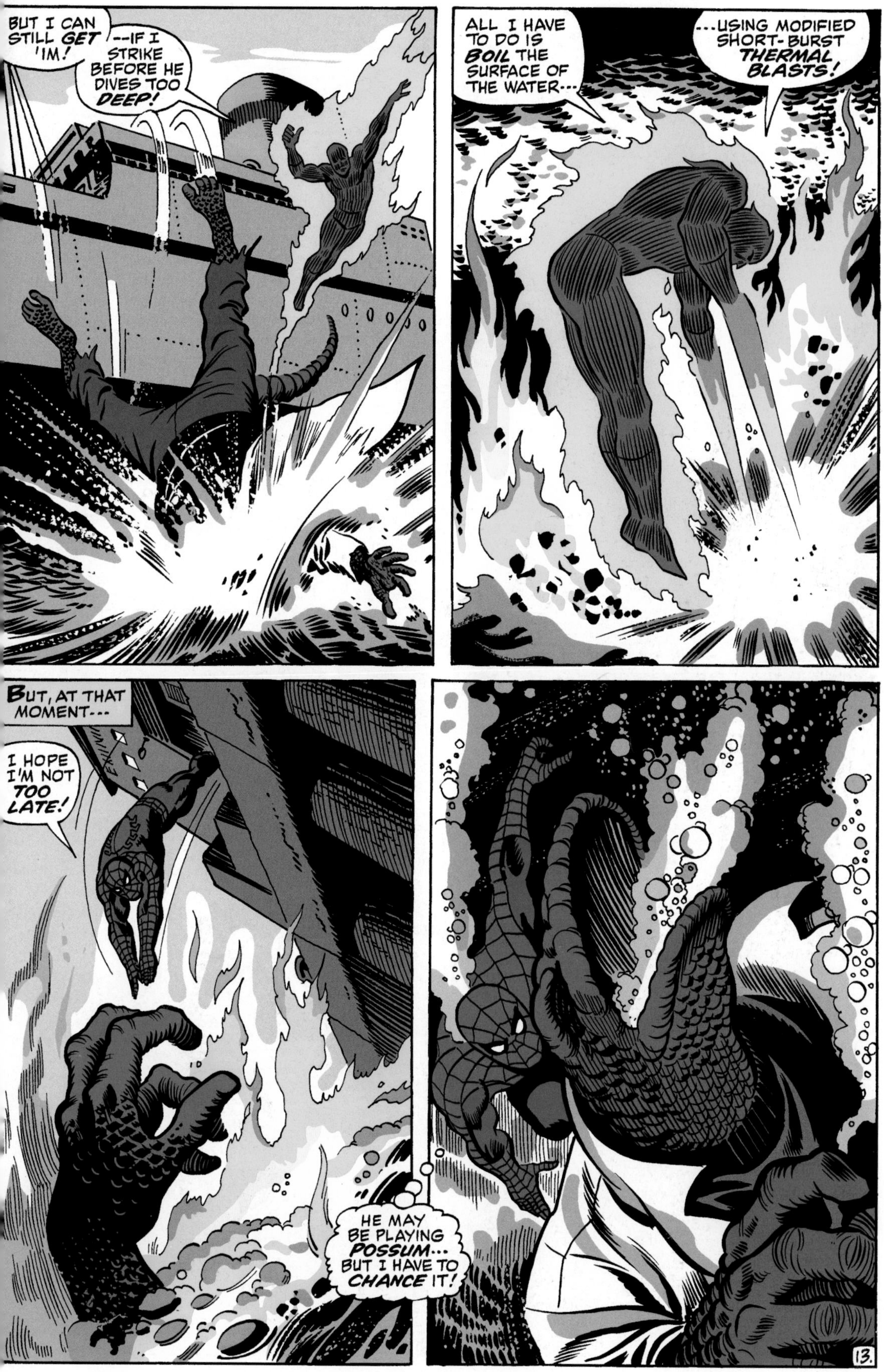

BUT I CAN STILL GET 'IM!
--IF I STRIKE BEFORE HE DIVES TOO DEEP!
ALL I HAVE TO DO IS BOIL THE SURFACE OF THE WATER---
---USING MODIFIED SHORT-BURST THERMAL BLASTS!
BUT, AT THAT MOMENT---
I HOPE I'M NOT TOO LATE!
HE MAY BE PLAYING POSSUM... BUT I HAVE TO CHANCE IT!
13.

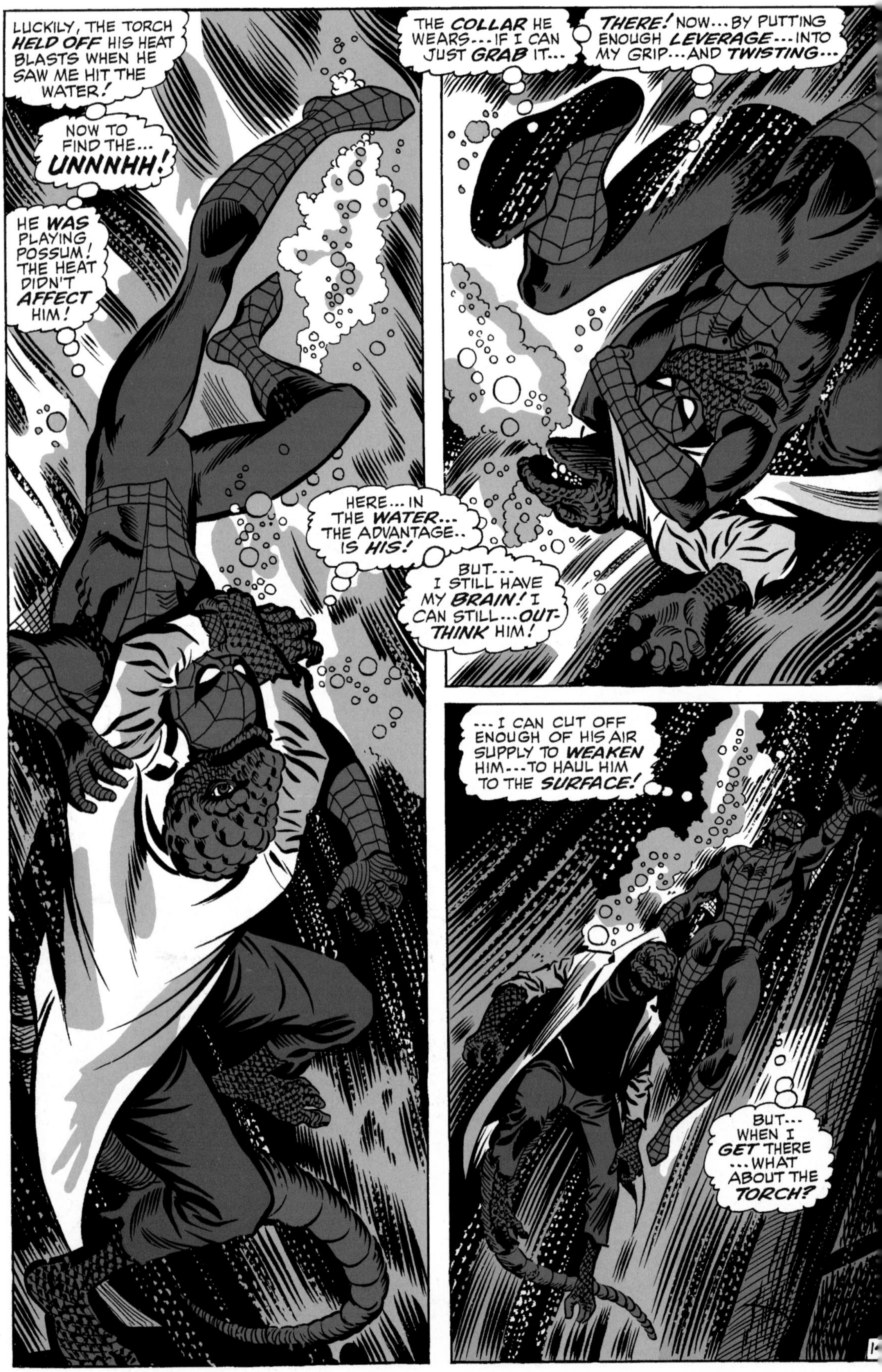

LUCKILY, THE TORCH HELD OFF HIS HEAT BLASTS WHEN HE SAW ME HIT THE WATER!
NOW TO FIND THE... UNNNHH!
HE WAS PLAYING POSSUM! THE HEAT DIDN'T AFFECT HIM!
HERE... IN THE WATER... THE ADVANTAGE.. IS HIS!
BUT--- I STILL HAVE MY BRAIN! I CAN STILL...OUT-THINK HIM!
THE COLLAR HE WEARS---IF I CAN JUST GRAB IT...
THERE! NOW...BY PUTTING ENOUGH LEVERAGE---INTO MY GRIP---AND TWISTING...
---I CAN CUT OFF ENOUGH OF HIS AIR SUPPLY TO WEAKEN HIM---TO HAUL HIM TO THE SURFACE!
BUT--- WHEN I GET THERE ...WHAT ABOUT THE TORCH?

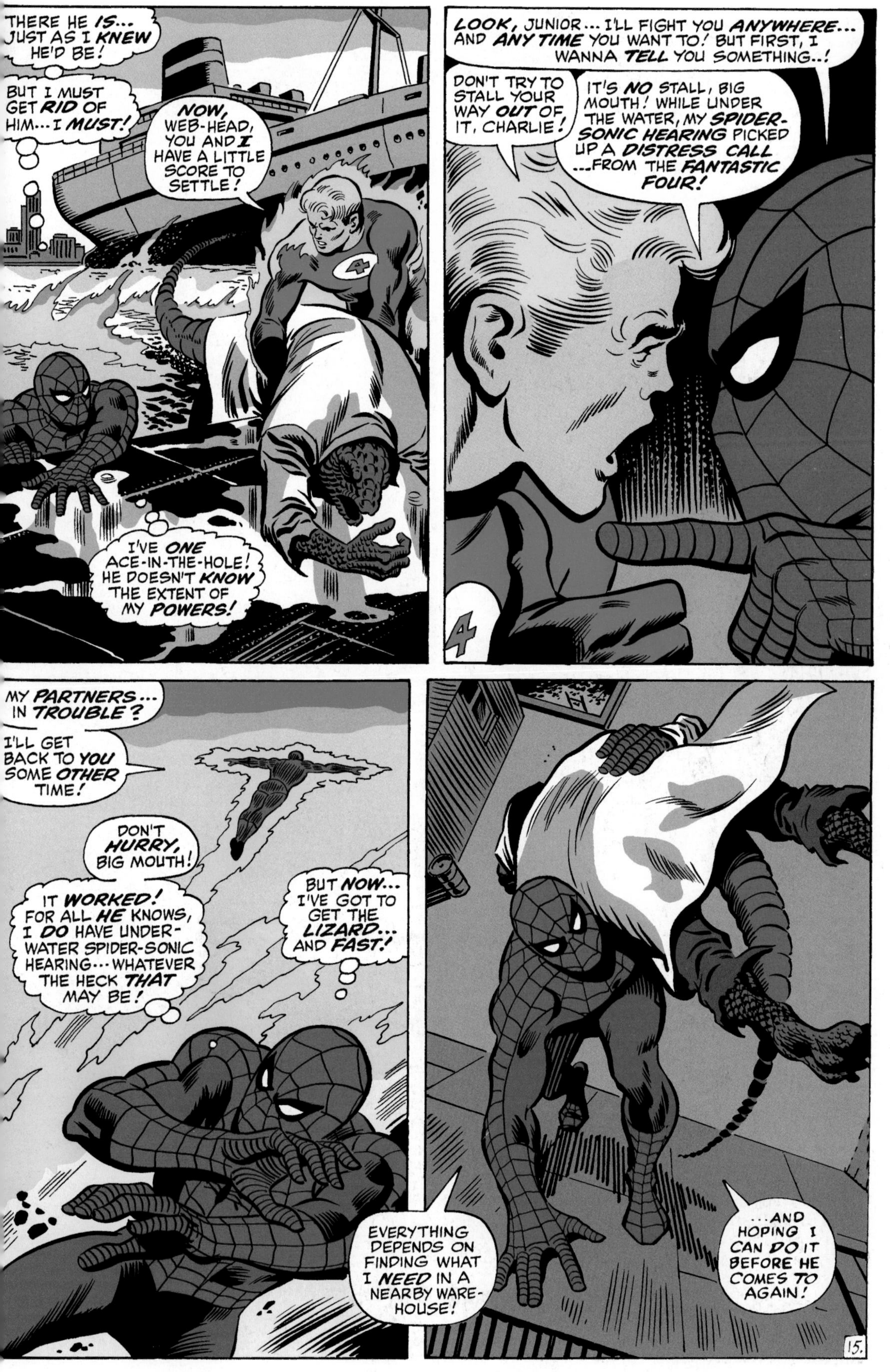
THERE HE IS... JUST AS I KNEW HE'D BE!
BUT I MUST GET RID OF HIM... I MUST!
NOW, WEB-HEAD, YOU AND I HAVE A LITTLE SCORE TO SETTLE!
I'VE ONE ACE-IN-THE-HOLE! HE DOESN'T KNOW THE EXTENT OF MY POWERS!
LOOK, JUNIOR... I'LL FIGHT YOU ANYWHERE... AND ANY TIME YOU WANT TO! BUT FIRST, I WANNA TELL YOU SOMETHING..!
DON'T TRY TO STALL YOUR WAY OUT OF IT, CHARLIE!
IT'S NO STALL, BIG MOUTH! WHILE UNDER THE WATER, MY SPIDER-SONIC HEARING PICKED UP A DISTRESS CALL ...FROM THE FANTASTIC FOUR!
MY PARTNERS... IN TROUBLE?
I'LL GET BACK TO YOU SOME OTHER TIME!
DON'T HURRY, BIG MOUTH!
IT WORKED! FOR ALL HE KNOWS, I DO HAVE UNDER-WATER SPIDER-SONIC HEARING... WHATEVER THE HECK THAT MAY BE!
BUT NOW... I'VE GOT TO GET THE LIZARD... AND FAST!
EVERYTHING DEPENDS ON FINDING WHAT I NEED IN A NEARBY WARE-HOUSE!
...AND HOPING I CAN DO IT BEFORE HE COMES TO AGAIN!
15.

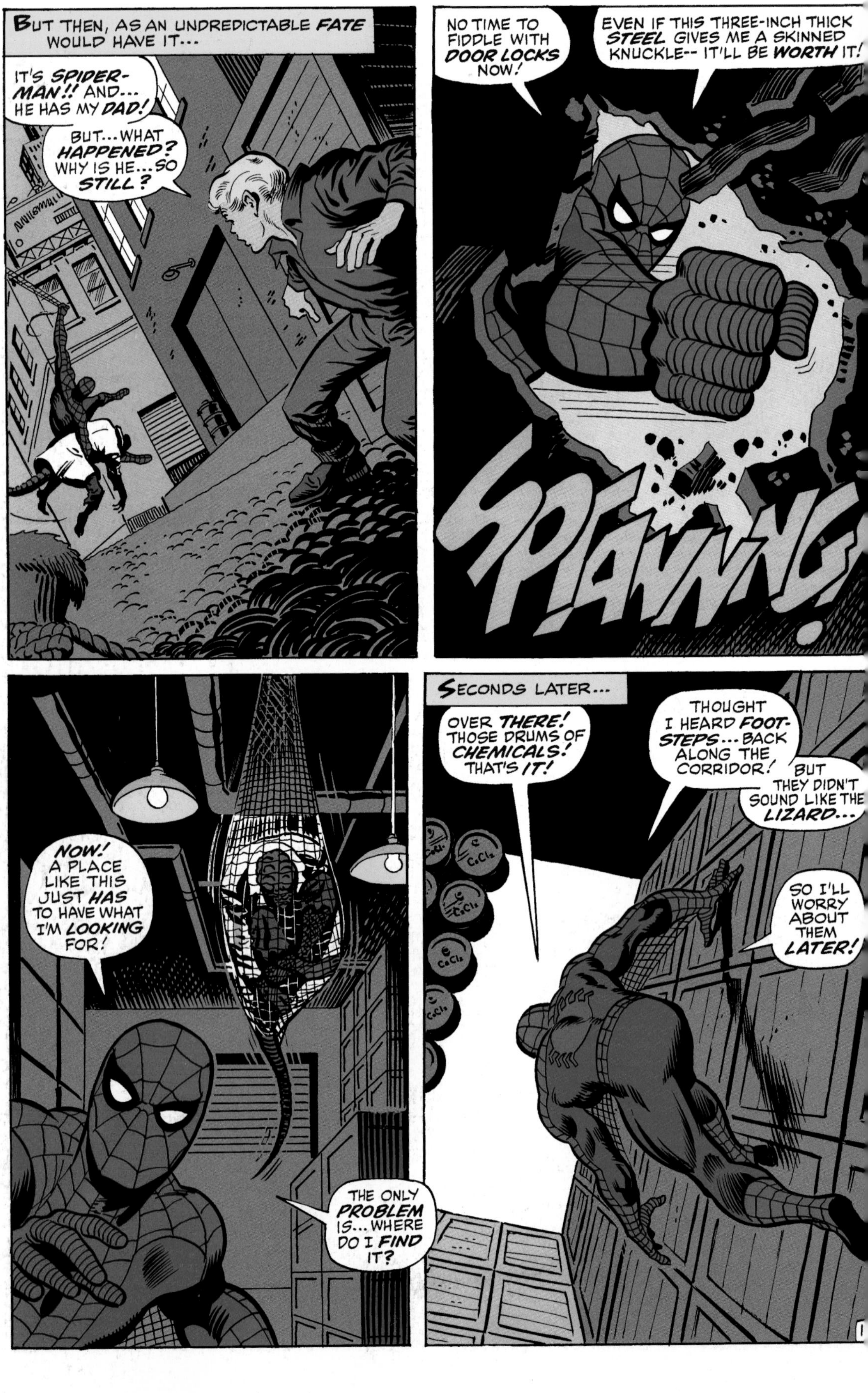
BUT THEN, AS AN UNDREDICTABLE FATE WOULD HAVE IT...
IT'S SPIDER-MAN!! AND... HE HAS MY DAD!
BUT...WHAT HAPPENED? WHY IS HE...SO STILL?
NO TIME TO FIDDLE WITH DOOR LOCKS NOW!
EVEN IF THIS THREE-INCH THICK STEEL GIVES ME A SKINNED KNUCKLE-- IT'LL BE WORTH IT!
SPTANNNG!
NOW! A PLACE LIKE THIS JUST HAS TO HAVE WHAT I'M LOOKING FOR!
THE ONLY PROBLEM IS...WHERE DO I FIND IT?
SECONDS LATER...
OVER THERE! THOSE DRUMS OF CHEMICALS! THAT'S IT!
THOUGHT I HEARD FOOT-STEPS...BACK ALONG THE CORRIDOR!
BUT THEY DIDN'T SOUND LIKE THE LIZARD...
SO I'LL WORRY ABOUT THEM LATER!

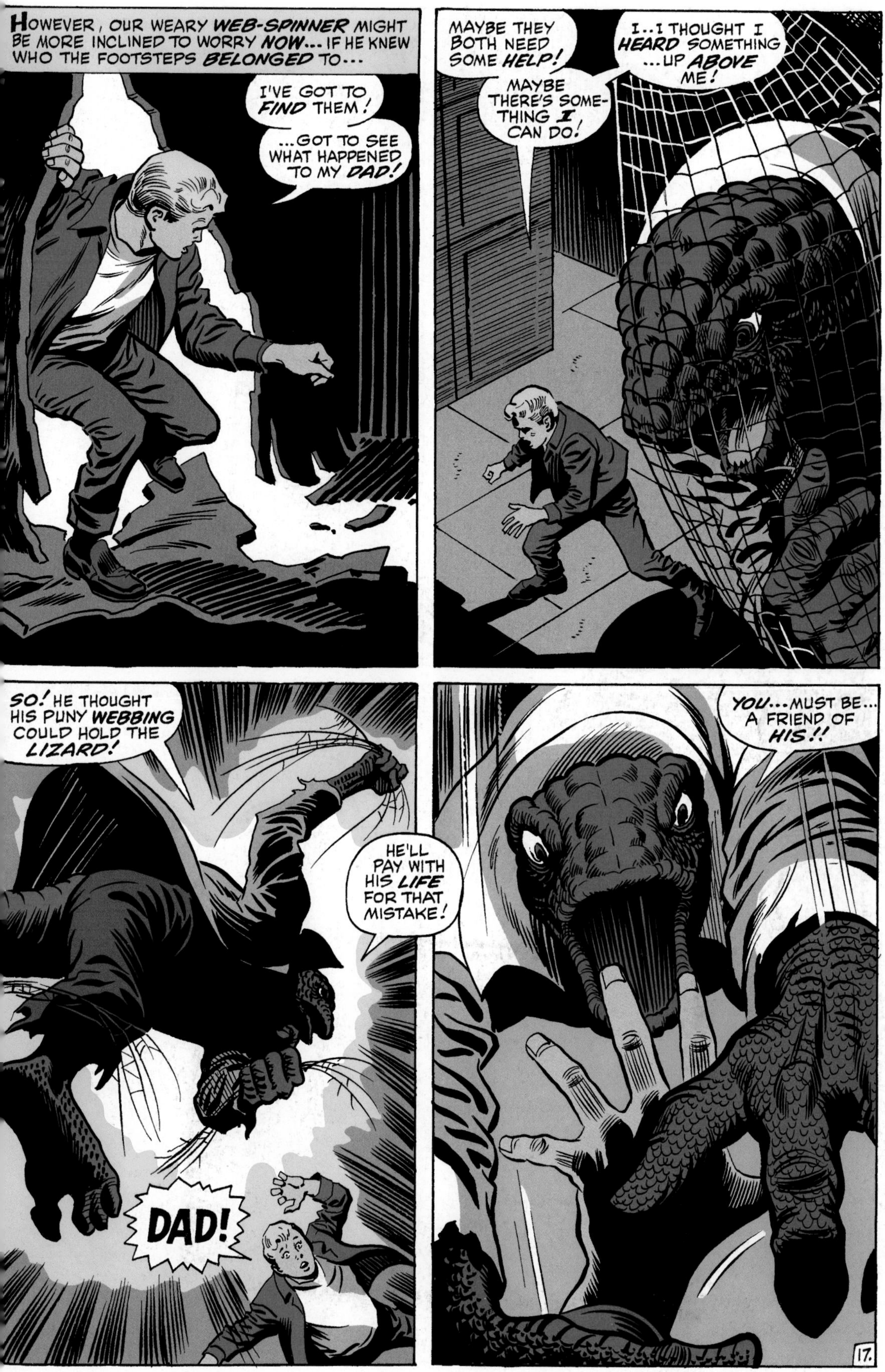
HOWEVER, OUR WEARY WEB-SPINNER MIGHT BE MORE INCLINED TO WORRY NOW... IF HE KNEW WHO THE FOOTSTEPS BELONGED TO...
I'VE GOT TO FIND THEM!
...GOT TO SEE WHAT HAPPENED TO MY DAD!
MAYBE THEY BOTH NEED SOME HELP!
MAYBE THERE'S SOMETHING I CAN DO!
I..I THOUGHT I HEARD SOMETHING ...UP ABOVE ME!
SO! HE THOUGHT HIS PUNY WEBBING COULD HOLD THE LIZARD!
HE'LL PAY WITH HIS LIFE FOR THAT MISTAKE!
DAD!
YOU...MUST BE... A FRIEND OF HIS!!
17.

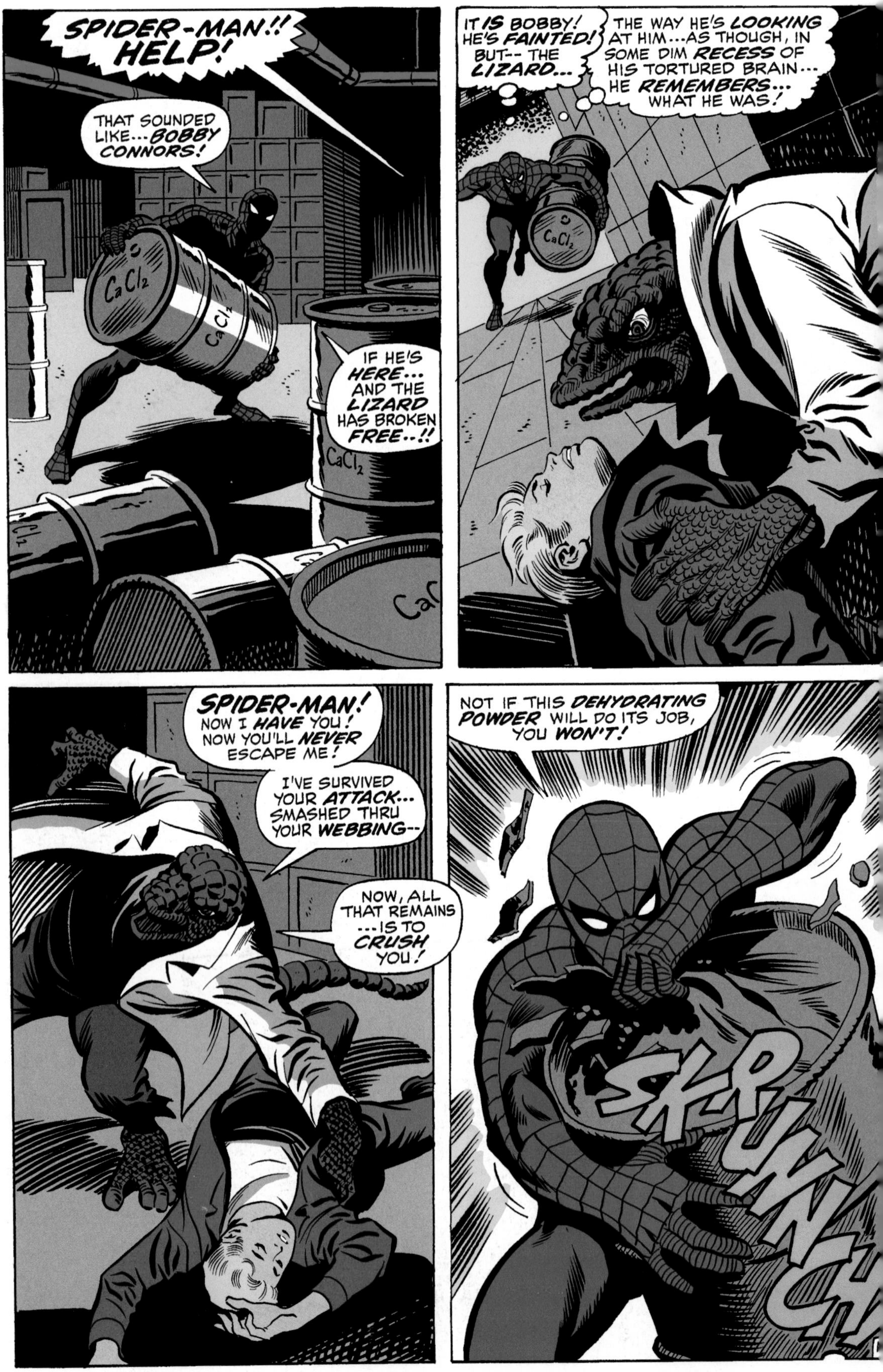
SPIDER-MAN!! HELP!
THAT SOUNDED LIKE... BOBBY CONNORS!
IF HE'S HERE... AND THE LIZARD HAS BROKEN FREE..!!
IT IS BOBBY! HE'S FAINTED! BUT-- THE LIZARD...
THE WAY HE'S LOOKING AT HIM...AS THOUGH, IN SOME DIM RECESS OF HIS TORTURED BRAIN... HE REMEMBERS... WHAT HE WAS!
SPIDER-MAN! NOW I HAVE YOU! NOW YOU'LL NEVER ESCAPE ME!
I'VE SURVIVED YOUR ATTACK... SMASHED THRU YOUR WEBBING--
NOW, ALL THAT REMAINS ...IS TO CRUSH YOU!
NOT IF THIS DEHYDRATING POWDER WILL DO ITS JOB, YOU WON'T!

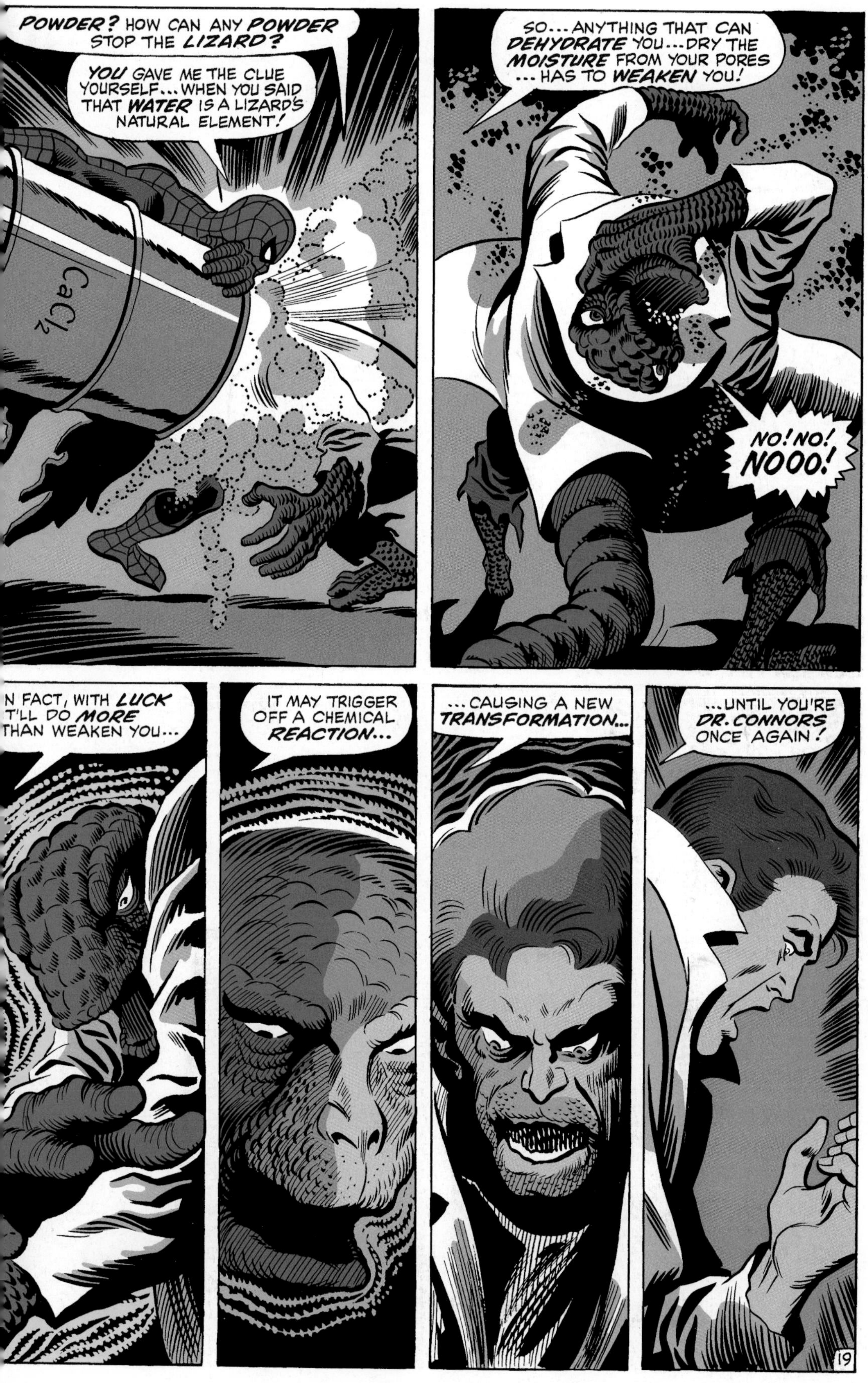
POWDER? HOW CAN ANY POWDER STOP THE LIZARD?
YOU GAVE ME THE CLUE YOURSELF... WHEN YOU SAID THAT WATER IS A LIZARD'S NATURAL ELEMENT!
CaCl2
SO... ANYTHING THAT CAN DEHYDRATE YOU... DRY THE MOISTURE FROM YOUR PORES ... HAS TO WEAKEN YOU!
NO! NO! NOOO!
N FACT, WITH LUCK T'LL DO MORE THAN WEAKEN YOU...
IT MAY TRIGGER OFF A CHEMICAL REACTION...
...CAUSING A NEW TRANSFORMATION...
...UNTIL YOU'RE DR. CONNORS ONCE AGAIN!
19

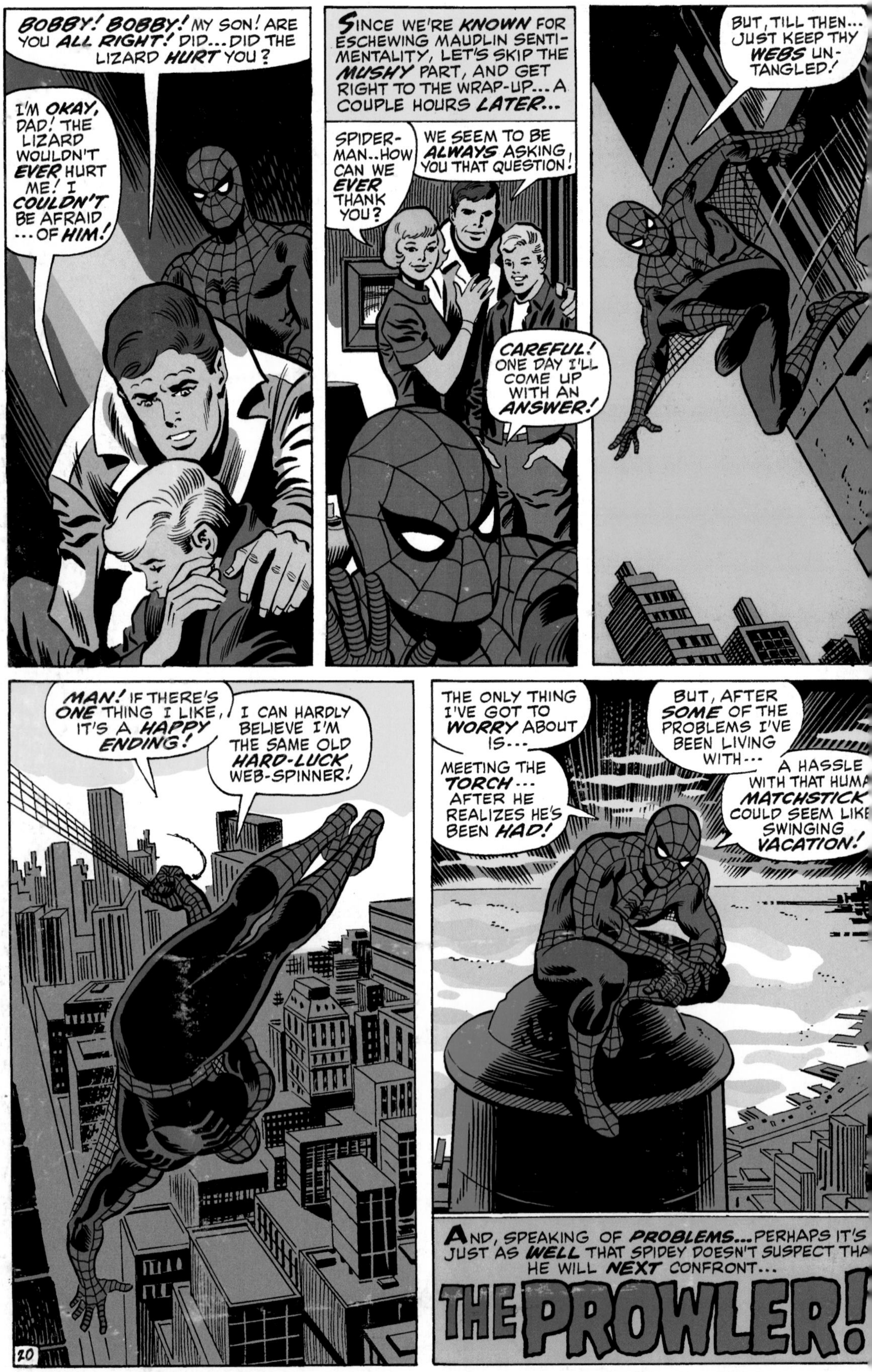

BOBBY! BOBBY! MY SON! ARE YOU ALL RIGHT! DID... DID THE LIZARD HURT YOU?
I'M OKAY, DAD! THE LIZARD WOULDN'T EVER HURT ME! I COULDN'T BE AFRAID ...OF HIM!
SINCE WE'RE KNOWN FOR ESCHEWING MAUDLIN SENTIMENTALITY, LET'S SKIP THE MUSHY PART, AND GET RIGHT TO THE WRAP-UP... A COUPLE HOURS LATER...
SPIDER-MAN..HOW CAN WE EVER THANK YOU?
WE SEEM TO BE ALWAYS ASKING YOU THAT QUESTION!
CAREFUL! ONE DAY I'LL COME UP WITH AN ANSWER!
BUT, TILL THEN... JUST KEEP THY WEBS UNTANGLED!
MAN! IF THERE'S ONE THING I LIKE, IT'S A HAPPY ENDING!
I CAN HARDLY BELIEVE I'M THE SAME OLD HARD-LUCK WEB-SPINNER!
THE ONLY THING I'VE GOT TO WORRY ABOUT IS...
MEETING THE TORCH... AFTER HE REALIZES HE'S BEEN HAD!
BUT, AFTER SOME OF THE PROBLEMS I'VE BEEN LIVING WITH...
A HASSLE WITH THAT HUMA MATCHSTICK COULD SEEM LIKE SWINGING VACATION!
AND, SPEAKING OF PROBLEMS... PERHAPS IT'S JUST AS WELL THAT SPIDEY DOESN'T SUSPECT THA HE WILL NEXT CONFRONT...
THE PROWLER!
20